Map of Cryptozoology, 1998-99

1. *Pterosaur*, Greenville, South Carolina 1989
2. Big Foot, Patterson-Gimlin Film, Orleans, CA 1967
3. Thunderbird Abduction, Kentucky 1977
4. *Axolotle*
5. Chupacabra, Puerto Rico, March 1995
6. *Andrewsarchus mongoliensis*
7. Romantic Encounter with Mosasaurus, Acapulco 1970's
8. Deloy's Ape (*Ameranthropoides loys*) Tarra River, Columbia 1920
9. Mapinguari (*Mylodon*) Amazon Basin
10. Lake Van Monster, Eastern Turkey 1995
11. U-28 Sea Serpent, North Atlantic, July 30 1915
12. Mokele-Mbembe, Congo River Basin 1776
13. Loch Ness Monster "Surgeon's Photo" Loch Ness Scotland 1934
14. Loch Ness Monster "Flipper Photo" Dr Robert H. Rines, Loch Ness Scotland 1972
15. Woolly Mammoth (*Mammuthus timigenius*) Russian Fur Trapper, Siberia 1920
16. Qilin (Chimera) China 15th C.
17. Vu Quang Ox (*Pseudryx nghetinnensis*) Vietnam 1990's
18. *Diprotodon opiatum*
19. Globster, Hobart, Tasmania 1960
20. Okapi (*Okapia johnstoni*) Central Africa 1901
21. Ya-Te-Veo ("I See You") J. W. Buel, Carnivorous Tree of Central Africa 1887
22. Gold Dinosaur Statue, Ashanti People, West Africa 18th C.
23. "Tadpole" Sea Serpent, Hook Island ,Great Barrier Reef, Australia 1964
24. Zuiyomaru, Japanese Fishing Vessel, near New Zealand 1977
25. Trunko, Margate, South Africa, Dec 24 1924
26. Uncharted Territory

Around the turn of the millennium, using hyper-realist techniques like the ones he found in National Geographic and other glossy magazines, the artist Alexis Rockman painted big, disjointedly narrative pictures about ecological catastrophe, species loss, sea-level rise, and (in this one, from 1998) young survivors of apocalypse who are putting themselves "Back to School" (the name of the series). What exactly are these survivors going back to school to learn? Maybe that the map is not the territory—though without conceptual maps, territories lapse into incoherence. Or maybe they're learning that reality is an artificial construct, where the real-but-strange (extinct species like mammoths, existing ones like okapis) mingle with the imaginary-but-plausible (like Chupacabra or Bigfoot or the Loch Ness monster). Or maybe they're learning that knowledge is global, as signaled by the little boy's flags-of-the-world shorts. Or maybe they're learning that real education ought always to be an adventure, like Huckleberry Finn setting off on the river. In other words, the heroes of this strange, disjointedly narrative picture are learning in their own way some of the things that comparative and international education has been exploring for decades.

Brian G. McHale
February 16, 2025

Comparative and International Education

ALSO AVAILABLE FROM BLOOMSBURY

Grassroots Approaches to Education for Sustainable Development,
Radhika Iyengar and Pooja Iyengar

Rethinking Education for Sustainable Development,
edited by Radhika Iyengar and Ozge Karadag Caman

Affect Theory and Comparative Education Discourse,
Irving Epstein

Ecopedagogy, Greg William Misiaszek

Global-National Networks in Education Policy, Rino Wiseman Adhikary,
Bob Lingard and Ian Hardy

International Schooling, Lucy Bailey

Critical Education in International Perspective, Peter Mayo and Paolo Vittoria

Internationalization of Higher Education for Development, Susanne Ress

The Bloomsbury Handbook of Theory in Comparative and International Education, edited by tavis d. jules, Robin Shields and Matthew A.M. Thomas

The Bloomsbury Handbook of Method in Comparative and International Education, edited by Matthew A. M. Thomas, tavis d. jules, Michele Schweisfurth and Robin Shields

Education, Affect, and Film, Irving Epstein

Comparative and International Education

An Introduction

**Esther E. Gottlieb,
Radhika Iyengar, and
Matthew A. Witenstein**

BLOOMSBURY ACADEMIC
LONDON • NEW YORK • OXFORD • NEW DELHI • SYDNEY

BLOOMSBURY ACADEMIC
Bloomsbury Publishing Plc, 50 Bedford Square, London, WC1B 3DP, UK
Bloomsbury Publishing Inc, 1359 Broadway, New York, NY 10018, USA
Bloomsbury Publishing Ireland, 29 Earlsfort Terrace, Dublin 2, D02 AY28, Ireland

BLOOMSBURY, BLOOMSBURY ACADEMIC and the Diana logo
are trademarks of Bloomsbury Publishing Plc

First published in Great Britain 2026

Copyright © Esther E. Gottlieb, Radhika Iyengar, and Matthew A. Witenstein, 2026

Esther E. Gottlieb, Radhika Iyengar and Matthew A. Witenstein have asserted their right under the Copyright, Designs and Patents Act, 1988, to be identified as Authors of this work.

For legal purposes the Acknowledgements on pp. xvi–xvii constitute an extension of this copyright page.

Cover design: © Adam Johnson
Cover image © Alexis Rockman, Artists Rights Society (ARS), New York

All rights reserved. No part of this publication may be: i) reproduced or transmitted in any form, electronic or mechanical, including photocopying, recording or by means of any information storage or retrieval system without prior permission in writing from the publishers; or ii) used or reproduced in any way for the training, development or operation of artificial intelligence (AI) technologies, including generative AI technologies. The rights holders expressly reserve this publication from the text and data mining exception as per Article 4(3) of the Digital Single Market Directive (EU) 2019/790.

Bloomsbury Publishing Plc does not have any control over, or responsibility for, any third-party websites referred to or in this book. All internet addresses given in this book were correct at the time of going to press. The author and publisher regret any inconvenience caused if addresses have changed or sites have ceased to exist, but can accept no responsibility for any such changes.

A catalogue record for this book is available from the British Library.

A catalog record for this book is available from the Library of Congress.

ISBN: HB: 978-1-3504-1555-3
PB: 978-1-3504-1554-6
ePDF: 978-1-3504-1557-7
eBook: 978-1-3504-1556-0

Typeset by Integra Software Services Pvt. Ltd.
Printed and bound in Great Britain

For product safety related questions contact productsafety@bloomsbury.com.

To find out more about our authors and books visit www.bloomsbury.com and sign up for our newsletters.

For Brian G. McHale (July 27, 1952–July 27, 2025), fellow traveler

Contents

List of Figures xiv
Acknowledgements xvi
List of Acronyms and Abbreviations xviii

Introduction 1

1 Histories 7
    International Comparisons of Education 9
    1945 to the 1960s 11
        Textbooks and Institutions 12
        The Cold War 16
        Analytical Comparative Studies 17
    1968—When Everything Happened 18
    1970s to 1980 19
        Education Attainment and "Stages of Development" 20
    1980s to 2000 23
        Rethinking Developmentalism 23
        "Education for All" 25
    The Long 1990s 26
        Globalization 26
        Neoliberalism 27
    The 2000s 30
        International Education 32
        Life Matters in Development Education 34
    Academic Activities—Springboards 35

2 Theories 39
    Four Social Science Paradigms and the "Post" 40
    Functionalist Paradigm 41
        Development 42
        Modernization 44
        Human Capital and Social Capital 45
        Summary 48

Radical Structuralist Paradigm 48
    Marxist Theory and Colonialism 49
    Dependency 50
    World Economic System and World Culture System 52
    Imperialism, Neo-Imperialism, and Sub-Imperialism 53
    Cultural Capital 56
Radical Humanist Paradigm 57
    Critical Theory 58
    Phenomenology 59
    Existentialism 60
    Summary 60
The Interpretive Paradigm 60
    Transcendental Phenomenology 61
    Ethnomethodology 61
    Symbolic Interaction 62
    Summary 63
Theorizing in the "Post" Era 63
    Poststructuralism 64
    Postmodernism 66
    Postcolonialism(s) 68
    Post-socialism 69
    Posthumanism 70
    Intersectionality and Affect Theory 72
Conclusion 73
Academic Activities—Springboards 76

3   Methods 79

Functionalist Research Methods 80
    Tension 1: Developed and Under-Developed 80
    Nation-State Unit of Analysis 84
    Human Capital and Rate of Return on Education 87
    Research on School Provision and Success 88
Radical Structuralist Studies and Methods 90
    Transfer and Borrowing Research Methods 92
    World-Systems and the Rise of Mass Education 93
Radical Humanist Methods and Studies 95
    Tension 2: Outsider–Insider Perspectives 95
    The Transition from Quantitative to Qualitative 97
    Decolonizing Methods 98
    Critical Ethnographic Methods 99

Interpretive Methods and Studies 102
    Tension 3: Context, Contextualizing 102
    Participatory Action Research 106
    Discourse Analysis 107
    Photovoice 109
Cross-Paradigms Methods 110
    Gender/Feminist Studies 112
    Data Visualization and Social Cartography 114
Conclusion 121
Academic Activities—Springboards 123

4 Practices 125

Time, Spaces, Directions, Shapes 125
Time 127
    Past Practices 129
    Past Present 133
    Conclusion 134
Spaces 135
    Where CIE is Practiced 135
    Colonial Space 136
    National and International 139
    International and Global 141
    Beyond Globalization 143
    Conclusion 145
Directions 146
    Directions and Orientations in CIE Practices 146
    West-East and East-West 147
    North-South 149
    North-South, South-North Comparativist 150
    South–South 151
    BRICS: New Development Practices? 153
Shapes 155
    Shaping the Global Order 155
    Southern Theory 155
    Re-Shaping 157
    Buen Vivir, *Ubuntu*, *Vā*, and *Tā-vā* 158
    Indigenous Culture and Education 159
Conclusion 160
Academic Activities—Springboards 162

5 Building Blocks 165
Introduction 165
Building a Research Library for Comparative Education 166
Organizational Building Blocks 167
    Professional Associations 168
    Professional Journals 169
    Organizations and Foundations 171
    Academic Careers in CIE 173
    Ethics in CIE Research 174
Future Building Blocks 177
    Sustainable Development Goals and Education 178
    Just Transition and Green Skilling 180
    Digital Learning and AI Prospects 182
Conclusion 186
Academic Activity—Springboards 187

6 Conclusion 189
"We Are All Comparativists Now *and* Internationalists" 189

Illustrations/Reflections 195
Introduction 195
Iris BenDavid-Hadar: *Education Finance, Equality, and Equity* 197
Gerardo L. Blanco: *Internationalization and Global Education* 202
Irving Epstein: *Affect Theory and its Contribution to Comparative Education* 205
Caroline "Carly" Manion: *Sharpening Girls' and Women's Education Agenda: Gender Responsive and Gender Transformative Approaches* 208
Fazal Rizvi: *Geopolitical Shifts and Comparative Education* 213
Karen Ross: *The Implications of Commitments for Research Practice* 218
Kathan Shukla: *Driving Educational Change Through Capacity-Building of Government School Leaders: A Case of India* 221
Matthew A. M. Thomas: *New Approaches in Teacher Education, and New Ways to Research Them* 227

Christina Yao and Chrystal A. George Mwangi: *International Students and Education Abroad—Whether in Global or Virtual Engagements* 232

Illustrations/Case Studies Contributors' Affiliation 237
References 240
Index 260

Figures

Figure 1	Total Enrolment Rations by Levels and Stages of Development (Adams and Gottlieb, 2nd edition 2018, part of pp. 162–3)	22
Figure 2	After Burrell and Morgan (1979), four paradigms are represented by the quadrants of a 2×2 matrix scheme	40
Figure 3	Paulston's global mapping of paradigmatic discourses and territorial disputes in sixty comparative education texts. Paulston, R. G., ed. (1996), *Social Cartography: Mapping Ways of Seeing Social and Educational Change*, p. 15	75
Figure 4	Astrid Høgmo (2018), Holistic system thinking Distant Education landscape, comparison between South Africa and Norway. Høgmo, A. (2018), MA thesis, Department of Education, Stockholm University, p. 84	119
Figure 5	Phenomenographic/conceptual map of critical cartography. Reitz, T. (2022), "Back to the Drawing Board: Creative Mapping Methods for Inclusion and Connection," p. 335	120
Figure 6	Paulston's mapping of knowledge positions and communities constructing and debating comparative education (and related) discourses. Reproduced from Gottlieb (2009), "*Somewhere better than this Place/nowhere better than this place*" *The lifemap of Rolland G. Paulston 1929–2006* **Prospects** 39 p. 97	121

Figure 7	Information redrawn from Bristow, T. (1965), "The University of London Research Library for Comparative Education in the Institute of Education," *Comparative Education Review*, 9 (2): 213–18	167
Figure KS1	Educational Ecosystem in Government Schools	223
Figure KS2	School Climate Framework for Improving Holistic Schooling Experience	225

Acknowledgements

All three of us have experience in teaching comparative and international education and in writing academic papers or editing research. So, while we are motivated to embark on this project, writing a textbook or even co-authoring one has proven to be harder and involving greater commitment than any previous work we have been involved in. It takes far more time than writing a scholarly article and even more than editing most scholarly books. The commitment is long term, a lot of assistance is needed, and we are fortunate to have colleagues, friends, and family that gave us their support. Even writing a textbook proposal is generally more of a challenge than writing a proposal for a scholarly book, which is why we are so grateful to the three anonymous readers of this book's proposal and the useful feedback they provided.

We are fortunate that we had expert readers of our various chapter drafts of this book. Esther's colleagues Maria Fanis, Associate Professor of Political Science and International Relations at Ohio University, and Robyn Warhol, Distinguished Professor of English at the Ohio State University, insisted that we needed to think much harder about how each chapter is structured, what is included, and what stays out. They enhanced the textbook regarding how the vast materials are organized and the pedagogy we used to enhance learning. Two University of Dayton graduate students, Evan Englander and Paul Wojdacz, each read a chapter, so we also got feedback from students' point of view.

When it came to the many references, Preet Dhillon at The Ohio State University (OSU) helped early on and Jiatian Xu, a graduate student at Columbia University, once we drafted each chapter, contributed assistance to other parts of the manuscript. We came across two relevant studies and contacted the authors; both Astrid Høgmo and Talitta Reitz gave us permission to reproduce their illustrations in this textbook.

Esther Gottlieb's scholarly work was supported by Ohio State research grants, at the Office of International Affairs thanks go to Danielle White, Megan Lawther and the communication unit. Adam Johnson worked on all charts, tables, and text lineup as well as designing the cover. Alexis Rockman, the artist whose work appears on the cover, was easy to communicate with and so very generous in allowing us to use his Map of Cryptozoology, from the Back to School series, and its key. Every time we look at the cover or get compliments on the design, we know how important the connection with Rockman and Johnson are.

In addition to our own writing, we are grateful to our colleagues' contributions and to their own synopsis of their CIE research experiences, which added so much and contributes to teaching and learning. Thanks go to each of them: Iris BenDavid-Hadar, Gerardo L. Blanco, Irving Epstein, Caroline "Carly" Manion, Fazal Rizvi, Karen Ross, Kathan Shukla, Matthew A. M. Thomas, Chrystal George Mwangi and Christina Yao. Their contributions are invaluable.

This book project would not have come to fruition without Mark Richardson at Bloomsbury. As Mark can see, from our first correspondence to add Radhika Iyengar and Matthew Witenstein the book will be three years in the making as of October 2025. Those years are marked by the pandemic and two new members joining Mark's family. Nevertheless, his obligations and commitment to the field of Education and to works like ours, has only grown, and we are the beneficiaries. With Elissa Burns, as Editorial Assistant, we feel very secure in having a smooth production of this new CIE textbook.

We thank the expert reader for his constructive feedback, reminding us that with the closing of USAID we have embarked on a new era in comparative and international education, not just in the US, and our commitment to CIE scholars of the future is even stronger. We are grateful for the work of Kate Greig and Dawn Cunneen for their comprehensive copyediting and proofreading of our manuscript, along with Anne Hunt, Integra project manager, for playing a vital role in ensuring the quality and successful delivery of this book. Integra Software Services, with its UK office in Harrow, Greater London, specializes in content publishing, including education.

Finally, we would like to thank Brian McHale (Esther Gottlieb's husband) who stood by and over us, to make sure this book is being written, edited, and published. Brian did not live to see this book in print as he passed away on July 27 2025.

Acronyms and Abbreviations

ADB	Asia Development Bank
AED	Academy for Educational Development
AFRE	All for Reparations and Emancipation
AIDS	Acquired Immunodeficiency Syndrome
ASHE	Association for the Study of Higher Education
BA	Bachelor of Arts
BBC	British Broadcasting Company
BRIC	Brazil, Russia, India, and China
CCIC	Canadian Council for International Cooperation
CE	Comparative Education (UK)
CEDAW	Convention of the Elimination of All Forms of Discrimination against Women
CER	Comparative Education Review
CES	Comparative Education Studies
CIDE	Comparative, international, and development education
CIDA	Canadian International Development Agency
CIES	Comparative and International Education Society (USA)
CoP	Communities of Practice
CSO	Civil Society Organizations
DFID	Department for International Development (UK)
EdD	Doctor of Education

EFA	Education for All
EMIS	Educational Management Information Systems
ERIC	Educational Resources Information Center
FCDO	Foreign, Commonwealth & Development Office (UK)
GAD	Gender and Development
GATS	General Agreement on Trade in Services
GDP	Gross Domestic Product
GINIE	Global Information Networks in Education
GIS	Geographic Information System
GMR	Global Monitoring Report
GNI	Gross National Income
GPA	Grade Point Average
GPF	Gender Policy Framework
GTE	Gender Transformative Education
HEI	Higher education institution
HIV	Human Immunodeficiency Virus
IAU	International Association of Universities
IBE	UNESCO International Bureau of Education (Switzerland)
ICT	Information and communication technology
IDEP	International and Development Education Program, University of Pittsburgh (USA)
IDPs	Internally displaced persons
IE	International education
IEA	International Association for the Evaluation of Educational Achievement
IER	International Education Review

IISE	Institute for International Studies in Education, University of Pittsburgh (USA)
IJED	International Journal of Educational Development
IMF	International Monetary Fund
IT	Information technology
JCES	Japan Comparative Education Society
JEP	Journal of Education Policy
JSIE	Journal of Studies in International Education
KEDI	Korean Educational Development Institute
LICs	Least Income Countries
LMICs	Low- and Middle-Income Countries
MA	Master of Arts
MBA	Master of Business Administration
MDG/s	Millennium Development Goal/s
MICs	Middle-income countries
MOE	Ministry of Education
NAFSA	Association of International Educators
NGO	Non-governmental organization
NICs	Newly industrialized countries
NOCIES	Nordic Comparative and International Education Society
NPR	National Public Radio
NUFU	Norwegian Programme for Development, Research and Education
OECD	Organisation for Economic Co-operation and Development
OISE/UT	Ontario Institute for Studies in Education at the University of Toronto (Canada)

PhD	Doctor of Philosophy
Pitt	University of Pittsburgh
ISA	Program for International Student Assessment
SNA	Social network analysis
SSCI	Social Sciences Citation Index
TCR	Teachers College Record
TIMSS	Trends in International, Mathematics and Science Study
TVET	Technical and Vocational Education and Training
UBC	University of British Columbia (Canada)
UCLA	University of California, Los Angeles
UK	United Kingdom
UN	United Nations
UNICEF	United Nations Children's Fund
UNIFEM	United Nations Development Fund for Women
UNIDO	United Nation Industrial Development Organization
UNDP	United Nations Development Program
UNESCO	United Nations Educational, Scientific and Cultural Organization
UNFPA	United Nations Population Fund
UNHCR	United Nations High Commissioner for Refugees
UNPD	United Nations Population Division
UPE	Universal Primary Education
US/USA	United States of America
USAID	US Agency for International Development
VSO	Voluntary Service Overseas

WB	World Bank
WCCES	World Council of Comparative Education Societies
WID	Women in Development

Introduction

If you have picked up this book, or were assigned it for your studies, we are assuming that you are curious and that you may have questions about comparative and international education (CIE). Perhaps you would like to know, what *is* CIE anyway? How does it fit into and connect with the broader landscape of the field of education? What are some of the topics it covers? How do you go about doing research in education through a comparative lens? Aren't all education practices comparative and international?

If these are some of the questions you might have entertained about CIE, you have picked up the right book! This book is most useful to learners and instructors who want to obtain an overview of CIE as well as for seasoned practitioners and educators who would like to have a teachable textbook that addresses the full spectrum of theories, methods, and practices under one cover. It starts with CIE's successive historical phases, along with a wide range of fundamental concepts and components, and topical issues to give a contemporary sense of the depth and breadth of this discipline. You will learn about histories, theories, methods, and practices, with each of these topics constituting one of the main sections of the book. Illustrations, each written by an expert in the field, add to the main chapters a range of reflections, points of view, and additional references.

We have set out to enable access to a rich picture of the field's many ways of knowing. We question the history of CIE as a mainly Eurocentric discipline which developed into a field at a time when patterns of education were planned and implemented in colonial dependencies in the geopolitical context of imperialism. Neo-imperialism, also called "cultural imperialism," is even-more relevant to our contemporary hyper-speedy cross-continental connectivity. The foundations of the field were mainly Anglophone (written in the English language), and only recently have other, less Eurocentric histories of education planning and policies, other measurements of learning outcomes, and other global rankings of institutions been added to published research in CIE. Scholars from the "Global South"—the parts of the world where, historically, Euro-American-style education patterns were funded and planned by outsiders from the "Global North"—themselves typically educated in Western universities and publishing in English their accounts comparative education in, for instance, Japan, Indonesia, Siri Lanka, or Tanzania, were shaped and influenced by US, UK, or USSR scholarship. The entanglement and complicity of CIE with the colonial and postcolonial, imperialist and neo-imperialist transfer of Western education planning and policy, teacher education, and curriculum to the rest of the world is openly and frankly discussed in this textbook.

We hope to open avenues for the teaching, learning, and practices of CIE in a global perspective, all the while acknowledging our own reliance on English-language resources and publications is a limitation. We also examine contemporary reconfigurations of the field, including "Southern theorizing," South-to-South collaborations, education for sustainable development, and internationalization and global citizenship. While there are many challenges to hegemonic Eurocentric education transfer and the rethinking of the spatial dimensions, flows and vocabularies we use in studying, researching, and comparing education phenomena, there are also collaborations across the regions of the world that recognize the interdependence of our education futures reflected, for instance, in South–North collaborations (see Chapter 4), and in the seventeen Sustainable Development Goals (SDGs). The foundation of the SDGs—namely, sustainable development, environmental sustainability, peace and security, inclusive social development, and inclusive economic development—are closely related to the development education goals that emerged during the post-Second World War reconstruction, which sought to address the education needs of states newly liberated from colonization. The 2030 agenda for sustainable development has been agreed upon by almost all United Nations member states, which starkly contrasts with the situation of the divided Cold War world (discussed in Chapter 1) in which CIE originally arose. Nevertheless, the experiences, methods, and practices of CIE have a lot to offer to the implementation of education in the current global environmental and geopolitical tensions.

You will find that CIE encompasses a complex and diverse set of dilemmas and challenges, some of which we present in each chapter in addition to the illustrative cases contributed by invited scholars to support and broaden our understanding of the fundamentals. In this book we aim to give you a flavor of these international education topics researched by different scholars by taking you through a journey—not an exhaustive one, but surely an interesting array of topics relevant in the field. You may not be very familiar at first with the topics and their contexts, but we ask that you work through them as illustrations toward greater understanding of how we have woven the fundamentals to facilitate learning of the field's various dimensions, sometimes even reflecting conflict among the different trends, theories and methods that have historically governed the field.

This book is a foundational companion for teaching and studying the field of comparative and international education, covering theories and methods, past and present, and ideas about some of what is coming our way, illustrated by examples written by nine different scholars. You will be introduced to several CIE topics, methods of research, and ways of knowing and how they are treated by scholars with different understandings of what the field is and how to practice it. The main conceptual and theoretical chapters are chock-full of key references to a broad existing literature, and you can turn to them to build further on the knowledge you have gained from our text. CIE is also a highly applied field with a large corpus of multi-country studies. The learner as well as instructors will get a sense of how research is conducted and the ethical considerations of data collection. The book reviews big-picture conceptions of knowledge production as well as fine-grained examples of comparative education studies in different parts of the world, in the chapters that follow as well as in the illustrations. We intentionally take a participatory, human-centered approach to the practice of CIE; consequently, many of the dilemmas we present are relevant to many disciplinary researchers, both inside and outside the field. We seek to lay bare what and how CIE in the twenty-first century is presently studied and practiced and where it may be heading.

As you can see from the table of contents, the structure of the book follows from history to theories, to methods and to practices, and finally to "building blocks" for the discipline's future. Followed by experts' reflections, illustrating their own area of study and research.

- Chapter 1 reviews CIE's history, with particular attention to the development of the field. As in other fields, there is no one consensus history; therefore, we dedicated space to articulating some of the many critical dilemmas in historicizing CIE.
- Chapter 2 discusses the theoretical foundations of CIE, reviewing its use of theories adapted from other social science disciplines. Social science theories are not presented in the chronological order of their impact on CIE, but in terms of four broad social science paradigms,

as well as the "post" theorizing that comes after the dominance of the four paradigms, including theories that are neo-, anti-, and even post-post theories, reflecting the times and places as well as the world events that influenced theorizing.

- Chapter 3 provides an overview of research methods employed by CIE researchers within the four broad paradigms. Research methods underwrite observation and data collection, as exemplified by the studies we include that use these theories to frame their research. This chapter can also be used in methods classes. Besides CIE, general education students taking methods courses could benefit from the overview we develop in this chapter as a starting point, and as illustrations of their applicability.
- Chapter 4 gives an overview of the practice of CIE, which is informed by past practices but also reflects the multiple times and spaces in which knowledge is produced, and the different directions education knowledge-production is carried out and "travels" all over the globe. CIE has a robust applied component informing education planning and policy, so Chapter 4 includes an array of contemporary movements that are shaping and reshaping CIE practices. Influencing past and future directions of knowledge flows, the North–South flow now also includes South-to-South flows.
- Chapter 5 looks back to how CIE was institutionalized, but also forward to new developments. The building blocks of CIE's future include information communication technologies (ICTs), artificial intelligence (AI), just transitions, and sustainable development goals. We challenge readers to consider careers in CIE and the ethics of conducting research.

The book's treatment of these chapters includes abundant references for reading and learning from, and academic "springboards" (like the ones divers or gymnasts use), here designed to help you think further and engage in useful discussions. These "Springboards" at the end of chapters are our pedagogical contribution to a field in which teaching is central for assuring the training of the next generation of comparativists. They can be used for in-class discussions or as prompts for assignments, for online discussion forums, or for opening topics not necessarily covered in the chapters.

Following the chapters are what we are calling illustrations, contributions by nine comparativists each well-known for their research practice, contributing reflections on their research studies. Illustrations expose future comparativists to the way our colleagues summarize and think about issues they are experts on. We intend the illustrations to prompt readers' engagement with current CIE issues, providing some of the contexts where theories, method, and research are practiced. These illustrations were selected with an eye toward including a wide variety of topics and authors who have shaped the field through their research, writing, and practices. They each include a reference list for further reading and investigative learning. Methodologically we remain open to a variety of traditional and newer ways of knowing the multifaceted relations among education and social, political, economic, and cultural constructs. This means to be ready, using each one in their own historical context of both the production and reception of theories and methods and their practices.

The histories of education and schooling—its disputed development in the past in so many different, newly established states with uncertain futures—generates strong if divergent needs for CIE learning and research to build critical dialogues across its theories, methods, practices, and histories. Drawing from many studies and past and present accounts, we both describe and assess the field for the training of future comparativists. We envisioned that this book could be used in a number of different ways. Designed to be a fundamental textbook for learning CIE in related courses, this volume would also work if it were read in a different order, especially if instructors opted to use each section of the book as a standalone module in a graduate course.

We recognize that the different constituencies of our large audience of scholars, students, and instructors who are interested in exploring comparative and international perspectives in education are likely to want different things from this book. Our recognition of the range of our readers has influenced our choices in constructing the content, and we embrace the fact that readers will be using this book in a variety of ways. The book captures CIE at a moment in its history when the theories and methods of both comparative and international education are highly contested and when its practices are undergoing continual change. This includes political changes to international aid, most visibly in US political Foreign Aid, when on January 27, 2025, the USAID official government website was shut down and all foreign aid was frozen for a ninety-day review. Our book is assembled to provide a foundation, explorations of the field, its debates, and its ongoing yet unknown transformations.

1
Histories

This chapter engages with comparative and international education (CIE) histories, pluralized because we can only recognize CIE knowledge as constructed in other languages and their interaction with Western comparative education developments. Comparativists like Ruth Hayhoe for example, have researched education relations between East Asia, particularly China, and the West (2007). Websites for Japan Comparative Education Society (JCES) and South Korea in English show that CIE has multiple histories, but this chapter covers the conventional story that CIE courses in English and in other languages cover, as we all synthesize the same sources into a similar narrative.

This history is socially constructed and didn't develop linearly, another factor in its pluralization. Non-Western comparative education does exist, and more discussions of studies in non-English-language-based comparative education societies take place, but this exchange still happens in English, the hegemonic language of CIE. "Comparative Education" tends to refer to the divergent approaches that have emerged from the UK, European, and North American institutions, as the US professional origination, CIES (see Chapter 5), is now the international society, with over 4,000 members globally. Now we are a long way from 1956, when CIES was established and all jobs in the field (including journal editors) were held by white men. Because of traveling to other "developed" countries, meeting with other men like ministers of education, health and social affairs, and discussing funding, grants and loans, CIE was for many years a man's profession.

CIE practitioners, researchers, and teachers attach multiple meanings to the categories "comparative," "international," and "education," another reason why this overview is one among multiple "histories." CIE as a disciplinary field includes fierce debates on methodology (see Chapter 3) and on theoretical perspectives, mostly Eurocentric (see Chapter 2). We can see the history through the different positionalities that were regularly published in "state-of-the-art" collections, each looking at teaching and learning in a particular space and time. Every era struggled with the underlying geopolitics of practicing CIE at different points of colonialism, imperialism, neo-imperialism, and postcolonialism and neo-colonialities. Each era followed various disciplinary traditions including history, philosophy, sociology, and later anthropology, using area studies, scientific, and social science methods for comparing systems.

"To study education well is to study it comparatively" (Adams 1977) was the motto during the heyday of CIE. The chapters of this book—on the histories, theories, methods, and practices of CIE—continue to honor this principle. Note that all our sources are in English, as our graduate studies were in the United States. Like many others we were attracted to studying CIE in English-speaking institutions. Many international students were always present in the field (see Chapter 4), and continue today to acquire degrees in CIE. Some remained in the country they studied, teaching and researching their home regions from afar, while others returned to their home country to serve as educators or even directing the ministry responsible for education (Pakistan), and university president (South Korea). They teach at colleges and universities, international schools, and publish in English, helping us understand education systems comparatively by researching their home/land ways of knowledge transmitting.

This chapter covers almost eight decades, looking back from the perspective of the 2020s at what has shaped CIE, when and where it was conceptualized, and how it spread globally. We can contextualize the events within the times and the places where they were elaborated. Our book acknowledges that theories and methods of CIE are highly contested, and its practices are continually changing in the work of scholars in more than forty CIE associations around the world. A field like CIE, so closely tied to the global spread of Western education and of the interventions of national and international agencies in developing education in other countries, must view the past in the light of what we know today about colonialism and anti-colonialism, imperialism, and anti-imperialism, socialism/communism, and post-socialism, as well as other "antis" and "posts" (see Chapter 2).

CIE has always been an interdisciplinary field of study. This means that theories and methods are applied from various disciplines, following their changes over the twentieth and twenty-first centuries. CIE moved from the study of similarities and differences to the study of the implications of and the demand for education as an instrument of social, economic, and political development. In an attempt to show education's role in nation-building and economic prosperity, CIE used concepts and research methods from the social sciences: sociology, for studying social impacts of education on nation-building and political participation; economics for showing schooling effects on personal and national transformations, as nations moved from traditional subsistence food production and extraction of natural resources for the empires that occupied so much of the globe, into industrial agriculture, commerce, and services, generating new sectors, businesses, and jobs requiring new skills for the great movement of people, goods, culture, and technologies around the world.

International Comparisons of Education

Marc-Antoine Jullien, the "ancestor" of CIE, already in 1816 and 1817, published five articles outlining a method for investigating education in different countries. He suggested using standardized questionnaires to collect data and displaying findings in comprehensive tables to make differences and similarities apparent. Jullien's ambition for this new field to be an "almost-science" that considers factors outside the school to understand education was vigorously embraced in the twentieth century. Making systematic comparisons between education in different lands became the way to study education in the context of local (and thereafter global) social, political, economic, and cultural changes throughout the twentieth century.

Fraser and Brickman (1968) defined CIE as the analysis of education systems and problems of social, political, economic, cultural, ideological, and other societal and national dimensions, toward understanding the factors underlying similarities and differences in education in various countries. Comparative and international research involves the study of patterns and processes across two or more research situations, countries, or cases. The question is whether the characteristics of two or more elementary parts, two or more relationships, or two or more patterns can be said to differ or to be the same. Traditional comparative inquiry emphasized studying the interrelationships between the elementary parts (which are assumed to be interdependent within the whole), using two different strategies:

Providing an account of wholes and the need to describe holistic qualities
Dividing into parts, comparing, and examining the characteristics of an elementary part in two or more situations

These strategies reflect an orthodox or traditional view of CIE and distinguish between its two primary purposes:

Interpretive: historical, philosophical, qualitative
Analytic: data-generating, empirical, positivist, quantitative

International comparisons in education have been shaped by nationalist (and thus potentially imperialist) and religious (and consequently missionary) motives from the time of Julien to the present. The concept of a citizen who was to be educated so that he (not yet she) could participate as a loyal citizen of the nation-state arose in the aftermath of the French Revolution. This model gradually spread throughout Europe, where territories began adopting national constitutions that were usually followed quickly by new schooling laws and curricula aimed at implementing the established social order (Tröhler 2023). The newly independent nations arising after the Second World War provided opportunities for comparativists to work for development agencies and donor organizations and to advise newly formed governments on planning education systems. The outcomes were studied, including economic development, a new social order following liberation from colonialism, and the efforts to establish and grow citizens loyal to the new nation. The idea that economic competitiveness depended on education led to the study of how to teach citizens reading and writing and provide schooling to children, the first liberated generation. Development education's first objective was to achieve universal elementary education where all relevant age groups completed six to eight years of primary schooling and then moved on to increase participation in post-primary education; those students' outcomes were used to statistically analyze economic change and correlate "stages of development" to schooling attainment by grade level.

In this environment, research questioned not only which nation had the better (however that was defined) school system compared to others, but who and how to make comparisons among national systems to show how attainment of education is an agent of national and economic change. Such studies were done, and CIE was taught at some universities and research centers as early as the end of the nineteenth century in the UK, Germany, and the United States. As we will see, the most significant change to CIE as a disciplinary field came after the Second World War.

For about fifty years there has been an ongoing debate about whether "comparative education" and "international education" are one or two fields of study. For historical reasons, such as at the University of London's Institute of Education, these two program components and research projects have, until recently, been separated. CIEs added the "international" designation in the 1950s when work and research in the field flourished under developmentalism (see Chapter 2). Establishing Western-type education was supported by national aid agencies in the United States, the UK, Canada, and the Nordic countries, as well as international aid agencies, granting funding to university comparativists for education planning, policy, and assessment on behalf of agencies and foundations. CIE has always been *international* as it refers to scholarship studying education through international perspectives. Now, in the new millennium, topics that previously were at the margins, such as study abroad, global education, and international students coming with funding from their government or the host country. (For instance, the Soviet Union funded international students to study at USSR institutions, starting in the 1950s.) Now more than ever, comparative and international inquiry and practice moved to the center of education studies.

1945 to the 1960s

The years after the Second World War became the *formative years* of establishing CIE as the international study of schools or departments of education. What secured CIE's position in mainstream education research was its embrace of modernization in social thought (see Chapter 2). Throughout the Second World War many nations became independent, education became a matter of national development, and schools became public institutions free from the hands of religion and colonial powers. Colonial institutions continued to assist in rebuilding, and many private schools and universities became nationalized. As large a project as a national schooling system was a massive undertaking, beyond the capacity of many newly independent nations. Funding came from governmental agencies—such as the International Cooperation Agency, the predecessor to the US Agency for International Development (USAID), Department for International Development (DFID) and (DFIAD) and CIDA Canadian International

Development agency (closed at 2013), and international organizations such as the World Bank (established in 1944 for the reconstruction of Europe), Asia development bank (established in 1966)—and foundations like Ford, Carnegie, and Rockefeller, who had been funding education initiatives even before the war. After the war, with so many countries establishing independence, grants were given to plan education systems and open them to all. As the State department or UK development office did not have experts of their own, CIE professors were called upon to advise, help plan, develop, and research education in Africa, Latin American, and the Pacific (see Chapter 4).

Colonization has remained powerful throughout those years and down to the present, in both education systems and other civic organizations. Development projects ensured constant comparison with the models and the analytical frameworks used to understand education in the West; education planning remains closely identified with the patterns established under colonialism. When the structure and organization of schools reflects a "transferred" foreign model, this necessarily impacts the nature of education processes and outcomes. In most of the world, education policy and practices invoke comparison and contextualization in Western terms. Neocolonialism (see more in Chapter 2) does not involve direct political control. It leaves substantial leeway to the developing country; however, some aspects of domination by the advanced nation over the developing country are evident during this period, from the standpoint of today. "Neocolonialism is partly a planned policy of advanced nations to maintain their influence in countries, but it is also simply a continuation of past practices" (Altbach 1971: 237). This was specifically so in large education systems where the structure was not changed, as in India, where achievement at levels of education continues to be named with British terminology. From its inception to today, CIE has been entangled with the geopolitics of international organizations, national organizations, NGOs (non-governmental organizations), and private foundations, all working on nation-state building.

Textbooks and Institutions

Two newly emerging learning centers in North America at that time, Columbia and New York Universities, took a positivist view of conducting empirical comparative research on education's contribution to social and economic change, holding out the promise of putting CIE on an objective footing. What facilitated CIE's "objective" learning were the courses that students took in sociology and economics that were just then adopting quantitative methods to study social factors. CIE joined their quest to do "scientific" research on education and compare national achievements. While CIE was taught to more and more students in this period, there were no new textbooks, so texts by earlier twentieth-century pioneers were published and republished. Nicholas Hans's *Comparative Education: A Study of Educational Factors and Traditions* (3rd edn, 1958) was translated into Italian, Japanese, Portuguese, and Spanish. Isaac Kandel's *New Era in Education: A Comparative Study* was published in 1954, 1955, 1957, 1961, and digitized in 2006. George F. Kneller (1963) was translated into German in 2016. Comparativists adopted methods of functionalist sociology that gained prominence in the works of nineteenth-century sociologists who viewed societies as organisms, a complex system of interrelated parts that work together to promote stability and solidarity. Another example of scholars who advocated a scientific CIE in their research and textbooks are Noah and Eckstein (1969).

In Europe, the influence of the Frankfurt School's focus on cultural sociohistorical studies became evident in CIE. A tradition practiced and still influencing contemporary CIE is a large group of comparativists including Jürgen Schriewer (1992) at Humboldt-Universität zu Berlin. Trained as a historian, he and his colleagues produced many longitudinal international education studies. In addition to his vision of historical-comparative studies, he worked on delineating an alternative approach to comparative analysis. This approach adequately accounts for the complex causal relationships characteristic of macro-social configurations and the irrevocably historical nature of the social world (Streck et al. 2019).

In Britain, Brian Holmes (1981) invoked US pragmatic philosopher of education John Dewey's reflective thinking and the work of Austrian/British philosopher of science Karl Popper. Holmes aligned himself with the practice of education policymaking, reaching the conclusion that positivism/scientific methods were not a framework within which he wished to work. Despite the coherence of Holmes's "problem-solving approach" to CIE, other comparativists in the UK, such as Edmund King—editor (1972–1992) of *Comparative Education*, one of the three most influential CIE journals (see Academic Activity, end of this chapter)—objected to the scope of Holmes' perspective. King's own six-country study (1958) had compared Denmark, France, Great Britain, the United States, the Soviet Union, and India, using Hans's (1958) method of "factor and traditions." King revised his 1958 book in future editions; for example, in the 4th edition (1973), he included Japan in his comparison and added chapters on strategies of

CIE and reflections on research, planning, and development, moving from reporting on other systems to how to conduct CIE research in the context of nations' development.

In Japan, the Research Institute of Comparative Education and Culture was established at Kyushu University in 1953 to study Western types of education as part of Japan's massive study of histories, geography, and languages of other parts of the world. They used funding after the Second World War from Germany's Goethe Institute, the UK's British Council, and nations like France to teach their students the discipline of CIE, using Area Studies methods. The US occupation of Japan after the Second World War significantly influenced the education system, including teaching and research. The United States was interested in those Japanese Area Studies scholars studying East Asian countries for strategic reasons during the Cold War. The Area Studies method stresses multidisciplinary approaches to regional studies and the need for deep language and culture knowledge of the people under investigation, overemphasizing national particularities and attending less to the geopolitical context. This method was later criticized as imperialist and was re-novated in the 1990s under new Japanese CIE leadership (Miyoshi and Harootunian 2002).

Since 1949, Chinese CIE has been heavily influenced by political, social, and cultural changes. In the 1950s, the education system's organization and structure, education theories and practices, and even teaching curricula and textbooks were all patterned on the Soviet model. China's close relationship with the Soviet Union abruptly ended in the early 1960s, resulting in radical changes in all aspects of Chinese society, including education. In line with state ideology, Marxism, Leninism, and Maoism were taken as the guiding principles of CIE. Theories and methods in CIE of Western origin were rejected and criticized. Only during the period of recovery from the Cultural Revolution, purging remnants of capitalism, including the academy and traditional societal elements, from 1966 till the death of Mao Zedong in 1976, did academic life and CIE re-emerge (Hayhoe 2007). The Research Society of Foreign Education, later changed to the China Comparative Education Society (CCES), was founded in 1979; with rising membership, they were admitted in 1984 to the World Council of Comparative Education Societies (WCCES) and hosted the 2016 WCCES conference.

The earliest chaired university professorships in CIE were one in London and another in Hamburg, Germany. In the United States, the programs at Teachers College Columbia University and NYU, which had offered a CIE degree as early as 1899, were joined by the Comparative Education Center at the University of Chicago, founded in 1958. Its new director, C. Arnold, was a sociologist, and collaborated with Mary Jean Bowman, an economist, and Philip Foster, who had studied economics, sociology, and anthropology at the London School of Economics. Together, they established a prominent new presence of "comparison" in education. Their students produced one of the most significant early bodies of research emphasizing social scientific applications, in particular, the role of education in economic development (Anderson 1961; Bowman 1969). These universities opened CIE programs as Europe, the UK, and the Far East were still reconstructing after the Second World War and decolonization. Stanford practiced CIE in Latin America and other parts of the world through their program "International Development Education Committee," showcasing CIE as a collective, collaborative study. US public universities followed in the footsteps of those private institutions, including Syracuse University's Center for Development Education, the University of Pittsburgh's International and Development Education Program (IDEP), and centers at other Midwestern public institutions such as Kent State University, University of Michigan, the University of Wisconsin, SUNY Buffalo, and later SUNY Albany.

The names of these centers are revealing. The words "development" and "international" appear in most of their titles. The growth of CIE teaching and research in the United States and of professors' consulting for development agencies attracted students from ministries of education around the world, funded by their own countries or by donor agencies and foundations active in the newly independent countries. Compared to the UK, Europe, and Germany, which were still recovering from the Second World War and the loss of their colonies, the United States and the Soviet Union were actively working to develop education in societies that the imperial powers had formerly colonized.

Increasingly, US institutions took up CIE. Teachers College, Columbia University (TC) was among the first to build CIE. They won two grants to develop education in East Africa. One was an initiative of the Kennedy administration, launched in February 1961 and funded by the International Cooperation Agency (renamed later USAID). The other was a Carnegie Corporation grant to form the Afro-Anglo-American Program in Teacher Education. Teacher education was and still is essential to influencing/changing education systemically (see the Illustration by Thomas at the end of the book). Believing CIE to be a way to promote world democracy and international understanding, TC was doing its part to "win" the so-called Cold War against Communist influence on the newly decolonized nations.

The Cold War

The histories of CIE and the Cold War are inextricably linked. As we have been arguing, the proliferation of programs and their institutional building (see next section) resulted from CIE's becoming connected to the project of economic development following the Second World War; the winners divided the world into two spheres of influence, that of the "West" and that of the "East." The "West," led by the United States and its allies, promoted democracy and capitalism. The Soviet Union was given the Eastern Bloc of Europe, where it promoted communism and economic dependency on the USSR. The war between them was "cold" because its beginning manifested mainly in "soft" power, even as proxy wars between "West" and "East" raged well into the twenty-first century. Education became a powerful weapon in the Cold War between the Western capitalist and the Eastern communist bloc, each giving economic support; funding students' higher degrees; sending food, weapons, and war supplies; and building financial, social, and education systems in countries under their sphere of influence.

In 1960, "international education" was the term used for the sub-field that facilitated the "borrowing" and "transfer" of patterns of education from the so-called developed countries to the newly decolonized, so-called underdeveloped or developing countries. Traveling educators and agency consultants aspired to transfer education patterns and policies from the so-called First World (the West) to the "underdeveloped" countries, the so-called "Third World." Those terms are derogatory now and have been replaced by "The Global South" even as "development" and "developing countries" are still widely used by scholars, as in *Six Decades of Development: The Impact of Structural Adjustment Programs on Education in Developing Countries* (Espinoza and McGinn 2023).

CIE writings from the Cold War period are full of dichotomies between rich/poor, educated/illiterate, capitalism/socialism, imperialism/liberalism, and developed/undeveloped, helping sustain the division of the world. The so-called "First World," capitalist, Western Europe and North America. The so-called "Second World" The Soviet Union and the countries behind the metaphorical expression "Iron Curtain." The political, military, and ideological barrier separated Soviet-controlled Eastern and Central Europe from Western Europe after World War II. The rest, countries in Africa, South Asia and most South America, were called the "Third World"—the so-called "undeveloped" or "underdeveloped." Those terms still come up as Escobar (1995; 2nd ed. 2012) documented. This marks the coloniality of knowledge that produces, disseminates, and funds education patterns congruent with each block's ideology.

Education after Sputnik

For an extended period, the Soviet Union and the United States were regarded as having world-class education systems and served as an orientation for reform in many "developing" countries. The US education system's accomplishments were highly criticized in the "Sputnik era." Sputnik was the first orbital satellite the Soviet Union launched into space in 1957, demonstrating their scientific and technological superiority over the West, further reinforced in 1961 when a Soviet cosmonaut became the first man in space. Sputnik provoked anxiety in the United States about the relative backwardness of its education system, resulting in massive reforms of teaching and learning that emphasized math and sciences in schools, as well as increased federal funding for research and development (R&D) at universities and the setting up of more national research laboratories. The National Aeronautics and Space Administration (NASA), responsible for the US space program, also received a considerable boost in federal funding, some of which was devoted to education programs in engineering and technology.

Analytical Comparative Studies

During the 1960s and early 1970s, CIE experienced a growing interest in education's potential for solving the world's economic and social problems. Throughout the 1960s, *The World Yearbook of Education* selected topics for comparative analysis and commissioned articles to provide education research information worldwide. Topics included teacher education (1963), the growing use of new communication media in education (1964), and questions relating to the so-called "education explosion" (1965). The 1966 *World Yearbook* was devoted to church and state in education, a controversial issue for CIE since religious organizations were involved in colonial education. Considered new in a comparative perspective were sharing research on economics and planning of education (1967), education within the industry (1968), examination systems (1969), urban education (1970), and higher education (1971). These volumes took up themes based on substantial research not previously analyzed in CIE, inspiring further research.

While all the above topics continued to be necessary to CIE in this era, *The World Yearbook of Education* was no longer the only source of analytical comparative studies. Up to the 1960s, international agencies such as UNESCO, the International Bureau of Education (IBE) in Geneva, and the Council of Europe had been collecting scholarship on school systems, using models derived from the United Nations Declaration of Universal Rights (1948) and European–North American education models. The IBE *International Year Books* brought together statements by member governments about the aims of policy, the present state of their school systems, and trends in their development; some of those were detailed and highly political. UNESCO, meanwhile, had built up statistical data and, in a series of *World Surveys of Education,* had collected systematic information about the school systems of member states. Introductory articles described development trends in primary, secondary, and higher education and administrative systems. The creation in 1961 of the Organization for Economic Co-operation and Development (OECD) brought new dimensions to CIE. One of the main tasks of the OECD was to help member countries adapt education policies and join the so-called "modern world." OECD's early comparative studies of education paid great attention to how education could be regarded as a form of economic investment and how education systems should be allocated financial resources. While at UNESCO human rights took precedence, in this phase of the OECD's work, economists and social scientists dominated the comparative methodology. As described in Chapter 3, the cost-benefit studies and analyses of education as the residual cause of economic growth occupied the attention of CIE research. Both Chapters 2 and 3 explain how theories and methods were developed to show that investment in education would bring both individual and societal economic rewards.

1968—When Everything Happened

The "Prague Spring," on January 5 with the first elected secretary of the party, was brief, as Soviet armed forces invaded and occupied Czechoslovakia in August, reinstituting hard-liner Communist rule.

During the Tet Offensive, January 30–31 of the lunar new year (Tet), North Vietnamese and Viet Cong forces launched attacks on Saigon and key targets in South Vietnam. This surprised the United States; the Vietnam War was the first televised war brought to the TV screens of 56 million homes, so 543 killed in action and 2,547 wounded in one week in February did not go unnoticed.

Students protested the Vietnam War on the campus of Columbia, occupying university buildings. A wave of student activism swept the globe, including mass demonstrations in Poland, West Germany, Mexico City, Paris, Italy, and elsewhere.

On "Bloody Monday," as May 6 is called, students and police clashed in Paris with hundreds injured. The protest was joined by millions of striking French workers and the occupation of universities and factories. France's economy slowed, leading President Charles de Gaulle to dissolve the National Assembly and call for immediate elections.

Robert F. Kennedy announced he would challenge President Johnson for the Democratic nomination on the same day (though it would not be revealed until the following year) that US ground troops killed more than 500 Vietnamese civilians in the "My Lai Massacre."

Martin Luther King Jr., the leader of the US civil rights movement, was assassinated on April 4 in Memphis; his murder sparked rioting in dozens of cities across the United States.

Robert F. Kennedy was assassinated the night the California primary put him in reach of the Democratic presidential nomination.

President Johnson, criticized for his handling of the war, announced he was not running for president. His vice president, Hubert Humphrey, ran and lost to Nixon.

The 1968 democratic convention in Chicago was met by thousands of students, antiwar activists, and other demonstrators; TV cameras captured the violent police response, "the revolution will be televised."

This period was especially active in development education, as the events of 1968 confirmed what CIE already believed: that education is important, and institutes of higher education do not just form opinions, but students also die for them. On May 2, 1970, the Ohio National Guard killing four and wounding nine unarmed Kent State University students at an antiwar protest brought the point home.

1970s to 1980

Theoretical and political shifts in the late 1960s and 1970s called into question the significance of concepts like modernization, which we now see as "meta-theory" or "master narrative," all-encompassing for understanding the reality of newly independent countries worldwide. Other theories, like dependency, inequality, World-Systems theories, Marxism, and neo-Marxism (all elaborated in Chapter 2), shifted research focus in many fields, including CIE. Although the comparative focus was still prominent on economic development, more researchers and practitioners working with local governments and non-governmental organizations (NGOs) began to take local context into consideration. This context in the newly independent nations throughout Africa was not well known in the US academy outside anthropology. Hence the United States during the Second World War found itself with no experts that understood or spoke the languages of islands in the Pacific. The US State department invested in Area Studies at US universities; this funding moved to the Department of Education in 1980 to move languages, geography, and culture to a less political undertaking. In the 2000s with wars in Iraq and Afghanistan, the 2020s support for languages acquisition are again a matter of national security.

The 1970s unofficially started in 1968, when worldwide events were formative for the next two decades. As geopolitical events closely influence universities and their students, it is worthwhile to read them all (Kurlansky 2003). We will highlight a few that followed the civil unrest in Eastern Europe, protesting the Vietnam War around the world, and the civil rights movement, all greatly influencing development education.

Education Attainment and "Stages of Development"

The World Bank, a significant actor in funding education for economic development, followed their economists, Hollis Chenery and Moises Syrquin, who in 1975 defined a pattern of development as a systematic variation in any significant aspect of the economic or social structure associated with a rising level of income or another index of development. This is how we ended up with stages of economic development as measured by change in the size of a country's economy over a period, as measured by the total production of goods and services, or "Gross Domestic Product" (GDP). Initially, economic activities and jobs were based in the agricultural sector, a phase US State Department economist Walt Rostow called "pre-takeoff" (1960). In "take-off," the share of agriculture in GDP decreases as employment shifts towards industry, especially manufacturing. The move to industrialization, knowledge society, and technological advancement is the "post-take-off" stage. Non-economic institutions such as social institutions and education must also be mobilized, according to Rostow (an economist at US State Department), to move to a higher economic developmental stage.

Don Adams and his students at the University of Pittsburgh statistically analyzed newly industrialized countries' total student enrollment levels to map these three stages of economic development as measured by GDP, showing causal relations by regression analysis. As Figure 1 shows, they found that primary education levels have the highest enrollment level during the economic "pre-takeoff." Enrollment ratios at secondary schooling rise during economic "take-off" while post-secondary and tertiary education vary at "post-take-off." Higher education is the most expensive level for national investment, boosting research and technology. From what we know today, Korea and Brazil are excellent comparisons, even though their economies are of very different sizes. In the mid-1970s, they were at almost the same degrees of industrialization and per capita income levels. But in 1980 Brazil only had 10 percent of the relevant age group attending higher education, while Korea already had 37 percent; the next twenty years showed the difference as Brazil's economy stagnated for twenty years, with political, social, and financial crises affecting education while Korea continues to grow, moving from industry to a knowledge economy. From 2000 to 2012, Brazil's annual GDP growth rate averaged over 5 percent, making it one of the world's fastest-growing economies; when Brazil was the world's sixth-largest economy, they invested in development education, with funding for higher education and paid for a year abroad for 100,000 students. The economic growth didn't last but the concern with higher education did continue. In 2024, in collaboration with UNESCO, Brazil launched "CRES+5" expansion and improvement of higher education in Latin America and the Caribbean, highlighting the importance of universities and federal institutes of education in supporting democracy, civic political and economic development.

As that study showed, "developing" countries between the 1960s and 1980s, such as South Korea, Thailand, and Singapore, achieved universal elementary schooling, over 50 percent secondary enrollment, and about 20 to 30 percent higher education enrollment. Such correlation data reinforced the assumption that higher participation in education attainments of the appropriate age group increases national economic development as measured by GNP.

UNESCO (2011) notes that each extra year of a mother's schooling reduces the probability of infant mortality by 5 to 10 percent, and an extra year of female schooling reduces fertility rates by 10 percent. In sub-Saharan

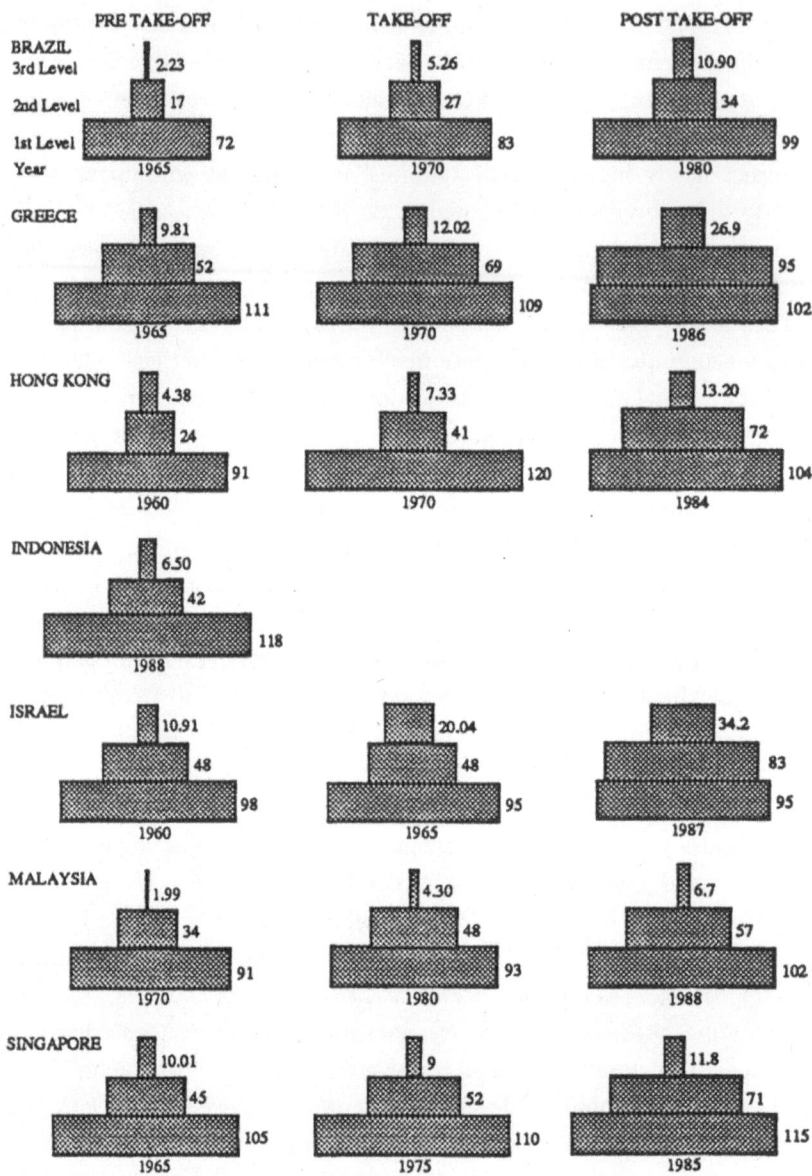

Figure 1 Total Enrolment Rations by Levels and Stages of Development (Adams and Gottlieb, 2nd edition 2018, part of pp. 162–3). Reprinted with permission from Routledge, London.

Africa, an estimated 1.8 million children's lives could have been saved in 2008 if their mothers had at least a secondary education. In this context, the CIE literature generally offered popular explanations of education's role in development. Modernization theory posits that educated people are more often assigned roles necessary to build and run complex new economic, political, and social institutions. As we will see in Chapter 2, "modern society" is characterized by clearly identifiable specific roles acquired through achievement criteria (e.g., level of education) and oriented toward universalistic norms. Modernization in both its social and individual dimensions is, so the theory claims, powerfully influenced by education, i.e., Western education. The spread of Western education was thought, for many years, to hold the key to economic development, as it was considered to teach the appropriate value orientations for joining the global economy, i.e., socialization to a rational society and normative preparation for political elites. This is how Western education came to hold the key to prepare people for an advanced industrial and technological society's norms, commitments, and obligations (Meyer et al. 1975).

1980s to 2000

Rethinking Developmentalism

Beginning in the early 1980s, theories of development education that went hand in hand with modernization theory and calculation of "human capital" (how much investing in one's education produces economic returns) have come under greater scrutiny. The already rich countries enjoyed economic growth, while Africa was still the poorest part of the world in 1980. The continent with the youngest population in the world, Africa, is still impoverished, and per capita income declined over the 1980–2002 period. Latin America, too, has experienced little economic growth since 1980. There was also the significant social and economic transition of Eastern Europe following total collapse due to economic stagnation and the overextension of the military of the Soviet Union in 1991.

Until the fall of the wall that separated West and East Berlin after the Second World War, Hans-Georg Hofmann, president of East Germany's GDR Comparative Education Society, argued that comparison should only be exclusively applied for "intra-system" comparison, that is, for comparison with other socialist countries and particularly with the Soviet Union, as having attained the highest level on the socialist path of development. In the 1990s the Eastern bloc acknowledged that the focus of interest was shifting to new education models, in particular the achievements of systems such as those of Japan, France, and Austria, but also Czechoslovakia, the People's Republic of Korea, and Cuba (Mitter 1992).

Once the Soviet "union" collapsed, symbolized by the fall of the Berlin Wall in 1989, the fifteen constituent USSR republics declared independence. Most adopted more liberal political systems and were in a deep economic crisis associated with a significant transformation from industry to services, as they returned to native languages and reconstituted past cultures. While the newly independent East European countries wanted to democratize their systems, education components like retraining teachers, creating new curricula and textbooks, and establishing administrative patterns took time (Kelly 2020). In the 2000s, CIE research showed that post-socialist patterns have not changed much.

South Asia at this time achieved high economic growth rates, though not as high as China's. India achieved average per capita growth as high as 3.5 percent per year, and even higher since the mid-1990s. Southeast Asian countries like Indonesia had relatively rapid economic growth. They adopted development education with greater involvement of CIE consulates with funding from USAID. South Korea's education system, modeled on the United States, was ahead at all levels and had an impressive average economic yearly growth rate of 5.9 percent between 1980 and 2002.

Quality of education rather than access and development of post-secondary education became significant issues from the 1980s on. OECD changed its mission along with UNESCO and other agencies with development education agendas when, in the mid-1960s, they started to collect national statistics.

Statistical methods and quantitative research dominate large-scale achievement comparisons among nation-states' education systems. The development of complex statistical analysis increasingly led comparativists to gather a vast amount of data to compare education outcomes across countries, leading to the advancement of international testing. Countries collect data for the Program for International Student Achievement (PISA), Trends in International Mathematics and Science Study (TIMSS), and Progress in International Reading Literacy Study (PIRLS) to publish cross-country comparisons. As these tests have gained influence worldwide, they influence national school systems' planning, curricula, and funding. They also attract criticism for developing international education indicators that promote comparing national education achievement without contextualization (see Chapter 3).

"Education for All"

Further evidence of CIE's role in geopolitics was the worldwide campaign for education initiated by international bodies such as the World Bank; US, UK, and Nordic AID agencies; and the United Nations, among others. In 1948, Article 26 of the UN's Universal Declaration of Human Rights stated that "Everyone has the right to education." For more than seventy years, UNESCO had advocated for more and better education, and universal primary education was high on the agenda of all postcolonial countries throughout the 1970s. The UN's declaration of the right to "education for all" in 1990 represents a breakthrough in national and international support for primary education, specifically for girls. The documents signed in the 1990s at the Fourth World Conference on Women (1995) identified the education disparity between boys and girls. In addition, the internal dynamics of the education system, with its upward pressure for growth, created increasing demand for secondary and higher education. This self-generating demand was further legitimated by policies anticipating future labor needs. The special needs for high-level peoplepower (then called "manpower") were apparent in all newly industrialized countries as both industrial and knowledge economies increasingly engaged in high-technology development and application. Currently, UN Sustainable Development Goal number 4 identifies inclusive and equitable quality education for all as a goal, and all 191 UN member states agreed to work toward achieving it by 2030.

"Education for all" establishes the importance of education globally and locally as a universal social good. Still, it does not set a threshold for inclusion, as in some countries, students with disability, for instance, are not included. In some countries (e.g., Saudi Arabia), cultural prohibitions prevent boys and girls from studying together beyond preschool (Aljabreen 2017). The Australian state of Victoria has enacted a policy of "education for all" as a solution to marginalization of students who are "at risk" or "disengaged." This identification has set up a false distinction between a supposedly problematic minority needing "education for all" versus a "normal" majority that is already included (te Riele 2006).

The Long 1990s

The 1990s were "longer" because so many major events took place between the dismantling of the Soviet Union (end of the Cold War) and the beginning of the War on Terror after September 11, 2001, see below. The 1990s began with the fall of the Berlin Wall in 1989 and the dismantling of the Soviet Union in 1991, this ended the so-called Cold WarFor the next ten years, Western Europe and the United States concentrated on the educational development of the liberated state from Soviet communism The joining of so many economies to capitalist global trade was named "the new global order." More concretely, this interaction affects and is reflected in the education system, the labor market, migration, the mass media, micro- and macro-power, gender, ethnicity, and social class. Globalization has affected many transformations in education and CIE research and practices (Stromquist 1995).

Globalization

The end of the Cold War in the early 1990s transformed the world into a new global order fueled by rapid technological transformations, with faster movement of goods, people, and culture, including education. "Globalization" describes economic developments at the world level. The concept of globalization has proved helpful in exploring world-level processes behind the spread of Western education (see Chapter 3) and the exchange of education ideas and practices from one system to another. Increased mobility across borders has led to an unprecedented rise in international students from China, Korea, India, and other Global South countries attending English-speaking universities, as well as enhanced scholarly exchanges and collaborative research.

CIE practice and research were most affected by a worldwide economic restructuring of science, technology, and culture. Computer and software technologies increased labor productivity worldwide and redefined relations among nations and their education systems. This new global economy, late capitalism, has multiplied fluid, flexible markets and lines of power and decision-making. Education needed to adjust, from producing a disciplined, reliable workforce to preparing workers to quickly acquire new skills. Education, formerly considered a vehicle for social transformation, shifted to serving the needs of productivity in the globalized economy. For example, African countries increasingly turned to international funding that came with ideas, values, and reform directives on how education should be managed and targeted. This form of globalization integrated African political economies into a world-system (see Chapter 2) on terms set outside the continent.

CIE attention to education systems has increasingly focused on efficiency, quality, and school "improvement" (Samoff and Stromquist 2001). This coercive process universalizes a particular idea of education, placing it in the service of social and economic development that distributes power and resources according to criteria that privilege a small minority at the expense and through the exploitation of a majority. Through education and social relationships, populations are socialized into thinking that the order is normal and natural and that there is no alternative (Freire 1996).

Multinational institutions involved in education funding, including the World Bank, the United Nations Development Programs, and the Asian Development Bank (ADB), among others, directly address education as a tool for economic growth and poverty reduction. Comparatists who work for those agencies and banks and university professors who consult for those organizations research the issue. This puts CIE research at the center of multinational funding agencies' decision-making in countries that need it most. UNESCO, World Bank, and ADB and the data they collect are used to shape education policy and practice by providing loans only for bank-specified programs, establishing conditions that must be met before loans can be implemented, hiring Western consultants to plan and execute projects, overseeing training and implementing education policies at approved donor agencies programs, organizing exchange and "what works" in various countries, and using sponsored research to justify recommendations for specific programs (Samoff and Stromquist 2001). Globalization and education research and development loans and policies conform with the neoliberal movement that reduced the state's power in favor of free markets, privatization, and deregulation of public services such as electric power and water supplies, housing, health, and education, among others.

Neoliberalism

The growing power of "the market," spread worldwide through globalization, changed not just the economy but all other spheres of society as well. Rooted in a belief that markets are the most efficient mode for decision-making and the optimal way to promote human welfare, neoliberal policies seek to reduce the state's role in market regulation, while globalization promotes free-trade agreements, lowering barriers to the movement of goods, labor, people, and cultural products. Neoliberalism favors property rights, free-market and choice policies, privatization, and deregulation of services, including education.

Neoliberal education reform programs use international comparative student assessments to inform policy, borrowing from the more successful performers to improve less successful models. The primary vehicle for mobilizing education towards economic purposes has been marketization. This has led to increased individualization and competition, replacing the equal treatment through one-size-fits-all approaches that dominated previously. Political alignment with European Union (EU) quality standards has been critical to the Baltic States and others aspiring to join the EU, spurring reforms in school structures and pedagogy. In education, the term "neoliberalism" has become an identifier of market-oriented policies' responsibility for a wide range of socio-political reforms based on economic outlooks. "Neoliberalist" is strongly pejorative in critical scholarship examining education models driven by free-market policies (Venugopal 2015).

Education has traditionally been regarded as a common good and a site of local control. Under neoliberal governance, education policies and reforms have weakened the long trend toward expanding and universalizing education participation. Under neoliberal education policies, school boards become appointed leadership rather than elected representatives, and district public schools in the United States, for example, are replaced by charter and private schools. School resources, such as curricula, testing, and even the training of teachers, are increasingly provided by vendors or projects, as in the case of Teach for All (see Thomas' Illustration in this volume) Neoliberalism frames the purpose of education in terms of investments made in the development of students' "human capital" (see Chapter 2). The value of education is determined relative to students' prospects for future earnings. This narrowed conception of education's purpose raises important questions about the relationship between schools, public institutions, and state governance, all topics researched by CIE.

Neoliberalism has implications for CIE on a global scale, with multiple contested meanings that result in serious problems when used as an explanatory device for education policy planning and reforms. While neoliberalism first emerged as state policy in Chile in 1973, when a

CIA-backed coup against the socialist government of Salvador Allende brought General Pinochet to power, it was most notably adopted by Deng Xiaoping for the Chinese economy in 1978–80; in Great Britain by Prime Minister Margaret Thatcher, 1979–90; and by US president Ronald Reagan, 1981–89. It has traveled worldwide as a neocolonialist strategy, particularly to the former Soviet Union States and the Global South, through international agencies' aid for economic and public services (Connell and Dados 2014).

In the course of its global reach, neoliberalism has morphed and shifted, adapting itself to local histories, politics, cultures, and institutions and taking on a hybrid, localized nature, giving rise to variations from place to place: social democratic versions in Canada, Australia, New Zealand, and Germany; the "neoliberal developmental state" in Singapore; and a version in the United States are examples of humanist ideals being co-opted by and entangled with neoliberalism. Apart from these spatial variations, neoliberalism has also shifted within different locales over time, so varieties of neoliberalism have been enacted in various ways since the 1970s, involving diverse networks of actors whose purposes differed concerning the role of education in social restructuring (Apple 1996). Despite this recognition of its multiplicity and complexity, references to "neoliberalism" in the literature on education tend to imply "globalized" despite the evidence of local variations, timely shifts, diverse motives, and the lack of agreement concerning all of its ramifications.

Neoliberal education reforms are legitimated, disseminated, sometimes enforced, and indeed sometimes bundled and sold together with an aid package by powerful and persuasive agents and organizations such as the OECD, the World Bank, the World Trade Organization, the International Finance Corporation, the EU, and Brazil, Russia, India, China, and South Africa (BRICS). Together with market-leaning think tanks, consultancies and planning entrepreneurs, these organizations set education targets to be achieved. Such "benchmarks" are borrowed from other education systems: a good example is the World Bank funding to develop early childhood education in Ethiopia, a country with a tradition of children following their mothers in fieldwork or tending cattle. Even urban parents there use domestic help rather than sending young children to private early childhood institutions. The World Bank's targets for Ethiopia are not achievable, as only 27 percent (2016) of rural children aged seven to twelve years old complete six years of primary education. Referring to the above section on "stages of development" and its high correlation to education level attainment, Ethiopia is reported to have only 5 percent participation in post-secondary education (2016). This rate is reported for the age group fifteen to twenty-four, using Western standards for students' age of attendance, whereas in law-income countries, or those with mandatory army services, the average age of undergraduate students is twenty-seven years. One other observation about the Ethiopian data: It is not reported by the Ministry of Education but by FHI360, a US non-profit supported by grants from USAID or other donor agencies to do such studies in countries without capacity, rather than giving the fund to the country to develop analytical capacity.

Another example is education in Mozambique. In the late 1980s, when the funding from the Soviet bloc ended, they started implementing structural adjustment policies imposed by the IMF. This paved the way for neoliberal economic policies. Liberalization of education in Mozambique since the 1990s ushered in private schooling for emerging middle-class families. As in the larger national economy, education became an area of investment from foreign institutions. Current assessments are that, despite significantly expanded access to primary education since 1975, there is a "learning crisis" or "schooling without learning" and "weak state capacity" due to dependence on external aid, advisors and implementers, and limited community involvement in schools (Chisholm and Chissale 2024) (see more in Chapter 4).

The 2000s

Robert Cowen acknowledged in 2000 the methodological and epistemological plurality of CIE—i.e., how the field is practiced and what counts as knowledge in it—and suggested the term "comparative educations" (335) in the plural to signal that contemporary CIE engages with a range of topics, phenomena, and perspectives. It encompasses research and reflection on how education interacts with nationalism, national character, population trends, economic and cultural dependency, neo- and postcolonialism, and a range of international topics the education discipline is interested in developing and researching.

"War on Terror" is what was termed the US policy in response to September 11, 2001. The coordinated terrorist attacks involving four hijacked airlines destroyed the World Trade Center in New York City, damaged the Pentagon in Washington DC, and crashed a passenger jet in Pennsylvania, causing thousands of deaths. These events changed forever the idea of social cohesion and "education for all" as an equalizer for societies and ushered in the stronghold of globalization and neoliberalism enforced by grants and funding development education. The legacy of Western colonialism included the arbitrary division of former colonies into unstable and warring nations (Lebanon Syria and Iraq are good examples) leading to a series of violent conflicts in the Middle East, US coalitions invading Iraq, Afghanistan, Syrian civil war since 2011 backed up by Iran and Russia, civil war in Yemen since 2014 and Sudan since 2023, and the Sahel regions of Africa witnessed a wave of coups d'état in seven countries, escalating conflict and violence, food insecurity, and people displacement. In 2023, more than 240 million children and adolescents worldwide had their education disrupted by war and violent conflict. While conflicts and inequalities have unfolded around the world, the power of Western education to eradicate poverty has increasingly been called into question, making room for globalization of economics, technology, culture, and politics.

In the 2000s, CIE is changing, taking what we describe in the next chapter as the "turn" in the social sciences from scientific to interpretive methods involving collaboration, recognition of how knowledge is produced, and awareness of the rhetorical devices used to build education ties to economic development, as well as lack of contextualizing of the "global" to the "local" (see Chapter 4). This turn follows the humanities' use of linguistic and interpretive methods to understand its "master narratives" which all encompass theories such as modernity and developmentalism. Many of the "post" theories, the ones that come after, like postmodernism, poststructuralism, postcolonialism, and post-socialism, were explored earlier but came into CIE disciplinary focus in the 2000s. They have challenged CIE to stop operating within meta-narratives of progress, modern urban life, education's role in an endlessly developing economy, and the subordination of traditional ways of knowing to modern ones.

Anglophone production of CIE knowledge was and is based at universities and organizations shaped by individuals who were both teachers and consultants in many postcolonial countries receiving funding from governments, banks, and organizations (see Chapter 4). There were comparativists that did research in former colonies and saw education as cultural imperialism, like Gail Kelly's work in West Africa already in the 1970s (1979). In the 2000s, comparativists intensified the debate over how development education is entangled with neocolonialism, neo- and sub-imperialism, racial disparities, exclusion of immigrant minorities, and an education-to-prison pipeline of students that cannot be mainstreamed (Bodkin-Andrews and Carlson 2014).

International Education

When "international" was added to "comparative education," it meant that research and planning were done internationally in the context of other countries. But the question of international students studying abroad has existed at the margins of CIE. In the postwar period, the countries that implemented US models of education, such as the Philippines, Japan, Korea, and Indonesia, sent the most international students to the United States, the UK, and Australia for further education. Sending the best undergraduates to get higher degrees in Russia, the United States, or Europe was one of the "development" strategies each political bloc took after the Second World War, with public funding for this cross-border education. In the 2000s, many new topics addressing the economic and cultural benefits of students' moving and learning abroad are being explored.

In the context of globalization, international education has moved closer to the center of education research in general, so CIE finds itself in the mix of other "international" fields of study like internationalization of higher education, international schools, international research on teaching and teacher education, and internationalization of K-12 education—all in the context of the global political, economic, social, and cultural shifts of the 2000s. The term "international education"—which has been part of CIE since the 1960s—has moved closer to the center of education research in general, no longer just at the conferences and journals of CIE. Of course, the term is used in multiple ways throughout the world. In 2023, the American Council on Education found that colleges and universities were under increasing pressure to demonstrate that their research was international. University research offices with diminishing internal funding tend to support international collaboration and grant writing with partners abroad. In the 2000s, global economic forces were driving the practices of international education, from the pressure to recruit international students to bolster declining state support for higher education worldwide to the growing interest in recruiting students from other countries so that Chinese students do not make up most of the non-domestic student body.

In the twenty-first century, most of the international students in the United States, UK, and Australia come from China and India. Countries like South Korea, Indonesia, and Brazil also established mobility programs for their students. For example, the Brazil Scientific Mobility Program (BSMP), a government initiative, has provided 100,000 one-year university scholarships; this stands to reason, as during Brazil's economic "take-off" in 1980 only 10 percent participated in higher education. These students are the future of the Global South. They return to their home countries to become the architects, planners, and managers of their education systems, or they stay in the West and bring diversity to industry and academia. In Europe, students take advantage of the Bologna Process, a series of agreements among European countries allowing all students to study at member institutions in other countries. As multinational companies employ more and more graduates, the education market has expanded from 2 million international students in 2000 to 6.4 million in 2021. In Australia international students account for 26 percent of the country's student population. Universities UK report that the economic benefit of international students rose from £31.3bn to £41.9bn between 2018/19 and 2021/22. International students in Glasgow, London, Sheffield, Nottingham, and Newcastle are among those that deliver the greatest financial contributions. In 2019, 500,000 international students generated 5 percent of the total budget for all higher education, UK students pay or get stipends for £9,535 tuition fees, which increased by three percent, in August 2025. The British Council, states that international undergraduate tuition fees vary from £11,400 to £38,000, and "A UK education opens doors, wherever you go in the world." While CIE scholars do investigate the economic impact of international students, they also study the circulation of people and culture, as well as the influence of international students on the whole system. Though students are not just a source of revenue, they also contribute to the economy and culture of the town, city, or region, and many seek temporary or permanent work in the country where they study.

Other topics explored by CIE include comparing the experiences of international students with those of local students and studying the policies and education economics of host countries. CIE scholars compare studying at offshore campuses (for example, Australian universities' branch campuses in South Africa, NYU's branch in Saudi Arabia, or the University of Michigan's in Shanghai). Comparing the curriculum of those universities' branches to that of their home campuses, they tested the contention that US or Australian university branches are selling a lesser degree in other countries. Scholars found that they operate by employing local instructors who teach in regional languages, so the curriculum is different. In addition to providing the capacity to accommodate many more students, the Northern universities' branch campuses, compared to universities in the Global South, also "have a prestige and power—due to their domination of the curriculum and of scientific discourse—that is rarely questioned in the contemporary academic marketplace" (Altbach 2004: 20). See the Illustration by Yao and George-Mwangi at the end of this book.

Life Matters in Development Education

The aftereffects of the 2021–2023 global pandemic, worldwide demonstrations for Black Lives Matter, and the ongoing threat of environmental degradation all cast new light on CIE studies as we scrutinize education's contribution to "endless exponential economic growth" (Dhara and Singh 2021). Black Lives Matter protests around the world helped focus attention on the erasure of the topic of racism from studies of the development of education and education's role in poverty, policing, and criminalization of Black and brown students (Strong et al. 2023). Early CIE research and postcolonial theories can help us understand the continuity of education's racialized exclusions in the liberated colonies and in schooling under the Anglophone and European systems, but as of 2025 in the United States and around the world there is a struggle over the meaning of race and the willingness to talk about it in public discourse and in academic research. Thinking of race as a defunct social category consigned to the past, as if contemporary societies are "post-racial." The contributors of *The Bloomsbury Handbook of Theory in Comparative and International Education* (jules et al. 2021) did not write as if social analyses should be "color-blind." They suggest an analytic focus on racial formations and racialization, one that will address the potential blind-spot of postcolonial theory which can often center around East/West or North/South distinctions (386). Researchers in CIE ought to pay greater attention to matters of race and racism in education comparisons.

Understanding the relative success or failure of minority students' social adjustment and academic performance is to recognize that there are different types of minority groups—autonomous, immigrant, involuntary, or caste-like, or what is now called indigenized. Ogbu (1990) found that a denial of equal opportunity in the job market has been the experience of generations of Black people and other minorities, whose education qualifications were not rewarded with positions and wages commensurate with their training and ability. This discouraged minorities from investing their time and effort into pursuing education. Minorities have also been harmed by the prevention of equal access to good education.

Research in the early 2000s into the US "school-to-prison pipeline" moved CIE scholarship to examine the relationship between school discipline and increased school failure of students deemed different—Black, brown, indigenous, refugee, queer, trans, or disabled—who dropped out and tended to experience higher rates of incarceration. Scholars compared involuntary minorities and indigenous students in the United States, Canada, Australia, New Zealand, and South Africa to study how race, politics, and other social institutions intersect with schooling to exclude people (Ogbu 1990). Findings include inadequate and unequal rewards for education to be part of the institutionalized structure of discrimination. Western types of education seem to be incapable of eliminating dropouts. These studies found minoritized people using means other than schooling to get ahead under the groups' particular circumstances. Such alternative or "survival" strategies appear to adversely affect their pursuit of Western mainstream education (Durst and Bereményi 2024). As Elizabeth Sumida Huaman (2022: 391) has observed:

> The schooling of Indigenous peoples has historically tended to reflect everyone else's values, standards, and objectives but our own.

In this chapter, we have sought to summarize what can be learned about our disciplinary histories by reflecting on its past in the light of the present, thereby, we hope, enabling students and scholars of CIE to envision and be ready for changes still to come in the future.

Academic Activities—Springboards

Springboard A

Review:
Kandel's selected "*problems of education*" (1933: xviii) were as follows:

- What is the place of private education and of private schools?
- What is the scope of post-elementary or secondary education?
- What should be the curriculum in each type of school
- How are teachers prepared and what is their status?
- How can standards be maintained? What should be the place of examinations?
- Who shall formulate curricula and courses of study?
- What is the meaning of equality of educational opportunity?

Reflect:
Comment on each question from your own experience: How relevant is each question Kandel posed in 1933 to what you know about education today?

Springboard B

Read & Reflect:
Edmund King 1914–2002: After graduating BA and MA, having won three Open Prizes and a graduate research scholarship at the University of Manchester, Edmund King taught Classics in grammar schools in London for ten years before entering university teaching, initially in Extra-Mural Studies at the University of London, then, from 1953, as Lecturer and subsequently Professor in Comparative Education at King's College, University of London, where he remained until his retirement. He was the author or joint author of eight books and many articles and papers, including some for the Council of Europe, OECD, and UNESCO. From 1978 to 1992, he was Editor of *Comparative Education*, of which he had been with A. D. C. Peterson and W. D. Halls, a co-founder in 1964.

Additional Reading: King, Edmund J. (1981), 'A Selected Bibliography', *Compare*, 11 (2): 125–7. https://doi-org.proxy.lib.ohio-state.edu/10.1080/03057928110110202

Reflect:
What can we learn about CIE as an academic field developed by scholars like King's qualifications; see also his books in our reference list.

From reading this chapter and our reference list that includes so many articles published in *Comparative Education*—one of the three major journals of CIE—can you comment on the influence someone like King as the co-editor for fourteen years had on the development of CIE.

Springboard C

What can we learn about the history and practice of CIE from the content of special journal issues devoted to the state of the art of the discipline in a few different eras?

1977—'The State of the Art.' *Comparative Education Review,* 21: 2–3. https://www.journals.uchicago.edu/toc/cer/1977/21/2%2F3
  —'Comparative Education: State and Future Prospects.' *Comparative Education,* 13: 2.

Comment:
What do you think, from what you learned from Chapter 1—is the point of view in those two issues?
  Read:
  The content of each of the above issues.

In the 2010s—(2017), 'Contesting Coloniality: Rethinking Knowledge Production and Circulation in Comparative and International Education', *Comparative Education Review,* 61: S1; (2018), 'Origins and Traditions in Comparative Education', *Comparative Education,* 54: 1.

Reflect:
On those two different CIE in the 2010s: while CER is looking to rethink CIE knowledge production and circulation in 2017 with postcoloniality, **Comparative Education** is looking back to CIE origins and *traditions* in order to look forward. Which of the two is a more attractive way and why?
  What do we learn about the history of Comparative Education from: a) the titles of the articles?; b) who the authors are (easily searched online) and their institution affiliations.

Note: The difference between the 1977 and later issues by the names and affiliations of the contributors.

Higher Education—If this is one of your interests read the content of this special issue: (2022), 'Making Worlds in Research on Higher Education: Different Pathways to the International and Global', *Oxford Review of Education,* 48: 4.

Reflect:
What do we learn about the history of CIE from: a) the titles of the articles?; b) the names, editor and the contributors a (easily searched online) and their institution affiliations.

2

Theories

Comparative and international education (CIE) has seldom originated its own theories. Typically, CIE studies have used theoretical concepts, frameworks, and methods adapted from the social sciences, especially sociology, political science, economics, and anthropology, as they were shaping during the late nineteenth century and continued to undergo fundamental changes, sometimes referred to as "turns," throughout the twentieth and twenty-first centuries. As CIE works within social science, theories and shifts and turns of those theories have influenced how education systems were researched for planned, and policy formation by CIE scholars and donor agencies.

As Martin (2003) has observed, "Many of the most contentious issues between rival research traditions in comparative education evolve around disputes between divergent *ontological* and *epistemological* underpinning" (105). Different worldviews or paradigms, each with their own view of what *is being* in the world (ontology) and what counts as *knowledge about* what is (epistemology).

In this chapter we present a comprehensive review of theories in basic paradigms (worldviews) within which the theories have been developed. One indurating categorizing scheme for these paradigms was elaborated by Burrell and Morgan (1979), by classifying interrelated theoretical assumptions about the nature of being and what knowledge is.

This chapter is organized by a close cover of major theories in four paradigms and "theorizing in the 'post' era," theories that "come-after," working outside, or across, the four social sciences paradigms.

Four Social Science Paradigms and the "Post"

Figure 2 shows Burrell and Morgan's (1979) 2×2 matrix scheme. On the horizontal axis, this matrix distinguishes between *subjective* (individualistic) theories and *objective* (structural) theories. On the vertical axis, it distinguishes between sociologies of *radical change* and sociologies of *regulation* (i.e., maintenance of the *status quo*). The four paradigms are reflected in the quadrants of the matrix:

Functionalist paradigm (objective-regulation): This has been the primary paradigm CIE has developed, as shown in Chapter 1. It assumes rational human action and believes one can understand society behaviors and education phenomenon through hypothesis testing.

Radical structuralist paradigm (objective-radical change): Based on this paradigm, theorists see inherent structural conflicts within society that generate constant change through political and economic crises. This has been the fundamental paradigm of Marxist and socialist theories, influencing alternative development education during the Cold War.

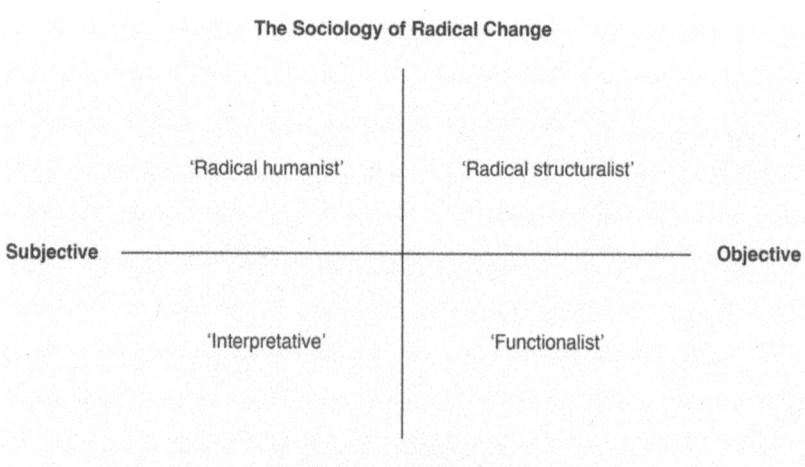

Figure 2 After Burrell and Morgan (1979), four paradigms are represented by the quadrants of a 2×2 matrix scheme.

Radical humanist paradigm (subjective-radical change): Theorists in this paradigm are mainly concerned with releasing social constraints limiting human potential. They see the current dominant ideologies as separating people from their "true selves." It is largely an anti-social organization, so it can be used to justify the desire for revolutionary change.

Interpretive paradigm (subjective regulation): Theories in this paradigm "[seek] to explain the stability of behavior from the individual's viewpoint." Researchers in this paradigm try observing "on-going processes" to better understand individual behavior and the nature of the world in which systems such as education operate (Burrell and Morgan 1979: 34–6).

Theories in the "post" are not just looking ahead but also looking back to the past, when theories have been massively translated from one language to another and theorizing was not limited to a few West European centers. To theorize in the "post" era amounts to theoretical shifts, it involves intervening in existing paradigms through a cross-disciplinary remaking of theory.

There are many theories bearing the "post" prefix, we will summarize the ones used or influencing practices of CIE: *post*-structuralism, *post*-colonialism, *post*-modernism, *post-humanism* and *post*-socialism and intersectionality and affect theory. This especially includes theorists that have explored the aftermath of Western colonialism and the collapse of the Soviet-Union, when CIE was established and practiced within modernization and developmentalism (see following). *Post* and/or *coming-after* signal the twilight of an entire ontological and cultural condition. As Moraru et al. (2002) observed "the world-systemic makeup of theory" (3), conceivable along the lines of cultural world-system (Wallerstein 1990; see below), coincides with the rise of antagonistic models, of *anti-*, *meta-*, or *neo-*alternatives: *neo-* and *anti-*imperialism, *neo-* and *anti-*racism, etc. A vast repertoire of the "mushrooming" transdisciplinary ethos of the "post" regime (Moraru et al. 2002: 37).

Functionalist Paradigm

This paradigm provided CIE with the dominant worldview for academic development studies, in the quest for economic development of the states newly liberated from colonialism, the so-called "developing" or "underdeveloped" nations, together refereeing to them, for many years, as the so-called "Third World," terms no longer acceptable. It accounts for the greatest volume of CIE research under development theory and development education's main framework from the Second World War to the 1990s, during the Cold War period. This paradigm embraces different sociological schools of thought, each occupying a distinct position relative to the paradigm's assumptions about the nature of science, on the objective side of the Burrell and Morgan matrix (with the subjective on the other side), and the nature of society, on the regulation change side of the matrix (with radical change on the other side). All schools of thought in functionalism reflect the dominance of positivism in social studies, in their quest to be scientific. Functionalism assumes the social world is composed of relatively stable and regulated order, and any change would be followed by incremental adjustments to restore the equilibrium. This encourages a belief in the possibility of an objective, value-free research, where the education comparativist keeps their distance from the scene, place, institute, which is analyzing through the rigor and technique of the quantified scientific method. The science that underlines this paradigm emphasizes the possibility of objective inquiry, based on empirical evidence, which provides explanatory and predictive knowledge of the external reality of human affairs. The example, in Chapter 1, of national level of education attainment and its correlation with economic development stages, developed under this paradigm, had an enduring impact on comparing states' education attainment in relation to economic development (see Figure 1).

Development

Development is the name for a collection of theories conceptualized within the functionalist paradigm, but as you will see, it is also theorized in other paradigms. Developmentalism looks at the processes of change in society and how best to achieve desired economic and social changes. Practicing under such theories draws on a variety of social science disciplines and approaches adopted by CIE scholars and transferred from one nation to another as tools to study education systems in the context of political, social, and economic change (development). Economic development is different under different systems (capitalist vs. socialist), just as social development, and education systems, differs under different political systems (authoritarian vs. democratic).

Within CIE, development seems to be one of the most enduring discursive practices, with impactful consequences for more than 100 years.

Development the way CIE has researched, studied, and documented is most clearly anchored in Western-type economy, with its systems of production, power, and signification. Escobar (1995: 10) suggests that we think about development as a historical experience that created a dominant mode of thought and action along three axes:

Forms of knowledge through which it came into being and is elaborated into objects, concepts, and theories.

Systems of power that regulates its practice, and

Forms of subjectivity that are fostered by this discourse, through which people come to recognize themselves as developed or underdeveloped.

The construct "social development," less used than "economic development," never acquired boundaries of its own, since it remains quite unclear when an intervention is economic and when it is social (Adams and Adams 1968). The United Nations Research Institute for Social Development used "social" (1966) in a broad way—"everything that refers directly to the conditions in which people live"—working with a composite "level of living" index (made up of social welfare indicators). This equated social development with the improvement of social services, frequently found in governmental and international reports, still used, to classify societies as *traditional vs. modern*. Hence, "social" has little to do with people's wellbeing as defined by them, their families, and their own community.

Within the development discourse, public education's expansion has been understood as a quest for modernity. Education became the means through which Western (modern) concepts and forms of knowledge could be used. Already under colonial regimes, the means of reforming the "poor," "illiterate," and "underdeveloped" areas of the world was to introduce Western schooling systems (Cortina 2019: 465). Development was defined in terms of a culturally specific Western system of knowing, which in turn discredits and delegitimizes other, local ways of knowing (epistemologies) such as *Buen Vivir and Ubuntu*, see Chapter 4.

Moreover, this is not some antiquated development discourse left over from the Cold War. The UN, in 2023, listed 45 countries as "least developed" (https://unctad.org/topic/least-developed-countries) in which level of development is measured in terms of poverty (GNI per capita less than $1), human resources (nutrition, health and education), and economic vulnerability. This classification is firmly entrenched in economic thought backed by geopolitical power and donor agencies, like national development agencies and World Bank(s). This CIE approach has resulted in the construction of a dominant view to introduce Western patterns of education and workforce training to a new generation in countries freed from colonialism, as in need of vast projects "to develop." Within the discursive development education practices, the expansion, planning, and investment in "education for all" has been understood as a quest for modernity that brings individual, and national, welfare and poverty alleviation.

Development theories have been used by comparativists to frame their research and consulting on developing education programs worldwide. We need to keep in mind how such division, and classification of countries into "developed," "developing," and "underdeveloped," which now are replaced by the use of low-income countries (LICs); lower-middle-income countries (LMICs); and middle-income countries (MICs), are still active discursive practices (Grant 2017).

Modernization

Functionalism was particularly influential in shaping modernization theory, one of the major theories behind CIE practice during the twentieth century. "Modernization" entailed guiding societies in a linear process toward achieving modernity, meaning advanced industrial, technological, and bureaucratic capacities and a pluralist society modeled on capitalist or socialist societies. Studies carried out during the 1950s and 1960s by social scientists like Talcott Parsons and Daniel Lerner defined modernization variously, yet always within an evolutionary perspective, which involved a multilinear developmental transition from traditional to modern society. While structural modernization is commonly understood as moving away from traditional society toward capitalism, industrialism, rationalism, urbanism, etc. Process of change toward those types of societal, economic, and political systems are the ones that have developed in Western Europe and North America. Modernization theory frequently uses dichotomous constructs (traditional vs. modern) and concepts like "social differentiation" and "social system," emphasizing the ability to adapt to gradual, continual change as a typical condition of stability. Modern, advanced societies had the goal of personal and social change, no matter what local or indigenous systems were in place and how much "modern" processes disrupted local values, wellbeing, education of the young, and ways of life.

Clearly expressed within the substantial CIE studies shaped by modernization theories was the role of education, which was to change the economic, social, and cultural systems of traditional societies. Modernization in its social and individual meaning and in its theoretical claims strongly impacted education at all levels and practices, from instruction to curriculum to policy. Education, from the perspective of modernization theory and practices, instills appropriate "modern" values, including personal efficacy, socialization to a rational society, and orientation toward the norms, commitments, and obligations of participation in a modernized society. Education as an agent of social change thus became an obvious focus of attention, and the way was opened to such powerful constructs as *individual modernity*.

"Making Men Modern"

In the 1969 Harvard University-funded project "Making Men Modern," Alex Inkeles used questionnaires as well as interviewing 6,000 men from six "developing countries" to study the impact on the individual of his exposure to, and participation in, the process of national and economic modernization. To a striking degree, the same syndrome of attitudes, values, and ways of acting—such as openness to new experience, independence from parental authority, and taking an active part in civic affairs—defines the modern man in each of the six countries and in all the occupational groups of cultivator, craftsman, and industrial worker. Education is the most powerful factor in making men modern ... (208).

The data was used to produce a scale to measure modernity, the typical "modern man." The fact that education was found to be "the most powerful factor in making modern men" (women were not part of Inkeles's study), was further statistical proof for CIE consults to borrow what worked, to transfer education systems from the Global North to newly established independent countries. Projects funded by nation agencies (USAID, UK, and Nordic aid) and international foundations (IMF, World Bank[s]).

Human Capital and Social Capital

Modernization theory is compatible with human capital theory, developed in the 1960s yet salient today. Early work on education and economic development concentrated on establishing education as a means of increasing the productive quality of labor, while in other theoretical views education is a consumer good and input. In a series of studies, Theodore Schultz developed the idea that education expenditure was not consumption, but rather an investment in increasing the capacity of labor to produce goods (Schultz 1961). This revolutionized the investment in and spread of Western schooling systems. Further research looked at education as an investment, calculating inputs in education as output in economic results. CIE studies started to estimate the social, societal, and individual returns associated with education and other human-capital-related expenditures, comparing populations with different education attainment in different countries and statistically correlating them with indices of national economic development.

The core of the human capital argument rests on the idea that education, health, and training are investments with anticipated future individual and social returns. Education is viewed primarily as a system for endowing the labor force with knowledge and skills to make people more productive. Drawn from economics and given impetus by the urgent search for capital formation and means of economic development in the so-called developing countries. Human capital theory, more than any other theoretical social construct, had a profound influence on concepts of the place of education in the newly established states. Modernization and development processes provide a rationale for expansion and funding of Western types of schooling.

"The human investment revolution in economic thought," as Mary Jean Bowman (1966) the education economist called it, took over the study of the investments in education with surprising rapidity (111). Although it was already known that resources devoted to the human component of capital could be considered investments, how to measure it was an open question of economic analysis. The view of education as an investment in future income was elaborated during the 1960s with formulas and calculations, thus making it scientific (see Chapter 3 on "rate of return"). The major methodological procedure in estimating the education value of human capital remains that of Schultz (1961). Education is conceived of as an indicator of modernization (as in studies of individual modernity) and a nation-building parameter, an indicator of further social and economic growth. We already mentioned that this is an antiquated theory, but it is used and practiced to this day, such as the 2017 study commissioned by UK DFID (department for international development):

> We would like to commission a rapid review on available evidence on the contribution of education to economic growth (beyond private returns, including productivity, social and economic returns, etc.). We would like a written report—a concise overview of the available evidence, a sense of how reliable the evidence is, and any significant gaps. We are not looking at any particular region. It would be useful if evidence from LICs, LMICs and MICs

could be split out. And we are interested in education overall, evidence split by basic, secondary, tertiary (and TVET if possible).

(Grant 2017: 1)

To further justify the accepted fact that education plays a significant role in a county's economic development, this study, as well as many others, quote the UNESCO 2012 report:

For every US$1 spent on education, as much as US$10 to US$15 can be generated in economic growth. If 75% more 15-year-olds in forty-six of the world's poorest countries were to reach the lowest OECD benchmark for mathematics, economic growth could improve by 2.1% from its baseline and 104 million people could be lifted out of extreme poverty.

(Grant 2017: 2)

The enduring "human capital" discourse is used by many Ministries of Education and donor agencies around the world. The above report did add TVET, Technical and Vocational Education Training, as "TVET needs to support the country's medium and long-term targets for human capital development, crucial for achieving not only the Sustainable Development Goals but also, economic growth" (UNESCO 2020: 2). Researching the Indian government's application of TVET programs toward women's upskilling, an important initiative in its twelfth five-year plan, Iyengar and Witenstein (2019) studied women's access to and interest in participating in these vocational programs from the women's own point of view (see methods in Chapter 3).

Social capital is defined by the Organization for Economic Co-operation and Development (OECD), an intergovernmental organization of member countries, as networks together with shared norms, values, and understandings that facilitate co-operation within or among groups.

"Networks" are the links between groups or individuals. Less concrete than social networks, "norms" are society's unspoken and largely unquestioned rules. "Norms" and "understandings" may not become apparent until broken. "Values" are more open to question, while schools and institutions often debate what their values are, what they should be, whether their values are changing, etc. These networks, like schools, universities, teachers' unions, etc., generate understanding and trust, and enable people to work together and gain social capital. Sociologist James Coleman (1988) defined these intangible resources as embedded within interpersonal relationships or social institutions. They can be as strong as that of family members, friends, colleagues, or fellow students, or as far as distant "LinkedIn" online connections.

Summary

Education was of major significance within functionalist theories of modernization, as the site for inculcation of new values and for reforming society under colonialism and post-independence. The functionalist distinctions between macro-level theories, related to large-scale issues and countries' populations, and micro-level theories, those that look at very specific relationships between individuals or small groups, tended to obscure much more important assumptions about what model of society theorists use to underwrite their analyses, including assumptions about ontology (being) and epistemology (knowledge).

In the context of the familiar functionalist CIE discourse, the terms "education" and "schooling" sustain a network of meaning-relations with other key terms and phrases, including "self-fulfillment," "intelligence," "skill'/skilled," "self-improvement," "personal development," and "liberation." These terms are connected to other sets of discursive practices: "equal opportunity," "horizontal mobility," "economic productivity," "employability," "external rewards," "material security," and "happier life." Ultimately, these terms refer to the individual. Other terms and phrases in this same network have a more broadly social referent that CIE research and practices had to contend with, including "social equality," "modern society," "social development," "economic growth," "increased per capita income," "valuable input," "increased material output," (improved) "income distribution," (increased) "political participation," etc. (Gottlieb 1989: 134). As part of working within functionalism those constructs are not just words, they are the content available for researchers, comparativists, Ministries of Education, donor agencies, and of course CIE students, to learn what constructs are being used within the functionalist paradigm to produce knowledge, that is turn is use for planning and education policy.

Radical Structuralist Paradigm

Any venture outside the realm of the dominant functionalist conceptualization of social change in the team of the "problem of order" inevitably encounters the "problem of conflict." Marxist theory was apparently forgotten in the 1960s when sociologists pronounced the order-conflict debate over. Academic sociologists and Marxist social theories worked in isolation from one another, especially in the United States. By the end of the 1960s, with functionalist developmentalism not showing the expected economic elevation in the newly decolonized nations aligned with the West, Marxist theories enjoyed a comeback in academic theorizing, and in relation to development, a radical Max Weber analysis of contemporary society, and conflict theory were elaborated. Michael Apple is a well-known critical Marxist educator who has focused on how power relations and inequality are manifested in education (Apple 1979, 1996).

The radical structuralist paradigm, accordingly, includes theories that advocate a sociology of radical change from an objectivist standpoint, based on an ontology that emphasizes the hard and concrete nature of reality that exists outside peoples' minds. Contrary to the claims of liberal theorists and educators that education offers possibilities for individual cognitive development, social mobility and political and economic opportunities, radical theorists have argued the main functions of schools in capitalist societies are: (a) the reproduction of dominant wealth and power patterns and their forms of knowledge; and (b) the transfer of skills needed to reproduce the social division of labor (Bowles and Gintis 1976). In the radical structuralist perspective, schools as institutions can only be understood through an analysis of their relation to the state and the economy at large (Carnoy 1974).

Marxist Theory and Colonialism

Marxism is a comprehensive worldview, a body of philosophical, economic, political, sociological, and scientific principles all interrelated and together largely forming an independent, self-sufficient intellectual structure. Marxist theory is an objectivist approach to social sciences; it is realist in ontology (i.e., the material world is the only reality), positivist in epistemology (i.e., we can achieve reliable, true knowledge about the world), and determinist in its view of human nature (i.e., we are fundamentally shaped by our material conditions). The sociology of Karl Marx and his followers is one of radical change and for disrupting the status quo.

While Marx never developed a theory of colonialism, his analysis of capitalism did emphasize its inherent tendency to expand in search of new markets. In his classic works, Marx predicted the bourgeoisie (the property-owning class) would continue to create a global market and undermine local and national barriers to its own expansion, a necessary product of the core dynamic of capitalism: overproduction.

The practice of Marxism in the US was mostly not a political practice; it has influenced postcolonial theory and anti-colonial independence movements around the world. Marxists have drawn attention to the material basis of European political expansion and developed concepts that help explain the persistence of economic exploitation after the end of direct political rule in the colonies (i.e., neo-colonialism, see following). Modernization processes according to this theory are entirely negative because people are poor due to low wages, and heavy taxation to support colonial rule and neo-colonial exploitation, and they must endure economic upheaval.

Development

The radical structuralist paradigm exerted a continuous, paradoxical influence on theories of development, making the state a primary focus of the analysis of education's economic relations. In their discussions, attention to the capitalist economy and state apparatuses reveals how schools function as agencies of social and cultural reproduction—that is, how they legitimated capitalist rationality and sustained dominant social practices (Aronowitz and Giroux 1985). Marxist theory's view of social change means it cannot be applied like other approaches or strategies to development. From a Marxist perspective, the kinds of societal models that other approaches promote can only be achieved as a consequence of a revolution.

Dependency

Dos Santos describes dependency as "a situation in which the economy of certain countries is conditioned by the development and expansion of another economy to which the former is subjected" (1970: 231). The notion of dependency relations among countries under international capitalism were discussed for several years by Marxist thinkers, but not until the late 1950s, when the UN Economic Commission for Latin America analyzed the "peripheral" status of Latin America countries in relation to the advanced industrialized countries, would a dependency theory of development come to be elaborated. The steady march from one stage of development to the next (see Chapter 1, Rostow's "stages of economic growth"), leading ultimately to dependent countries being incorporated into the global economic network, was called into question by dependency theory, which rejected the foundational premise of development theory and modernization. The emerging critique of modernization was not restricted to trade relations alone but included a whole "structure of dependence," as argued by Santos (1970: 234). Theotônio Dos Santos, Andre G. Frank, and Samir Amin contributed significantly to the dependency scholarship. They focused on the relations between countries located in the "core" (the so-called "developed") and those identified as peripheral (the so-called "under developed" or "law income") relationships that are inherently unequal and exploitative. Frank (1966: 18) argued:

> Historical research demonstrates that contemporary underdevelopment is in large part the historical product of past and continuing economic and other relations' such as between colonial countries and the Empire just that now they are metropolitan, or economically strong countries.

Prospects: The review of education, XV (2) in 1985 was devoted to dependency theory(ies) following the fifth World Congress of Comparative Education (WCCE) held in Paris rather than in Latin America (where it was planned). The papers show that the sociological literature produced in dependent countries, particularly in Latin America, insists that the liberal theories of Europe and the United States do not adequately explain the phenomenon of dependence or feasible solutions for overcoming the situation of economic dependence. Already in the 1960s the theory of dependency began to be applied to education, in opposition to the developmentalism based on the economics of education. Benno Sander (1985) asks what is the role of comparative education in the reciprocal relationship between education and society in the context of the reciprocal relationship between dominant society and dependent society? He thinks the answers to these questions are a direct function of the historical perspective, positioned in space and time, rather than social theories and methodologies without specific historical conditions; they do not have universal validity for explaining education phenomena and processes that occur in different geographic situations. This seriously questions the transplantation, transfer, or unidirectional adaptation of theories and methodologies and of educational forms and contents from the dominant society to the dependent society. We have referenced the many CIE transfer and borrowing studies (see Chapter 3).

Dependent society denies the unidirectional or vertical determination of the dominant society over the dependent society. It assumes that the dominant and dependent societies limit one another reciprocally and construct one another dialectically. In this process of reciprocal limitation, one can only conceive of a place for comparative education in the dependent society, if it is designed to play a mediating role in order to overcome economic, political, and cultural dependence (Sander 1985: 201).

World Economic System and World Culture System

According to dependency theories, a worldwide system emerged, perpetuating international power and economic imbalance—a world economic system. Like dependency theory, World-Systems suggests that wealthy countries benefit from other countries and exploit those countries' citizens. In contrast with dependency theory, this theory recognizes the minimal benefits enjoyed by low economic status countries in the world-system. Sociologist Immanuel Wallerstein originated the theory (1974), which suggested the way a country is integrated into the capitalist world-system determines how economic development takes place in that country. World-Systems theory is a macro-sociological perspective seeking to explain the dynamics of the "capitalist world economy" as a "total social system," replacing the study of states as the unit of measurement, used by large comparative studies of students' achievements (see Chapter 3).

Wallerstein joined the attack on the then-dominant approach to understanding development, based on modernization theory, by proposing an alternative explanation providing a new theoretical guide to investigating the emergence and development of capitalism, industrialism, and mass education systems. He saw the world as an economic system and cultural system divided into:

> *core*—countries that were dominant, capitalist countries characterized by high levels of industrialization and urbanization which have the most power in the world economic system.
> *periphery*—countries dependent on that core for capital, less industrialized and urbanized. Some are still agrarian, some with lower literacy rates and primary education participation, and even lower secondary. They supply natural resource to core countries.
> *semi-peripheral*: countries sharing core and periphery country characteristics. Higher participation in all three levels of education (see Figure 1). According to Wallerstein, they are the buffer, economically, between core and peripheral countries.

The primary mechanism of this "unequal exchange" is achieved by transfers of surplus value across the word economy, maintaining the structural inequalities, the inequitable development of geographical areas within the word economy, and the endless accumulation of capital. International dependence as part of a World-Systems theory has implications well beyond economic structures, giving rise to globalization and neoliberalism, discussed in Chapter 1.

World Culture Theory extended World-Systems to theorize the transmission of ideas, meanings, and values around the world from core to peripheral countries in a way that extends and intensifies social transfer, including education structure and curricula transfer. Nowadays, this system is referred to as Cultural Globalization, encompassing processes marked by the common consumption of cultures diffused by international travel, student and scholar exchanges, and popular culture media including movies, streaming television, email, YouTube, Facebook, Instagram, TikTok, and a myriad other social media and connective technologies, like WhatsApp.

Imperialism, Neo-Imperialism, and Sub-Imperialism

As both Chapter 1 and this chapter have so far made clear, CIE disciplinary studies are not divorced from geopolitical affairs that take place in the countries we teach and study. The creation and flourishing of the study of education in relation to political, economic, and social development is embedded in larger world affairs such as colonialism, and postcolonialism and imperialism. Imperialism, as distinct from colonialism, is a broad term referring to economic, military, and political domination achieved even in the absence of significant permanent settlement like the European empires. Most Marxists focus on the economic motives generating capitalist imperialism. Galtung (1971) shows that imperialism takes as its point of departure from:

a. the tremendous inequality, within and between nations, in almost all aspects of human living conditions, including the power to decide over those living conditions; and
b. the resistance of this inequality to change.

The example Galtung uses to illustrate how the "core" was ruling the "periphery" is by asking how could "a small foggy island in the North Sea

(Great Britain) rule over one quarter of the world?" This is how he thinks it was achieved:

By isolating the Periphery parts from each other; by having them geographically at sufficient distance from each other to impede any real alliance formation; by having separate deals with them so as to tie them to the Center in particularistic ways; by reducing multilateralism to a minimum with all kinds of graded membership; and by having the Mother Country assume the role of window to the world (90).

The point about "graded membership" applied to education as well; there was Western schooling in the colonies, it was just that access was controlled, both in independent states from colonization, like in India, and the Eastern Bloc independent states after the fall of the Soviet Union. When it comes to education, there was a rush to institute Western schooling and democratic principles, supported by donor organizations. Reforming whole systems is not just costly, but also cannot happen quickly (Silova 2010). This is where it is easier to fall back on the old education institutional patterns of the past socialist regime; after all as we mentioned in Chapter 1, right after Sputnik, the United States, followed by many other countries, regarded the Soviet education system as superior. See more below on post-socialism.

Neo-imperialism is more often connected with the projection of European and North American economic and military power in reaction to the perceived threat of the spread of international socialism. In the absence of political or any other direct control (of the kind exercised in countries that were colonized), power intervention, in the newly independent nations to maintain free trade, was named Neo (new) imperialism. An early good example of the United States exercising such geopolitical power is the 1956 Suez Canal crisis. Egypt announced the nationalization of the Suez Canal, a valuable waterway that controlled the moving of two-thirds of the oil and other goods, owned and operated by the British and French (since it was constructed in 1869). The United States, worried by the emergent influential Egyptian power backed by the Soviet Union, brokered a diplomatic settlement with the help of the UN, where the British–French troops withdrew, and the Canal moved to be operated by eighteen of the world's leading maritime nations. This is a good example of how neo-imperialism works: the United States, which did not have colonies, exercised its power showing the imperial powers (British–French) how from then on they could not act on their own. This relation was mirrored in education reform and policies when the US system is being transferred and borrowed where before the Empire's education system was the model.

Although that historical event was a long time ago, already then, and now, education and CIE are practiced within such geopolitical forces, and this 1956 event helps us understand many other past events, e.g., the 1991 Gulf war, 9/11, the Iraq and Afghanistan wars, as US State and UK government departments contract education NGOs to reconstruct education in Iraq and Afghanistan, in the hope of economic and social change. With the 2024 events in the Middle East, the Suez Canal crisis helps us understand the airstrikes by the United States and UK against the Houthi in Yemen (backed by Iran), in response to Houthi attacks on ships in the Red Sea, interrupting international commerce sailing, during the Israeli war with Hamas in Gaza and Hezbollah in Lebanon, and Iran in 2025. Those examples show that North America, UK and Europe, Russian, China, and Iran, among other world actors, supply weapon, military training, economic and social support, such as scholarships to acquire higher degrees, as well as sanction threats, coups, invasions, and "color revolutions," which happen frequently enough to remind, independent governments how neo-imperialism operates.

Sub-imperialism was already outlined by Ruy Mauro Marini (1972) with the case of the Brazilian imposing those relationships on their own people. They did so after the economic crises of 1962 and 1967, which led them to power by offering partnership to foreign monopolies in the exploitation of the Brazilian worker through an unrestricted alliance with foreign capital. Those imperialists accepted participation but imposed their own conditions. Big Brazilian industry was de-nationalized; the exploitation of raw materials such as iron was monopolized. Brazil developed these lines of production while imposing more intense capital accumulation, which made it necessary to "suppress the dependent country in the process of converting its imperialism to subimperialism" (17). It is relevant to recall Figure 1 (Chapter 1) where Brazil in 1965 had only 2.25 percent of the relevant cohort completing higher education, 17 percent attainment of secondary school, and only 72 percent completed primary school. Thereafter (see Chapter 4) the World Bank imposed education reform and primary schooling as part of a loan for social-economic development.

Now more generally sub-imperialism names projects and countries that declared their intentions to promote new development practices that could lead to a socially just, and environmentally sustainable model. But what they do offer is another kind of imperialism. While analyzing the (relatively) new blocs alliance, Brazil, Russia, India, China, and South Africa (BRICS) using their own foreign direct investment (FDI), trade, especially in Africa, Latin

America, and the Caribbean, in the name of reversing historical, unequal trade and investment relations between the "core" and "peripheries," Bond (2023) found BRICS countries are in an uncomfortable middle ground which "sub-imperialism" fits best, as they fail to promote new development practices. BRICS countries appear to be reinforcing old patterns of underdevelopment amplified by natural resource extraction, reinforcing elite's education, resulting in adverse impacts for local communities, workers, and nature.

Chisholm and Chissale (2024) explore the question of geo-political dynamics, and their significance for education by examining the applicability of the concept of sub-imperialism to education relationships established by South Africa with Mozambique funded by BRICS (see Chapter 4).

Cultural Capital

Cultural Capital is another sociological concept referring to the social assets people possess that can help them achieve success and social mobility. These assets can be tangible or intangible, including education, other non-financial belongings, skills, knowledge, social values, and ideas.

Pierre Bourdieu and Jean-Claude Passeron (1977) coined and defined the term "Cultural Capital." Bourdieu's cultural capital theory, often used by CIE research, was influenced by Marxist identification of economic accumulation as a power and agency in capitalist society. They argue that different kinds of capital owned by individuals can determine their education attainment, and positions in the social stratification that can further influence patterns of social behaviors and standing like employment. In his account, there are three forms of capital: economic, social, and cultural which includes education. Bourdieu's theory of the reproduction of social hierarchy describes the reproduction systems, mainly on the basis of preconditions in demographics, like education and inheritance on just material property or legal titles, that comes with class, both from home and schooling that develops know-how, taste, and social connections. Bourdieu's work is often a fundamental reference for studies about education systems, calling into question the promise of education, to democratization. His anthropological work on the education system showed how education reproduces the social structures students bring from home, and other community institutions. Useful illustrative research is in Willis's (1979) ethnography on how working-class kids end up getting working-class jobs. Bourdieu's theory demonstrated that pedagogical communication functions less as the transmission of culture and more as the legitimizer of a particular culture; that is, educational institutions promote a certain "cultural connivance between the school and the ways (of living, speaking and thinking) characteristic of the ruling class" not the class the students come from (Bourdieu and Passeron 1977: 42). They condemn all pedagogies that do not challenge the domination of the well to-do, with a lot of social and cultural capital.

Comparative education within the radical structuralist paradigm accepts neither the functionalist construction of the ways things are, nor the functionalist discourse in which it is constructed. The radical structuralist social educator re-contextualizes the familiar terms "schooling" and "education," integrating them into a new discursive context where their meaning is changed. To recontextualize terms in this way is creative, opening new language possibilities, with potential to create new knowledge. For instance, Carnoy's (1974) new metaphor "education as cultural imperialism" recontextualizes education in the context of dependency theory and the "free-trade colonialism" experienced in the de-colonized countries, such as Brazil or Peru. Similarly, education is asserted to be a tool of "internal colonialism" in the United States (Bowles and Gintis 1976). Moreover, World-Systems and World Cultures Systems theories were used by comparativists to research mass Western education spread by diffusion and adoption from the core to the periphery (Meyer et al. 1992). The methods for studying the worldwide spread of Western education policies and practices are reviewed in Chapter 3.

Radical Humanist Paradigm

The radical humanist paradigm comprises the subjective and objective idealist strains of thought, which have their origins in German idealism. Existentialism differs from phenomenology in its vigorous humanism and political commitment to the desirability of change in the existing social order. The intellectual origins of this paradigm are found in the idealist notion of the spiritual rather than material reality, including the social world. The social world according to this view does not have an independent existence, as in the materialist ontology of radical structuralism. The notion that individuals create the worlds they live in is shared by the radical humanist and the interpretative paradigms (see next), with an important difference that the radical humanist theories use this notion not just to understand schooling and education reality, but also to critique it. The knowledge that radical humanist discourse constructs for education research is shaped by the crucial category "the human" and by the gap between full humanity and people's actual present state of alienation, distorted communication, and dehumanization (see Freire 1996).

Critical Theory

Developed by the Frankfurt School, mentioned in Chapter 1 in relation to the development of practicing CIE in Germany, this school of thought in sociology and critical philosophy is associated with the Institute for Social Research founded at Goethe University Frankfurt. The Frankfurt school includes theories such as Theodore Adorno, Herbert Marcuse Jürgen Habermas, and Walter Benjamin. Critical theories differ from one another in their analysis of the cause of alienation: the four dimensions of alienation identified by Marx are alienation from: a) the product of labor; b) the process of labor; c) others; and d) self. While the philosophers differ in the nature and method of their specific critiques, they all share the purpose of achieving social change through human emancipation. Critical theory has been developed in comparative education as a way of rethinking the power dynamics that influence and work within schooling systems. As explored by Antonio Gramsci, often used in CIE references, there is a belief that all humans are capable of intellectual and rational faculties; see more in Chapter 3.

Critical theory in education was developed by Paulo Freire, still widely regarded as the foremost literacy expert and radical educator, who brought to the comparative study of education a revolutionary education thinking. Freire's work in Latin America corresponded with Liberation theology which aims to understand Christianity and religion through the process of liberation, while not stopping at reflecting on the world, but moves to transforming the world through education. People are encouraged to become active agents of their own destiny and in effect to liberate themselves from the confines of injustice. This theology extends beyond development education to liberation, representing the aspirations of oppressed peoples. "Consciousness raising," a key education practice for Freire, suggests that education cannot be judged for its economic and political effects but should be viewed as a means for understanding education's mechanisms of oppression and for exploring alternatives with the aim of making society more just (see Gottlieb and LaBelle 1990).

Critical theory is also a major drive in the development of the new sociology of education, critical educationists, like Michael Apple (1996), showing the relationship between cultural, political, and economic forces and the impact of those forces on the school. This critical turn in sociology of education comes through the distinction between reproduction and resistance. Rendering this distinction in education, reproduction theories see schools as mechanically maintaining unjust social structures, while resistance theories permeate teachers, students, and others in and around schools with the agency to fight that structure and make their own political realities (Backer 2021). CIE has used and elaborated critical research methods to find agency through critical theory by studying and teaching social inquiry that aims to transform the space of schools, the practice of teachers, the treatment of students, the sharing of diverse knowledge, and the improvement of society at large (see Chapter 3).

Phenomenology

Phenomenology, as a philosophy of experience, had a profound influence on radical humanist theorizing. In Greek, phainómenon, meaning "thing appearing to view," showing themself, flaring up. Understanding education phenomena, as they appear to, or experienced by others. German philosophers such as Kant, Hegel, and Brentano were the founders, but Husserl (1970) is the one that showed that phenomenology would be how the experience of phenomena can be studied. For phenomenology, the ultimate source of all meaning and value is the lived experiences; learning, as in education, is all about relationships and experiences. This means that philosophical systems, scientific theories, or aesthetic judgments of education have the status of abstractions useful to know. The task of researchers is to describe the structures of experiences, so knowledge generated on classroom size; number of students per teacher; relations between educators and their students; the situatedness of comparing education structures; and the place of schooling in society and history are all possible CIE research topics. Phenomenological thought contributes to the searching for experiential foundations on which CIE could ground their knowledge production.

Existentialism

Existentialism differs from phenomenology, from which it borrows many of its ideas in its humanism and political commitment to changing the existing order. It first emerged during the occupation of France by Germany during the Second World War. The philosopher Gabriel Marcel used "existentialism" in 1943 to describe the philosophy of Jean-Paul Sartre's *Being and Nothingness*, which was deeply rooted in the work of the German phenomenologist Martin Heidegger. Sartre and his intellectual and personal partner Simone de Beauvoir were part of the resistance to the Nazi occupation, when so many of their countrymen collaborated, believing they "had no choice." At the core of Sartre and de Beauvoir's writings was the idea that human consciousness was defined by an individuals' abilities to create their own selves, crucially through *making choices*. They took consciousness as their starting point, showing the ontological relationship between subjective and objective worlds. Seen as a philosophy of individual freedom in the face of totalitarian oppression, French existentialism contributed to the perennial debate about "free will."

Summary

We will come back to phenomenology and its critical approach to CIE research in Chapter 4. Heidegger's phenomenology was concerned with what it means to *be in* the world (ontology); he was driven by the question of the meaning of "being" and this focus on being-in the world lies in contrast to focus on what we can *know about* the world (epistemology). This is also a continuous debate in CIE theorizing. Conducting research grounded in this paradigm offers vigorous humanism and political commitment to the desire to change in the existing social order, which in CIE is about decolonizing knowledge production relying on new advancements of de-colonial ways of knowledge like those elaborated by de Sousa Santos's (2018) epistemologies of the South.

The Interpretive Paradigm

Interpretivism is based on the assumption that reality is subjective, multiple, and socially constructed. We can only understand someone's reality through their experience of that reality, which may be different from another person's shaped by the individuals' historical or social perspective. The interpretive paradigm shares with the radical humanist paradigm its roots in the idealist tradition of social thought. Like radical humanism, this paradigm involves the attempt to understand and explain the education social world primarily from the point of view of the actors themselves. As opposed to radical humanism, however, interpretive philosophers and sociologists seek to understand the very basis and source of social reality. Their commitment to the sociology of regulation means they are involved with such issues as consensus, cohesion, solidarity, and actuality (Burrell and Morgan 1979: 31). Based on the belief that reality is socially constructed through human interactions and interpretations, it has influenced CIE from the 1990s and further research in the twenty-first century focuses on understanding the subjective meanings and experiences of participants. The theoretical schools of this paradigm differ by their degree of concern with the subjectivity and intersubjectivity of their education research. There are multiple interpretive theories, some of which are summarized below.

Transcendental Phenomenology

Transcendental phenomenology adopts an extremely subjectivist ontological view. It is a philosophical framework emphasizing subjectivity and discovery, and it can help CIE understand how education is experienced in the everyday. As you'll see in Chapter 3, transcendental phenomenology theory will help with the exploration of the experiences of learners, teachers, administrators, parents, street children, and to gain an understanding of their being and learning from their own point of view. The task of knowledge generation is to explore and reveal essential types and structures of their experiences. The methods of "direct intuition" and "insight into essential structures" are offered as a principle means of penetrating the depth of everyday education affairs in search of subjectivity. To understand the interpretive schemes by which an individual endows their lived experiences with meaning, we must understand how such schemes are intrinsically intersubjective, and how they are affected by and oriented toward varied forms of social interaction. This account of intersubjective interpretive schemes even applies reflexively to social-scientific theorizing of education itself.

Ethnomethodology

Ethnomethodology begins with the assumption that everyday life is orderly and aims to study the methods people persistently use in constructing their social world. Harold Garfinkel (1979), a US sociologist credited with coining the term in his *Studies in Ethnomethodology*, led to its wider use. It seeks to identify the taken-for-granted assumptions that characterize social situations. Ethnomethodologists are interested in procedures and making activities rationally accountable and in the common-sense suppositions of everyday life. Ethnomethodology has as one of its principles that social reality is not studying fixed entities but interpreting and processing. The concepts that comparativists have studied in their documenting of society relationships are no longer shown to exist as part of the reality. Heyman (1979) has observed, "Ethnographic accounts of schooling come closest to ways of studying education to tackle the problem of when we talk about school/society relationships, from the standpoint of an ethnomethodology critic of comparative studies" (245).

Unlike functionalism, ethnomethodology does not explain ordered structures such as schooling or patterns of events or regularities in education affairs, but rather provides explanations of the way actors make evident and persuade each other that events and activities are coherent and consistent. In the history of comparative studies, the work in anthropology comes closest to understanding and trying to deal with the epistemological problems CIE anthropologists such as Vandra Masemann have long been interested in ethnographic studies in their efforts to describe and interpret school culture (1976).

Symbolic Interaction

Both ethnomethodology and symbolic interactionism follow the phenomenological tradition of attributing an ontological status to social reality. Covering largely the same ground as ethnomethodology, namely human conduct within a social order, symbolic interactionism focuses on how interacting selves cooperate in the construction of routine and taken-for-granted meaning. Symbolic interaction is a micro-level theory focused on meanings attached to human interaction, both verbal and non-verbal, and to symbols used in communication by which individuals create their social world rather than merely reacting to it. The work of Margaret Mead was analyzed using symbolic interaction theory (Blumer 1969). Unlike ethnomethodologists who restrict their focus to the actor's world, the interactionist treats the actor's point of view as only one aspect of the problem of order, seeking to relate it to a wider context.

Summary

As opposed to functionalism and radical structuralism, the interpretive paradigm urges that social sciences are based on people's social world. Theories in this paradigm assume that the social world is not a "hard" fact, concrete, tangible, and given-in-advance, but an emergent process, an extension of human consciousness and subjective experiences. This means this paradigm, in common with radical humanism, regards social affairs as rooted in subjectivism and recognizes the precarious ontological status of the social world, i.e., its contingent and immaterial mode of existence. However, by contrast with the radical humanist and radical structuralist paradigms alike, the interpretive paradigm shares with functionalism a common concern for the sociology of regulation. Interpretive theories present a perspective in which individual actors negotiate, regulate, and live within the context of the status quo. As we saw in the context of the radical humanist paradigm, the intellectual currents that radical humanism shares with interpretivism are the interpretation of language, whether written or spoken. To study institutions (political, economic, educational) means to study the people who act and interact by making meaning, through spoken and written language. Making language and meaning the topic of analysis presents some research problems because it means that the research tools are the same as the subject of research (Heyman 1979: 243). Such an analysis can be directed toward a critique of the status quo within education from the actor's point of view.

Theorizing in the "Post" Era

As this chapter has shown, CIE theorizing since the 1950s has been largely influenced by modernist, positivist, and functionalist theoretical approaches, and comparative education teaching, research, and practices have reflected this dominance. Theorizing in the period following the peak years of these dominant paradigms—the "post" era, as Moraru et al. (2022) have called it—is a matter not just of looking ahead to what comes next, yet also looking backward into the past, "specifically into the modern tradition of theoretical reflections" (p. 6). These theories of the "post" have been vociferously debated in CIE forums; they have influenced CIE methods (see Chapter 3) and impacted its practices (see Chapter 4). Theorizing in the "post" has provoked healthy skepticism about the universalized meta-narratives such as modernization and developmentalism, with their goal of endless economic growth. It has also called into question the Anglophone world's assumption that what we now call the Global South (and used to call the Third World) suffered from a "deficiency of modernity" which could only be remedied by Western-style education. Now, in the "post" era, theorizing *from* the Global South is increasingly articulated on its own terms, without reference to Anglophone paradigms. Along with advances in technology (e.g., cellular communication, online teaching and learning, etc.) and the freer movements of goods, people, and ideas that come with globalization, these theories of the "post" have helped shape late twentieth-century and twenty-first-century CIE.

We review some of the major "post" theories and their development in the humanities and social sciences: *poststructuralism, postmodernism, postcolonialism, post-socialism*, and *posthumanism*, and a couple that qualify as "post" theories even though they do not have "post" in their names (e.g., *affect* theory).

Poststructuralism

Poststructuralism is a group of theories of knowledge and language initially developed by Foucault ([1966] 1970) and Said (1978), followed by scholars we quote in different chapters, including Mohanty (1984) and Loomba (2002) among others. Michel Foucault, in *The Order of Things* ([1966] 1970), demonstrates how, within the discourse of a particular discipline, the objects, subjects, concepts, and strategies of research emerge and are structured. Form is as binding as content; this is how discourse not only shapes meaning but also constructs knowledge. In *Archaeology of Knowledge* (1982) Foucault examines the discursive traces and orders left by the past, in order to write a "history of the present." For Foucault, archaeology is about looking at history as a way of understanding the processes that have led to what we are today. Foucault uses the term "archive" to designate the collection of all material traces left behind by a particular historical period and culture. In examining these traces, one can deduce the historical a priori of the period and then if one is looking at science, one can deduce the episteme of the period. The idea of CIE archive work has followed Foucault in that these concepts do not have predictive value—they are all descriptions of limited historical orders.

Hence, it is an important lesson when analyzing past policies or long-range education planning.

Edward Said's "Orientalism" (1978) represents a monumental study through his analyses of histories, political treatises, and scholarly and literary texts, scrutinizing style, figures of speech, setting, narrative devices, and historical and social circumstances. Moreover, his analysis of *discursive practices* enabled Said to show how Orientalism re-presents the Orient. Said's analysis had uncovered how Western narrative has invented "the Orient" and this narrative/story has nothing to do with the places or people. This work is very relevant to CIE as the "developing" countries were invented by institutions such as development agencies and international banks. Chandra Talpade Mohanty (1984) showed how a particular cultural discourse about the so-called "Third World" was produced using economic and political hierarchies, with little to do with how people in emerging economies found themselves, or their traditions or culture. Once this was "invented," it began representing those countries. As mentioned earlier, Escobar (1995) has rendered the narrative hierarchy, where "underdevelopment became the subject of political technologies" (52). Relying on Foucault's work on the dynamics of discourse and power in the representation of social reality, Escobar compares Said's discourse on Orientalism to that of developmentalism where "developing" was not how the people saw themselves, where decision-making and management were entrusted to "development professionals" with little importance attached to the interpretation of each society's history and culture (see more in Chapter 4).

Poststructuralist theory calls into question accepted conceptual oppositions or hierarchies, including central vs. peripheral, developed vs. undeveloped, self vs. other, male vs. female, and school graduates vs. dropouts. The operation of exposing and overturning such oppositions and hierarchies emerged as *deconstruction*, a practice (rather than a concept); see Chapter 3. We use it here in a very broad sense to encompass many of the ways that poststructuralism has impacted CIE, as the example of deconstructing the concept "development."

The deconstructive method or practice spread throughout humanities departments in the 1970s and 1980s, and offered a serious challenge to traditional literary and cultural criticism dominated by textual objectivism (the assumption that a text is a stable object of analysis). A deconstructive reading would reveal profound unexamined assumptions in such research, for example, about the gendered nature of education and work (Peters 1998). What is most valuable in poststructuralist theory, from the CIE point of view, is its capacity to loosen our own worldview's hold on us by calling attention to the unrecognized fictional structures (e.g., developed, underdeveloped, developing), which CIE adhered to.

Postmodernism

Contemporaneously, critics of Continental philosophy used the term "postmodernism" to hold together a variety of thinkers often at odds with one another (e.g., Julia Kristeva, Michel Foucault, Jacques Derrida, Gilles Deleuze, etc.). These critics argued postmodernists believed that there were no such things as "facts," only modes of discourse forever impeding us from making truth claims about reality, and the term "postmodern" became a pejorative term to deride these thinkers as adhering to epistemological and moral nihilism.

Lyotard (1979) published in English in 1984, defines the postmodern as "incredulity towards metanarratives," where meta-narratives are understood as totalizing stories about history and the goals of people that ground and legitimize knowledges and cultural practices. Modernization and developmentalism are such "grand narratives" or metanarratives, large-scale stories that explain so much of the search of education for modernizing traditional societies and bringing about economic development, justify producing comparative knowledge and practices such as large numerical studies comparing Western school attainment (see Figure 1, Chapter 1) and students' academic achievements. Lyotard wrote that the contemporary world entered a new era where all metanarratives were obsolete. He argued modern science uses grand narratives, like emancipation narrative, or modernization to legitimize itself. In post-industrial societies, science's socio-political legitimacy is performative rather than emancipatory. Lyotard preferred a plurality of smaller narratives that compete with each other instead of the totalitarianism of grand narratives.

If we approach *postmodernism* as a historical concept, primarily associated with the Marxist literary critic Fredric Jameson (1998) who essentially names what comes after the radical experimentations of twentieth-century modernism, which is the meta-narrative of CIE's own history (see Chapter 1). Jameson identifies it as a moment of "late capitalism" in the political and economic sphere, insisting that *time* lost its domination on social thought and is dominated by space rather than time. Jameson extended this "spatial turn" that was already announced by Foucault in 1969; while recognizing the nineteenth century was obsessed with history (time), by saying that the present will be above all the era of space. This, known as the *spatial tune* in the social sciences, did produce some tensions when disciplines like geography for the first time, studied cultural geography, as a study of space.

The other major conception of postmodernism is associated with McHale (1989) arguing that postmodernism is defined best by a turn away from *epistemology*—questions about knowledge, the province of modern education—towards *ontology*, meaning a preoccupation with various modes or states of *being*: making or unmaking "the 3rd world," multiplying and juxtaposing worlds, developed, emerging, traditional, and or indigenist, see Chapter 4. A roughly parallel ontological turn in anthropology dispenses with the traditional (modernist) anthropological notions of culture, with what counts as knowledge (epistemology), and with worldviews. While CIE was slow to do any research using postmodernism as a method Gottlieb (2000: 171), in her overview of CIE concludes:

> The "post-modern turn" in comparative education, if and when it takes place, will most likely result in a [different] construction of knowledge. Destabilisation of the dominant modernist genres of discourse and the opening up of space for the actors' voices and authority will introduce indigenous knowledge and new categories into the semantic universe of comparative education, through the typical interpretive underlying metaphors of culture as text, dialog and game.

The ontological turn has generated interest in being in the world and accepting that different worldviews. CIE conceptualization of the Global South are not simply different representations of the same world, but a different world (Connell, 2007; Cottrell, 2010 and de Sousa Santos, 2018). The ontological turn entails a change in theoretical orientation, whereby differences are understood not in terms of a difference in world*views* but differences in *worlds*, and all these worlds are equally valid (see Southern Theory, Chapter 4). This is challenging to apply in practice in versions of CIE that cling to the idea of education empowering people to transition from one world (traditional) to another, more desirable one (modernity), instead of thinking of each people's own education as having equal validity. As Chapters 3 and 4 will show, in the case of studies of indigenous people uncovering their own past education in Africa, South America, Australia, or Canada, or juxtaposing education in the

United States and India, peoples' own words have not always been accorded equal validity, in education itself or in CIE research.

Postcolonialism(s)

The different understandings of colonialism and imperialism complicate the meaning of "postcolonialism," a term and a set of theories still debated. "Postcolonialism" cannot be used in the singular but only in the plural—"postcolonialisms"—because decolonization went on for three centuries and unfolded so differently in different parts of the world, including South America, Australia, and South Africa. The prefix "post" further complicates matters because it implies aftermath. A country and its education system may be *post*colonial, in the sense of formally independent, and at the same time *neo*-colonial, remaining militarily, economically, and culturally dependent, as Latin American dependency theorists in particular have argued. In an immanent critique of humanism, postcolonial and race theorists re-grounded the lofty claims of European Humanism in the history of colonialism and racist violence. They held Europeans accountable for the uses and abuses of this ideal by looking at colonial history and the violent domination of other cultures but did not fully reject its basic humanist premises. As we have seen, Edward Said (1978) exposed the "dismissiveness" of other cultures and civilizations and what was constructed as "the Orient" has nothing to do with the place, people, or cultures of that region. Postcolonial theory challenges the traditional practices of comparative education by questioning its inherent power imbalances, Eurocentric biases, and tendency to overlook the historical and social contexts of colonized nations when comparing educational systems (Soudien 2008). Soudien promotes a critical re-evaluation of how education comparisons are conducted, particularly when examining systems that have experienced colonialism, there is a need to consider the cultural and historical context of a country when analyzing its education system in comparison to Western systems. Can comparative research be conducted without reinforcing existing power hierarchies? Or how can CIE researchers decolonize their methodologies to ensure a more equitable analysis of educational systems? Those are basic questions Crain Soudien, from South Africa, poses for doing comparative research using postcolonial theory.

In a similar way to poststructuralism, postcoloniality can be understood as subversion and overturning of received oppositions and hierarchies, and it has come in for criticism. As it resorts to a language of critique serving to reinforce rather than challenge the dominance of Western interpretations of non-Western realities, there is a certain wariness on the part of intellectuals from the Global South toward postcoloniality. It is perceived as distant from situations in the South, and because of its supposed overlap with "post-modernism." Postmodernism in this view has a specifically Western malaise which breeds angst and despair instead of aiding political action and resistance (Loomba 1998: xii).

Another shortcoming of postcolonial theory is its focus on Global East/West or North/South distinctions and its underestimation of the role of race and racism. By conflating the West with whiteness and contextualizing it in terms of the civilizational encounter between "West and the Rest" postcolonial theory tends to efface racism internal to the West itself.

Post-socialism

If post-socialism was a historical time we could explore when it began and, respectively, when it may stop being useful, Ringel (2022) would rather ask this question from an analytical perspective: "What temporal reach does the concept of post-socialism have, and what kind of temporal phenomena does it help to describe?" (191). Some scholars have argued that as an analytical concept post-socialism has run out its course, the same way postmodernism did (McHale 2007). Yet for the last three decades the concept of post-socialism was productive and stimulating research because of its manifold temporal meanings. Education comparatives found it useful in their explorations, notably Iveta Silova's article (2010a) and her edited book *Post Socialism is Not Dead* (2010b)

By contesting a common expectation that post-socialist societies would inevitably converge towards Western norms, this book sees post-socialism as open, plural, and inevitably uncertain. When comparative research gives serious consideration, Silova writes on the historical, political, social, and cultural contexts of post-socialist transformations, assuming characteristics of complex, dynamic processes. The chapters (Silova 2010b) pose both theoretical and conceptual complexifications of post-socialism by raising a series of important questions. Like, what are the elements of continuities and discontinuities in various post-socialist settings and how do they interact in reshaping education policies and practices? What rationalities underpin the logic and define the purpose of education transformations in different post-socialist contexts? While we might not be able to answer all those questions or what influence the socialist past has on the post-socialist present and future,

Ringel (2022: 206) suggests we keep the term "post-socialism" for now as it is an invitation to think about time and human agency, and to reconsider our understanding of permanence and change. In this way, she writes:

> Presuming a link to the socialist past, either envisioned as a break with or a continuation of it, encourages us to be more specific about our informants' metaphysics as well as the temporal frameworks that we have in mind when thinking through what stayed the same and what did actually change after the downfall of state socialism and its incorporation into the global capitalist political economy.

Posthumanism

Posthumanism is especially associated with the foundational work of Donna Haraway, a feminist theorist and historian of science and technology. Her texts constitute a pioneering effort to explore connections between contemporary biotechnological sciences and the human and social sciences. The key site of this intersection is the posthuman figure of the *cyborg*, the cybernetic organism—both literal and metaphorical—where the organically human and technologically artificial converge. "Late twentieth-century machines," she writes:

> have made thoroughly ambiguous the difference between natural and artificial, mind and body, self-developing and externally designed, and many other distinctions that used to apply to organisms and machines. Our machines are disturbingly lively, and we ourselves frighteningly inert.
>
> (Haraway 1991: 152)

CIE is dependent on the very notion of "the human" who takes charge of their futures, using education internationally to advance the global economy personally and nationally for better futures. Contemporary market economies profit from the control and commodification of all that lives, they result in erasing categorical distinctions between the human and other species, seeds, plants, animals, and bacteria. This is complicated by contradictory redefinitions of what exactly counts as human. As shown above, the poststructuralist rejection of Enlightenment-based ideals of the human did not stop at the humanist image of "Man." In the twenty-first century, we acknowledge it is impossible to speak in one voice about a category such as "Modern Man" (see above), women, LBGTQ+ communities, indigenous people, disabled, and other marginal subjects. CIE studies human globally linked, and technologically mediated societies have blurred the traditional distinction between the human and its others. Braidotti (2019) helps us explore the extent to which a posthumanist move displaces the traditional humanistic unity and "Man" as the subject of education and development studies. Rather than perceiving this situation as a loss of cognitive and disciplinary self-mastery, Braidotti outlines new forms of cosmopolitan neo-humanism that emerges from the spectrum of post-colonial and race studies, as well as gender analysis and environmentalism, who have shown that human have become the major changing agents of the most physical process. Anthropocene, the current geological age, refers to the period of time during which humans have become the major planetary force of change. Human activity has been the dominant influence on climate and the environment, some date it as far as the Industrial Revolution. Comparativists have to revise many fundamental assumptions and procedures of "development" in the era of the Anthropocene. As Amitav Ghosh (2016) points out, "the climate crisis is also a crisis of culture, and thus of the imagination … This culture is, of course intimately linked with the wider histories of imperialism and capitalism that have shaped the world" (9–10).

This was the theme of the 2021 CIES conference. The challenge of a field like CIE is seizing the opportunities for studying new social configurations and community building, when they are the physical agents of change, while educating how to pursue sustainability and empowerment. Braidotti (2019) argues the posthuman helps make sense of our flexible and multiple identities and the escalating effects of post-anthropocentric thought, which encompass not only other species, but also the sustainability of our planet (see Chapter 5). Considering the implications of these shifts for CIE practice, this new interest has tied the fate of humanity to the fate of the planet, as Iveta Silova (2021) observed: "For comparative and international education, this entails searching for new vocabulary that brings to the forefront of our work the reality of the climate crisis … while learning new mutually recuperative ways of being with the Earth where everyone and everything (both human and more-than-human) are deeply interconnected" (593).

The de-stabilizing of the human by technologically mediated social relations in a globally connected world is also complicated by contradictory redefinitions of what exactly counts as human. Due to dislocating the centrality of the human in favor of the in-/non-/post-human in Western techno-sciences, Haraway (1991) stresses a dynamic web of interconnections or hybrid contaminations, such as the cyborg, which is the figure of hybridity par excellence. She refuses to succumb to the pitfall of the classical nature/culture divide: there is no natural order as distinct from technological mediation. Haraway argues the subject/object and nature/culture divides are ultimately linked to patriarchy, in opposition to it, as many CIE feminist scholars did and do work on patriarchy. She advocated for an enlarged sense of community based on empathy (see Affect Theory and Irving Epstein's Illustration). Haraway is very cautious about the term *posthuman*, giving priority instead to our accountability for historical aspects of Western culture, including colonialism and fascism, which are in open contradiction to our stated beliefs in humanist ideals and principles.

Intersectionality and Affect Theory

Other theories belonging to the *post* era not overtly marked by the prefix *post* include *intersectionality theory* and *affect theory*.

Intersectionality is understood in CIE as an interpretative frame of reference for viewing the social world, developed within the practice of social justice by grassroots social activists struggling for change. Broadly, intersectionality can be defined as the critical insight that race, class, gender, sexuality, ethnicity, nation, ability, and age operate not as unitary, mutually exclusive factors or forces, but as reciprocally constructing phenomena that in turn shape complex social inequalities. To put it simply, lives are always made up of multiple relations of social domination. Patricia Hill Collins (2015) argues that "intersectionality" is a crucial analytical tool for understanding how different systems of oppression, like race, class, and gender, overlap and intertwine to create unique experiences of marginalization. Critically important for CIE academic analysis and political action to achieve social justice and the need to consider these intersecting systems rather than examining them in separation from one another in isolation. Intersectionality is important both analytical and political for its "attentiveness to power relations and social inequalities" (Collins 2015: 3). This comes through in Iyengar and Witenstein's (2019) work in which women in a non-formal, upskilling center introspectively and collaboratively examine their hybrid worlds at the work-shed and at home in relation to their multiplicity of identities. When opportunities for engaging intersectionality arise, comparativists and the communities they are working with/in can more fully address dilemmas. Moreover, intersectionality has entered the forefront of CIE work as Call-Cummings et al. (2019) indicated, "destabilizing power and authority: taking intersectionality seriously" was one of the four plenary sessions at the 2017 CIES sponsored symposium Interrogating and Innovating CIE Research (p. 4). Further unpacking of intersectionality in CIE can be found in Manion et al. (2020).

Affect theory explores emotions and feelings both in their "hard-wired" physiological aspect (tears, expressions of disgust, fight/flight responses, etc.) and in their partly acculturated social aspect. Associated with critical theorists such as Eve Sedgwick and Lauren Berlant, affect theory spans a number of disciplines, including psychology, philosophy, psychoanalytic theory, gender studies, and art theory, appearing with different emphases and definitions in each discipline. Critical theorists and other scholars identify the role of affect in shaping social values, gender ideals, and group solidarity. Affect is seen as instrumental in events and symbols that produce shared identities and is therefore central in contemporary social and political studies that examine connections between education and nation- and society-building. The importance of assemblage to social movement formation and development, and its importance within the realm of interpersonal connection, is significant as a central component within theories of affect. Assemblage theory can indeed promote CIE scholarship, teaching, and practice in important ways, if its importance is understood as supporting the broader tenets of theories of affect (Epstein 2019). Affect also has a central role in capitalist systems, where it features in people's attachment to commodities and in the association of education with class mobility. The non-discursive and non-deliberative attributes of affect may produce social interactions and experiences that allow people to experience new modes of existence distinct from their main life circumstances (see Epstein's Illustration in this volume).

Conclusion

The structure of modernity as a metatheory and development space for individuals and for nation-building is fundamental for understanding the theoretical building-blocks of CIE in its past manifestations and contemporary changes. In modernity, the self was for the first time separated from the larger field of organized social forces that ascribed identity. For the first time in history, the social self was viewed not as ascribed to the individual but as achieved, developed, constructed, or fashioned. The social theories above were used by CIE research and advocate for national and international investment in education. This worldwide project after the Second World War to build and structure the new modern selves, for building the newly liberated, newly drowned boundaries by the colonized nation, came to absorb a large swathe of the academic social-science disciplines. The dissolution of the modernist project and the concomitant crisis of selfhood have driven the tendency of recent social science to reorganize, to look back critically at familiar social forms such as education, ethnicity, regionalism, religion, heritage, country of origin, and indigeneity. Questions have been raised about the education system's role, and about what has been transferred or borrowed from other systems and implemented through the power of international donor entities and their consultants, who advise, plan, and assess education outcomes and students' achievements.

The paradigms we surveyed in this chapter—functionalist, radical structuralist, radical humanist, and interpretive—frame the ways research is conducted into educational phenomena and the ways education systems are compared. The paradigms enable the social construction of knowledge. Each represents a distinct social-scientific reality with regard to the nature of knowledge and society. Therefore, educational planning, policy, and implementation is differently elaborated in each paradigm. These four broad worldviews employed social science theories, each with their methods (see Chapter 3), leading to the conclusion that what the paradigms of comparative education all share (or three out of four of them do, at any rate, the case of the interpretive paradigm being problematic in this respect) is the very category "education," which thus permits educators from different worldviews to continue their conversation with each other. Within the functionalist paradigm, education is seen as a liberating, empowering experience, contributing to individual modernization and national social change. Within the radical structuralist paradigm, by contrast, education is seen as assisting through screening and allocation, in the preparation of a compliant workforce for the modern economic sectors, leaving the "uneducated" in the non-modernized sectors behind. Here, education reproduces social inequality rather than affording the opportunity for individual social mobility. Within the radical humanist paradigm, development education is viewed as part of the alienating institutions that drive a wedge between people and their true consciousness. A "pedagogy of the oppressed" would seek to rehumanize education through dialogue and consciousness-raising. The interpretive paradigm has produced the most impact on contemporary methodological debate within CIE, shifting the ground away from "high" or "grand" metatheories, those that underpin modernization and developmentalism, to investigate the epistemological foundations of education sciences and the ontological status of social reality, not only in schools but in different types and ways of education, even children learning in the streets. In CIE's social theorizing this shift is evident in the renewal of interest in interpretation, active participatory ethnographic research, the production of open-ended dialogic work, and a focus on theorization and practices in the Global South.

We began this survey of social science theory with paradigms that compose and frame CIE and its research and knowledge production. We conclude this overview with Rolland Paulston's 1994 mapping "comparative education: paradigms and theories" changing the 2×2 schematic (see Figure 2) to rounded (world) plotting the theories we have reviewed in this chapter. As you can see below Figure 3, the theories are in the space of four paradigms with the arrows indicating how close or far a theory is from one worldview, and in relation to another. As you can see in this placement,

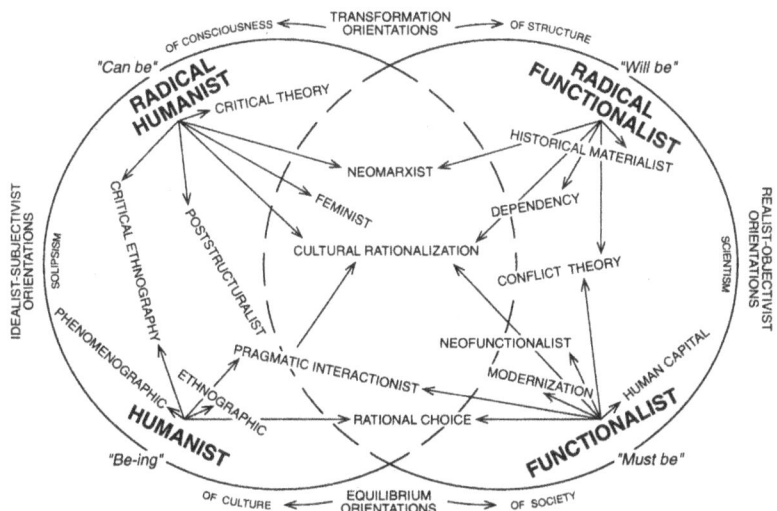

Figure 3 Paulston's global mapping of paradigmatic discourses and territorial disputes in sixty comparative education texts. Paulston, R. G., ed. (1996), *Social Cartography: Mapping Ways of Seeing Social and Educational Change*, p. 15, Reproduced from a paper presented at CIES, San Diego, California, 21–24 March, 1994.

Paulston associated radical functionalism with transformation of structure and a projection that the world "will be." Whereas the radical humanist is associated with the transformation of consciousness and a project the "can be." As the functionalist is close to equilibrium society "must be" with Human Capital theory at its very head. The humanist paradigm, as described above, shares with functionalism a common concern for the sociology of regulation, yet interpretive theories present a perspective in which individual actors negotiate their "being." Paulston believed that without such a "map" it would be difficult for CIE researchers with diverse views and way of producing knowledge to work and communicate as a worldwide community of scholars, whereas his "social cartography" (see Chapter 3) is a way he found to include all perspectives in one circular world (Paulston 1996: 298).

It would be simplistic to conclude that lack of firm academic institutional structures led to CIE's fragmentation, given its competing goals, theories, methodologies, and claims, and the role ambiguity that is inherent in the practice of CIE. Given the different worldviews they embraced as an initial point of dialogue, the question is whether this fragmentation indicated a commitment to diversity and an openness to competing worldviews, framing theories, and research methodologies. Chapters 3 and 4 will also address these questions, bringing the paradigms and theories to bear on methods and practices of doing research and scholarly investigations.

Academic Activities—Springboards

Springboard A

Read, Juxtapose & Comment:
Escobar, Arturo. (1992), 'Imagining a Post-Development Era? Critical Thought, Development and Social Movements', *Social Text*, 31/32: 20–56.

Arturo Escobar introduces:

The Demise of Development and the Problematization of Protest. For some time now it has been difficult—at times even impossible—to talk about development, protest or revolution with the same confidence and encompassing scope with which intellectuals and activists spoke about those topics in the 1960s.

CIES 2024 chose *The Power of Protest in Education* as the theme for the annual conference:

The power of protest in education lies in the fact that it is, by definition, a public act. Protest allows people facing injustice to generate power through collective action. As a community of Comparative and International Education researchers, teachers, activists, program developers or organizers, how might we engage with, and think generatively about, the histories, curriculum, theories and methodologies, and pedagogies that guide acts of protest? See more at CIES 2024 Conference in Miami.

Escobar views protest within social movement and in-did unbeknown to CIES, 2024 turned out to be **the year of protests**, a social movement all over Europe and United States this time about the war in Gaza.

Comment on CIES idea of "the power of protest in education." From your own view about education and from the reading of this chapter, what will bring people out to protest even without having a personal part in the cause.

Springboard B

Read & Comment:
Blake, Nigel. (1996), "Between Postmodernism and Anti-modernism: The Predicament of Educational Studies," *British Journal of Educational Studies* 44 (1): 42–65.

Nigel Blake highlights the urgent and radical questions and problems that postmodernism posed for education studies in general. He outlines and interrelates the legacies of modernism in social and cultural theory and contrasts the reactionary anti-modernism of the Right with traditionalism. A salient theme to this point is the variety of conceptions of the relationship between knowledge and power. The concept of the self in postmodernism and thereafter is described and related to new problems about ethics and a newly emerging importance of the aesthetic. Finally, the paper argues that while the fundamental issues for philosophy of education are unchanged—problems about instrumentalism and various issues of autonomy—these are radically recast and present new difficulties.

A. Are the 2020s political and economic context of education like political takeover of Boards of Education, to enforce curriculum changes and removing books from libraries in the United States; or violent protests, against Muslim immigrants all over Europe, a reaction against progressive education and liberal values?

B. Some of those who react declare that "they are traditionalists." Since in many walks of life keeping up tradition is regarded as positive. How do you view their reactionary acts in the name of tradition?

3
Methods

The theories outlined in Chapter 2 in four social sciences paradigms and theorizing in the "post" have influenced and even dictated comparative and international education (CIE) research methods. They have not done so in any chronological manner, some were "in fashion" earlier in the 1960s, years well-covered in Chapter 1, and some "came after," but our disciplinary studies are not static, they are used at different times, some come back, while others fade away. As elaborated on in Chapter 2, each paradigm has different assumptions about the nature of being, what it is to be in the world, ontologically, the philosophical study of being, as well as the assumption of knowledge, Epistemology, in Greek epistēmē ("knowledge") and logos ("reason"). Both ontological and epistemology underlinings, are especially important regarding methods, validity, and scope, of producing disciplinary knowledge.

We have framed the overview of the methods in this chapter, aligned with the theories we have covered in Chapter 2, also explored by Gunbayi and Sorm (2018), showing how functionalist, interpretive, radical humanist, and radical structuralist paradigms influence and guide the design of social research studies. They highlight how each paradigm carries different assumptions about the reality of being and therefore leads to distinct research approaches and methodologies. The methods CIE researchers use evolve in shifting assumptions, worldviews, that are used to anchor research questions and what lenses are used to conduct the analysis. This chapter also uses the idea of "tensions" as we discuss various methodological alternatives within one paradigmatic sphere. We have included references and descriptions of different research done in the different paradigms, the studies exemplify CIE research studies to learn from. As a researcher or an aspiring one, it is useful to ask yourself, what assumption does the mentioned study assume about "being" and what method(s) has it used to produce (new) knowledge? One other question when examining studies and the ways CIE methods operate is to identify the level the research operated on: macro, micro or meso.

The *macro level* corresponds to structures that are national, social, economic, cultural, or institutional—for example, countries and national or supranational organizations like the UN, NATO, or the European Union.

The *micro* level of analysis focuses on individual or small-group interactions. The unit of analysis typically consists of individuals, small groups, specific events or teaching method/s, or student-teacher relations of one grade level at one school system.

The *meso level* analysis falls between the macro and the micro levels, mid-range; Meso-level units of analysis include clan, tribe, rural schools, political parties, social movements, and schools, private or public. Meso level may also refer to analyses designed to reveal micro and macro-level connections.

By reading research studies, we can learn both the level of analysis, macro, micro, or meso, and about the method/s used (Wirt 1980). Most of all published work has a section called "method," which describes which and how a method was applied and what prior research has been done using this method. Most studies refer to other studies that have used the same method, as a way to anchor the chosen method, and rationalize why this method fits a given research question, or the objectives of the study. We all mainly use methods that researchers have used before us, quoting them, and the way/s they have used this method/s, and why it fits our research purpose or protocol. At different points in a research paper, you will find short abstracts of relevant research to the methods discussed, to know what methods were applied and how they have been appropriated to study education internationally.

Functionalist Research Methods

Tension 1: Developed and Under-Developed

Comparative research right after the Second World War was all about developing the so-called newly established states after colonization, under the regime of the all-encompassing modernization theory. As Chapter 1 has shown, CIE in the 1950s and 1960s was all about developing, development, and modernization. Once education was found to have highly statistically significance in such studies as the "modern-man" and the theory of Human Capital (see Chapter 2), the only missing part was how to calculate" rate-of return" on investment. As mentioned, Schultz (1961) invented the formula to calculate both the personal and national return on investment in developing human capital as before only physical capital investments had formulas to calculate their economic return. This discovery showed a clear path to eradicate the so-called "under-developed" investment in education in the quest for economic, social, and political development.

Research during this tension and the quest to "develop" was genuinely dependent on country studies sponsored by development agencies such as USAID, the UK Department for International Development (DFID), UNESCO, OECD, and the World Bank using societal models coming mostly from Western economics and sociology. Those were the base of CIE research methods to study different countries to advise on developing education systems, or reforms, that got funding. So as Chapter 4 will illustrate, the funding comes with advice (or directives) from the funding agency that will contract a study before deciding on funding. A good example is a 1989 World Bank (WB) working paper to offer India relevant international experience on why they should embark on primary education rapid development. This study was contracted out to two international education scholars, who were responsible for the findings, the Bank had no obligation to implement the recommendations. Colletta and Sutton's (1989) study starts with a review of the "current situation in India with regard to the goals, targets and constraints on realizing universal primary education" (UPE). Followed by one page, on the comparative international method, this method is based on a descriptive, primary education development in five selected countries. Reading the countries names it is hard to justify the comparisons, but here is their explanation: Countries that have made rapid progress towards attaining and sustaining UPE, to "derive lessons relevant to India from them," are Kenya, Tanzania, and Indonesia. They have gross enrolment ratios higher than 90 percent, fifth grade cohort retention rates of 60 percent or more, and primary enrolments have grown at an annual rate of 5 percent or higher, from 1960 to 1980. Because their progress is recent, "it has been attained in a global situation similar to that which exists for India today." Great justification but still questionable if we recall that Tanzania was supported by Soviet funds and curriculum and learning methods. Indonesia, the largest Muslim population in the world, is so different spatially (islands). The other two are Sri Lanka, which was selected for 'its sociocultural similarity to India" (what about size?), and China, which was selected "because it has approached provision for the largest, and among the poorest, child population in the world" (1); but what about such different geopolitical makeup? As you can see, Colletta and Sutton (1989) rationalized their comparisons choice, which is the most important factor when writing up your method. This is a typical comparative study for a country the WB is preparing a loan for, as this was the time when the WB believed in universal primary education for development and their funds were given for this purpose (Klees et al. 2012; Bonala et al. 2023).

As this example shows, the assumptions of "what works" and "best practices" used for "underdeveloped countries" in the Global South have been taking form models the World Bank has been using while working with different countries. Donors for many years used cost-benefit analysis, quantitative research methods, in determining which intervention is most effective in delivering education to support economic development. Even in 2017, Edwards Jr. observed a pushback of other methods that may be more contextually relevant and action/empowerment-focused that could be used instead of the favorable functionalist quantitative method.

Paradigm and Major Theories	Methods Within Those Theories	Example Studies
The Functionalist Paradigm Development Modernization Human Capital Social Capital	Empirical cross-national study of large amounts of data Social science concepts and techniques testing hypotheses: The relations between educational variables and political, economic, and social characteristics (Edding 1965; Foster 1966; Evans 1968; Lave & Kyle 1968; Asher and Shively 1969; Li 1971; Farrell 1979).	Inkeles (1969) and his Harvard project, 'Making Men Modern: On the Causes and Consequences of Individual Change in Six Developing Countries.' Schultz (1961) calculates human capital expenditure on education not a consumption but an investment in the capacity of labor to produce goods
	Collect official statistics data on social & economic indices of "development"	Bowman (1966), 'The Human Investment Revolution in Economic Thought.'
	Questionnaire responses to education parameters to compare countries	Farrell (1979), 'Some New Analytic Techniques for Comparative Educators.'

Paradigm and Major Theories	Methods Within Those Theories	Example Studies
	Index national and personal modernity	Eckstein (1970), 'On Teaching a "Scientific" Comparative Education.'
	Measure of indicators using formal deductive logical properties	Psacharopoulos (1982), 'The Economics of Higher Education in Developing Countries.'
	Rate of return on human investment in education; value-added method	Coleman's social capital case studies
	Direct observation of Education processes	

The table presents the functionalist paradigm, significant theories, and analysis methods. It shows the methods derived from the theories we encountered in Chapter 2 and references to CIE studies.

The functionalist paradigm uses statistical techniques to analyze data and compare results across countries. The studies in this paradigm use already collected data at a single point in time across multiple countries or also longitudinal data. Large data sets are also collected using official statistics, using questionnaires for education parameters, or direct observation of educational processes. Research using such scientific methods in CIE implies a functionalist worldview.

Counting, surveying, questionnaires collecting, and statistical analysis—those usually quantify the education phenomenon, like national levels of schooling attainment in a country to compare with another country or a few countries in a region or countries with the same gross national income (GNI; another statistically measured indicator).

Methods in this paradigm use theories such as modernization and developmentalism as a way of producing knowledge and practicing comparative education research. Unsurprisingly, a large proportion of empirical research in comparative education countries studies, e.g., costs or benefits measures, measuring individual modernity, workforce planning techniques, incorporates methods and techniques taken directly from neoclassical economics using quasi-experimental statistical analysis.

In education, most quantitative studies of the effects of educational inputs on outputs—or educational attainment correlations with outcomes such as income, unemployment, job satisfaction, or productivity—use regression analysis techniques; they do not show any causal relation. There are theoretical and empirical reasons to argue that such methods provide helpful information but remember that those are not cause-and-effect results (Klees 1986: 599).

Nation-State Unit of Analysis

Using the "nation-state" as a unit of analysis refers to studying education in countries, using each nation as an individual entity, where each country is considered a distinct political unit with a shared national identity. Those comparative education studies were the bases of CIE becoming a disciplinary field of study. In Chapter 1 we showed how research using the "state" as the unit of analysis has been criticized, as so many large countries have regions that are very different from one another, including language, culture, and implementation of Western education patterns. Analyzing 1157 articles in CER between 1957 and 2006, Wolhuter (2008) found that the most used level of analysis was the nation-state. The country or nation-state or national education system was traditionally the focus of comparative education research. Many were sure that globalization would change the focus of comparative education on the state as the preferred unit of analysis. We mentioned Holmes (1981) presenting a coherent theory of comparative education research based on a taxonomy for education problems. Holmes suggested that problems should be examined, and the outcomes of hypothetical solutions or policies should be tested under identified national circumstances. Those methods, distinctive mirror debate among social scientists in the 1970s, rejected induction or any interpretive methods, using qualitative research as not adequate in themselves. Although Holmes explicitly declared himself to be a follower of the importance of context in defining education systems as a starting point, he proposed a "scientific" method that, if applied with rigor, would overcome the difficulties making successful analysis of education borrowing possible (Holmes 1981). Statistical analysis became more rigorous with time, and coupled with other qualitative methods as we will see following, using mix-methods, took over. Other paradigms analyzing smaller than national levels comparatively, like classrooms, schools and districts, permitted observing processes and taking context into account, were less favored by US CIE research, at the time of planning or reforming the whole country system.

Large-Scale International Comparisons of Nations

As referred to a few times, the widely known international comparison studies that continue to use nations as the unit of analysis, making world news, every four years, about the ranking of nations on the bases of comparing students' academic achievements. The extensive international tests which use quantitative models—the comparison units are students' achievements in each country. International assessments evaluate students' knowledge of the curriculum and ability to apply their skills. TIMSS and PIRLS are grade-based, while the Program for International Student Assessment (PISA) tests are an age-based sample of fifteen-year-old students. PISA was launched by the OECD in 1997, first administered in 2000 and now involves over eighty countries. The PISA survey provides comparative data on students' performance in reading, mathematics, and science literacy. PISA also assesses the country's education system and emphasizes socio-economic and equity factors. Global comparisons have become improved by new information technologies, which has raised the impact of the data analysis resalts on international, national, and privet organizations funding decision-making.

The method used included statistical and psychometric approaches underlying the analysis of the TIMSS 2019 data using a program called "Item Response Theory" (IRT), a methodology frequently used in educational measurement that is also increasingly common in other applications of quantitative analysis of human response data such as patient-reported outcomes, consumer choice, and other domains. IRT allows controlling for a mode of administration effects on student performance and produces a latent variable scale representing student proficiency that is comparable across the paper- and computer-based assessments. For TIMSS 2019, in an attempt to provide more context, the mathematics and science items were collected from student questionnaires and parent questionnaires of fourth graders' attitudes and participation. This model combines IRT approaches and a regression-based approach that utilizes the context data as predictors for the deviation of a prior distribution of proficiency.

Researchers question this research: those tests are "measuring global standards or reinforcing inequalities" (Kell and Kell 2010). Following up on the new test results, countries scoring low on their student achievement tests look up and visit "them" countries with high scores. This search for cause and effect, continues international flows of reform, funded by national and international donor foundations and agencies, that look for "proven" education structures and content that "works." Government, and non-governmental agencies from around the world investigate the nation's education system that tested the highest in search of the "one factor" of its education accomplishments. Studying the testing results to isolate "what works" ignores the need to contextualize students' academic achievement. While those published results are influencing governments and Ministries of Education to reform, just what has produced the high scoring country's students, might not be replicated.

One powerful incentive for such borrowing is created by what Sellar et al. (2017) have called "PISA envy." Those international comparisons, like PISA, serve as a powerful lever for change; countries with poor comparative performance experience policy pressure through which ideas that previously seemed extreme, unfit for their local condition and cultures, enter national policy and attract attention and support implementing change. In turn, these might lead to new ideas that legitimate the pressure to adopt borrowed educational practices from high-performance countries. A good example is from the early 2000s when Finland scored the highest, and there were countries as far as Japan and Nigeria, in their education character, that were looking to copy Finland. Finland became the envy of the world, and education researchers sought explanations and lessons (Simola 2005). Just as Finland achieved hegemony in landing education teaching and learning to others, after the 2012 PISA administration, Finland found itself outside the top ten countries in math for the first time. Sending the country into a search for education solutions may be practiced by the new highest-scoring country. Why do some comparativists dismiss those studies as "international" and not comparative, even if they are used in planning and policy? As Gorur (2019) showed, no amount of "big data" can demonstrate a causal relationship between education and social-economic, political, and cultural development.

Even today, many comparativists assume that the nation-state is the relevant unit of comparison in that national cultural traits can explain education phenomena in each country. This assumption still underpins much comparative research but is ever more questioned in the context of globalization, cross-border migration, and transnational teaching and learning and educational organizations that operate across borders.

Human Capital and Rate of Return on Education

Education achievements, human capital, and different rates of return, nationally and individually, were measured for many years by statistical analysis of data collected on indicators such as: years of schooling, data inputs for education such as availability of classrooms, textbooks, pencils, teacher training, and salaries, use of radio, and/or television, (and more recently) school computers, and iPads, tablets, or phones, that teachers and/or students can use. They are then measured by conducting correlation and regression analysis. Another quantitative lens to compare education accomplishments was to calculate the rate of return, as part of the "Human Capital Theory" for which Theodore Schultz (1960s) provided a formulate to evaluate return on investment in education. Lifelong rate of return is mostly measured using the income approach (what is the expected earning for individuals). As discussed in Chapter 2, human capital was used to show that one of the most profitable investments to increase the overall economic productivity of countries (as measured by GNP), as well as individual social mobility was investment in education. Exactly what aspects of education contributed to productivity were unknown and unexamined; higher earnings were consistently associated with more educated workers and they were assumed to be more productive. Development education for years used a single explanation: that better-educated workers have more knowledge and skills, which translate into higher productivity (Levin and McEwan 2001: 159).

As we saw above this is what international comparisons use, the test scores and students' achievements; higher test scores reflected levels of skill and knowledge that increased productivity and earnings. Levin and McEwan (2001), among others, noted that human capital investment in education had no specific implications for what should be taught in school and how it should be taught. In other words, whatever the content of schooling, it showed high correlations between the amount of education received and earning. Levin's research into different disciplines and literatures shows that with technological advances this simple equation no longer works. Using the 1996 Third International Mathematics and Science Study to assess the relationship between examination results in mathematics with indicators of national economic performance for the forty countries they found no relationship. Nor was there any statistical relationship between scores from past studies and subsequent economic growth. In 1984 Kim used a qualitative method to show that schooling is the variable that accounts for about 17 percent of the variance in social achievement, and family and individual variables only explains 4 percent. Both Kim (1984) and many other studies of Henry Levin report on data that have been derived primarily from the traditional economic systems that have characterized most countries. While shifts are made to industries based on high-productivity workplace organizations and products and services, the question, does what schools teach makes a difference, is ongoing.

Research on School Provision and Success

A 1981 study in Nicaragua, reported by Jamison et al. (1981), examined the impact of radio use and availability of textbooks in improving mathematics education at the primary school level. Eight schools participated (with 3,000 pupils), with forty-eight of them in the experimental Group, and the remaining forty in the control group. Regarding textbooks, the control group did not have individual textbooks; texts were used exclusively as resource books for the teacher. In the experimental group, each student had access to a textbook. As for radio use, the control group was taught by teachers, whereas the experimental group was taught by radio. The results showed that the experimental group scored more significantly in mathematics on both counts than the control group. They further observed that radio and textbooks were more effective in rural areas (557).

Another study that looked at the relationship between academic achievement and the availability of books/furniture/classrooms in Botswana was investigated by Mwamwenda and Mwamwenda (1984). Their statistical analyses showed that pupils who belonged to schools with enough classrooms performed significantly better than those who did not have enough classrooms. They found that this held "true in their overall performance, mathematics, and social studies, except for their performance in English and science in which the difference was non-significant," i.e., low correlation (234). They also questioned teachers, and many in Botswana admitted that on numerous occasions they could not conduct their outside classes because of adverse weather conditions. Such pupils' performance at school cannot, with justice, be compared to that of pupils who are provided with classrooms.

These studies are not limited to the 1980s: Investigate links between students' achievement and several resource inputs in African primary schools were used by Lee and Zuze's (2011) study of four sub-Saharan countries that had in place legislation mandating free and universal primary schooling: Botswana, Malawi, Namibia, and Uganda. They used data from the 2000 Southern and Eastern Africa Consortium for Monitoring "Educational Quality" attributing it to multilevel modeling (hierarchical linear model); they reported high correlations which they called *strong links* between material and human resources and grade six students' achievement in reading and mathematics. Structural features such as school shifts and school size were *negatively associated (law correlated)* with achievement, although effects varied across countries. Please note these students' achievements were test scores. As noted above, Levin (2002) states that the forty-country comparative analysis he quotes reinforces the observations that examination scores seem to play a smaller role than popularly believed in accounting for the economic contribution of education. However, he thinks that what schools do does matter.

A long-term priority is to establish schools in which enrichment replaces memorization, student projects replace drill, and student assessment is based on what Sternberg has called measures of successful intelligence, not inert intelligence. Of course there would be provision for students to learn basic skills, but these would be integrated into the activities of a different type of school (Levin 2002: 149).

It would have been helpful to have such research. However, comparativists' using political science and economic research indicators have not answered those questions. Controlling for the usual factors does not explain many learning outcomes; for instance, a study in India found that the mathematics achievements of street children are not explained by the usual socio-economic control factors (Chowdhury 2017).

Radical Structuralist Studies and Methods

Paradigm and Major Theories	Methods Within Those Theories	Example Studies
Radical structuralist paradigm Marxist theory and colonialism Development Imperialism Dependency World-Systems theory Neo-institutionalism World Cultural theory Theorizing convergence: consensus model—Modernization transcended internationally Globalization Internationalization	Study the macro-relationship between educational systems and their social contexts Analysis of social hierarchy reproduction analysis Early ethnography systematic research protocol Studying societal models Measures of economic growth Network Meta-Analysis; Statistical Analyses Transfer & borrowing Western education worldwide spread Implement similar education systems & solutions and reforms borrowed to different national systems Understanding globalization by studying the convergence of education models Emerging global economic and communications	Bowles and Gintis (1976), 'Education in Capitalist America.' Foster (1970), 'Comparative Methodology and the Study of African Education.' Carnoy (1974), 'Education as Cultural Imperialism Knowledge Itself has been "Colonized."' Bourdieu and Passeron (1977), 'Reproduction in Education, Society, and Culture.' Masemann (1976), 'Anthropological Approaches to Comparative Education.' Carnoy (1985), 'Schools as Institutions Understood by Relation to the State and the Economy.' Wallerstein (2000), 'The Rise and Future Demise of the World Capitalist System: Concepts for Comparative Analysis.' Levin (1978), Altbach (1977), and Arnove (1980) compare how educational systems serve societal groups differently Jackson and Nexon (2002), 'Globalization, the Comparative Method, and Comparing Constructions.' *Comparative Education Review*, 46 (1) (2002) 'The Meanings of Globalization for Educational Change.' Crăciun (2018), 'National Policies for Higher Education internationalization.' Stein (2017), 'Considering the Case of Curriculum Internationalization.'

Paradigm and Major Theories	Methods Within Those Theories	Example Studies
	Internationalizing Higher Education: Students and visiting scholars: what was "brain drain" has become global "brain circulation."	George Mwangi and Yao (2021), 'U.S. Higher Education Internationalization.' Altbach (2013), 'Brain Drain or Brain Exchange: Developing Country Implications.'

Approaches of data collection in this paradigm include:

Collection of official statistics: Data on social and economic indices of "development" are collected from official sources to measure macro-level factors.

Cross-national comparative analysis: The study examines educational systems across multiple countries to compare and analyze relationships with social contexts.

Questionnaires: Responses to education parameters are collected via questionnaires to compare countries.

Index creation: Indices of national and personal modernity are developed to measure critical concepts.

Indicator measurement: Various indicators are measured using formal deductive logical properties.

Economic analysis: Methods like rate of return on human investment in education and value-added analysis are used.

Social capital analysis: Coleman's social capital framework is applied to examine relationships.

Case studies: In-depth case studies are conducted to provide qualitative insights.

Direct observation: The educational process is directly observed in some cases.

Large-scale data collection: The study gathers and analyzes large amounts of data across countries.

Hypothesis testing: Social science concepts and techniques are used to test hypotheses about relationships between educational variables and political, economic, and social characteristics.

When surveying and using global data to study and compare education systems, we can no longer use concepts like core and margins or center and periphery. Instead, as we saw in Chapters 1 and 2, in globalization economics, politics, culture, and education systems are studied to show transnational flows, regional and international networks grafted and plotted by computer programs. With qualitative and computation methods on the rise, the idea of the State as the unit of analysis becomes very weak.

Transfer and Borrowing Research Methods

"Foreign influences" or "educational transfer" from one system to another are so fundamental to comparative education studies that "transfer" has been considered the "unit" we can use to compare education systems. Overall, "educational transfer" can be defined as the movement of educational ideas, institutions, or practices across international borders. Although different scholars had different views about educational transfer, overall, they followed an interpretation of this process in which educational transfer was construed as responding to the following pattern:

A local problem was identified.

Solutions are sought in foreign education systems; and

A "tested" institution or educational practice (which had worked or was believed to have worked) was adapted to the new context and then implemented.

Transfer and borrowing of an education structure, policy, or practice were already used by travelers who came back from other parts of the world where they observed other ways of teaching and learning. Those processes intensified after the Second World War when so many liberated colonies restructured whole education systems that did not exist under the Empires that ruled them. As long as worldwide travel and communication systems were still slow, all development agencies used consultants, many of them CIE professors, to visit the country and to write a "country study"—an overview that helped the national and international donors make their contribution. Once the recommendations were made the country needed advisors to help with planning, and later with assessments of "returns on investment" (see more about this role of comparativists in Chapter 4).

Rappleye (2010) suggested identifying education transfer, both the volume and its consistency, as a legitimate CIE unit of analysis, concluding that transfer emerged as the "unit idea" in comparative education inquiry and scholarship (76). The Oxford group, which proposed and implemented this idea of mapping transfer, which Rappleye used for his dissertation to study Japan and Nepal (see below), explains how "a map gives us a means of underwiring questions that necessitate a historical and spatial reading of transfer" (2010: 74), as a map is not a locked analysis of transfer in a limited range of theoretical possibilities.

However, just because a transfer took place, local institutional and cultural factors determine *how the transfer is implemented*, including implementation, translation, transformation, and local conditions (Gottlieb 1991). A case study by Lee et al. (1988) examined a US teaching method called "inquiry teaching methods," transferred and implemented in South Korea. The focus of the research was not only on the source of knowledge transferred but also on its *uncritical acceptance*, as the study suggests:

> A critical posture implies an attempt to understand the limitations of the knowledge in question, including its technical quality, the assumptions underlying its production, and the extent of local relevance. It also implies consideration of the comparability of environments in which the production and utilization of knowledge take place
>
> (Lee et al. 1988: 243).

Plenty of other such research shows that transfer of methods has changed, in the context of the country or even the classroom, as the saying in teaching goes, when the teacher closes their door, they determine what and how they teach.

World-Systems and the Rise of Mass Education

World-Systems and cultural theories were used from the 1980s to explain the rise of mass education by analyzing the power relations of interest groups in societies. The complex interdependence among social units, whether seen as reciprocal and mutually beneficial or as asymmetric and exploitative, is believed to be the root of all other features accelerating the same education systems and policy worldwide as modernization has endured (Boli-Bennett et al. 1985: 146). World-Systems theorists have advanced a global convergence of education policy and practices as part of the emergence of an increasingly similar world culture. The shared values of international donor organizations, transnational NGOs, and the CIE scholarly communities in the scientific investigation of the nation-state as the unit of analysis have driven this macro research.

World-Systems theory has guided the research on mass schooling becoming a worldwide institution and the aspiration to achieve universal educational enrollment in all nations. Comparativists such as John Boli-Bennett, John Meyer, and Francisco Ramirez and their students published over fifty years of CIE research about the world expansion of mass education and how models are diffused from core nations to peripheral nations. Those scholars do not stop with classic theoretical arguments, which are functionalist accounts that stress variations in the internal characteristics of societies to explain educational expansion. They argue that in both the mainstream and the critical variants of functional theory, the expansion of schooling is a solution to societal-level problems:

> Such arguments do not easily explain the worldwide character of educational expansion. We argue that mass schooling made sense in so many contexts because it became a central feature of the Western, and subsequently the world, model of the nation-state and its development. Nation-states expand schooling because they adhere to world models of the organization of sovereignty (the modern state) and the organization of society as composed of individuals (the modern nation).
>
> (Meyer et al. 1992: 129)

Boli et al. were attentive to what is borrowed and what is implemented as only "loosely coupling" because education system transfer might be "a manual cut and paste process in which what exactly gets cut and how precisely it gets posted varies" (1985: 128).

In their 1992 study, Meyer et al. statistically analyzed enrollment data for over 120 countries from 1870 to 1980. Their event-history analyses indicate that mass educational systems appeared steadily before the 1940s and sharply increased after 1950. Pooled panel regression analysis shows that the expansion is endemic in the system. National variations are indications of national modernization or structural location in the world-system and have only modest effects on the expansion rate (Meyer et al. 1992). Opposing those large-scale studies using World-System theories state that local differences and cultural variations continue as a result of enduring social, cultural, religious knowledge and economic configurations, of international organization funding not just "distance education" in South Africa but also system thinking (see below, Social Cartography).

Radical Humanist Methods and Studies

Tension 2: Outsider–Insider Perspectives

The first issue that radical humanists would have concerning methods is the need to understand education phenomena from the actor's point of view—insider perspectives. This has implications, especially for CIE research methodology, both historical and contemporary. Where researchers from other countries within other cultures (most likely Western) bring their pre-established research categories, like "individual modernity," "social mobility," "cultural imperialism," "economic development," and "academic achievement," to just name a few, to the research site and construct methods, mostly qualitatively, it will yield data about those predetermined categories—the outsider perspectives. Researchers using radical humanist methods would attempt to observe the local through which members of the observed culture give meaning to their categories such as schooling or outcomes or achievement. This was the challenge of poststructuralism to the functionalist notion of a fixed, stable research subject: reshape educational inquiry by exploring how researchers can grapple with the complexities of meaning-making in education settings, recognizing the fluidity, acknowledging the role of language, culture, and power in shaping understanding (Lee 1992).

Such categories are not imported from the researcher or consultant worldview and imposed upon the research or phenomena observed but "negotiated" between the observer and the observed. Even this negotiation has the tension of the outsider versus the insider points of views. Social researchers nowadays clarify their personal motivation for their research, especially for those utilizing qualitative methodologies that require reflexivity, as a component of clarifying their role in the research, these researchers often position themselves as either "insiders" or "outsiders" to their research domain (Breen 2007).

Paradigm and Major Theories	Methods Within Those Theories	Example studies
Radical humanist paradigm Phenomenology Existentialism Critical theory	Ethnographic studies Discourse analysis and Discursive practices Critical discourse analysis Critical ethnography Resistance & accommodation studies Insider research "co-constructions" researcher and the participants Seeking to understand & reveal social reality Case studies Qualitative comparisons teachers' education Comparing vertical case studies	Beach and Larsson (2022), 'Developments in Ethnographic Research.' Gottlieb (1989), 'Discursive Construction of Knowledge.' Vavrus and Seghers (2010), 'Critical Discourse Analysis.' Anderson (1989), 'Critical Ethnography in Education.' Mirón and Lauria (1998), 'Student Voice as Agency: Resistance and Accommodation in Inner-City.' Kelly (2014), 'Intercultural Comparative Research: Rethinking Insider and Outsider Perspectives.' Robinson-Pant (2016), 'Exploring the Concept of Insider-Outsider in Comparative and International Research.' Jabbar (1976), 'A Critical Study of Educational Implications of Existentialism.' Crossley and Vulliamy (1984), 'Case-Study Research Methods and Comparative Education.' Gottlieb et al. (2022), 'When is an Academic Degree the Best Vocational Education?' Tatto (2022), 'The Need for Comparative Studies in Teacher Education.' Vavrus and Bartlett (2006), 'Comparative Vertical Case Studies.'

Methods used for studies within this type of critical ethnographic study of the macro relationship between educational systems and social contexts include:

Ethnographic fieldwork: Researchers conduct in-depth, immersive fieldwork in educational settings to observe and document practices, interactions, and cultural dynamics.

Interviews: Critical ethnographers conduct interviews with various stakeholders like students, teachers, administrators, and community members to gather diverse perspectives.

Document analysis: Researchers analyze curriculum materials, policy documents, textbooks, and other relevant texts using discourse analysis techniques.

Case studies: In-depth studies of specific schools, programs, or communities are conducted to provide rich, contextual data.

Comparative analysis: Data is collected from multiple sites or contexts to enable qualitative comparisons between different educational systems or approaches.

Participant observation: Researchers may participate in and observe classroom activities, meetings, and other educational processes, as both a participant (inside view) and observer (outside view).

Focus groups: Group discussions with stakeholders can provide insights into shared experiences and perspectives.

Archival research: Historical documents and records are examined to understand the development of educational systems over time.

Reflexive journaling: Researchers maintain reflexive journals to document their experiences throughout the research process, taking into account their positionality (from where they are coming) and what preconvections they have.

The Transition from Quantitative to Qualitative

In CIE, we can attribute moving from quantitative to qualitative due to the rise of globalization's impact on CIE. Marginson and Mollis (2001) narrate globalization's effect on CIE methods:

Analytical frameworks—scholars should locate nation-to-nation comparisons in broader frameworks. At the same time, they should note that global effects are contested and uneven and vary among nations, regions, and institutions.

Units of analysis—the traditional comparative studies in which all countries are ranked according to their level of development on a single scale, fail to explain power relations between nations, and they mask qualitative national differences.

Cross-border—like in the transfer and borrowing, in international education this has become an essential research object. Such trade raises questions about the identities of mobile students, and online teaching and learning produces tensions between pedagogical practices and national cultures.

Identities—globalization opens a new form of identity other than national identity due to worldwide circulation of cultural practices, educational participation, free courseware learning resourcing, and online degree awards. All contributing directly or indirectly to global citizenship identities, which is one of CIE research building blocks.

National/international: Modern education systems are still organized locally, and are subject to national regulation, but both K-12 and higher education went through internationalization of their students' learning experience. The increased mobility of students and scholars, which used to be a "brain drain" where Western countries recruited international students to stay in their country of study, is now more like "brain circulation" with graduate students and scholars moving and teaching, work, anywhere their specialty is needed.

Mixed methods: The mixed research design is a sequential design in which the first strand of quantitative research is prioritized. At the same time, the qualitative method is applied to supplement the first phase (quantitative data collection and analysis and then followed by qualitative data collection and analysis, and lastly, interpreted). The design of this method attempts to find the "why" questions by generally developing causal explanations or testing theory (Baran 2016). The researcher deploys mixed explanatory sequential research when the researcher and the research problem are more quantitatively oriented. The researcher knows the critical variables and has access to quantitative instruments for measuring the constructs of primary interest. The researcher interested in contextualizing their study can return to participants for a second round or choose some of them for qualitative data collection. The researcher develops new questions based on quantitative results that cannot be answered with quantitative data.

Decolonizing Methods

Critically looking at how we make research more radical, inclusive, and contextualized in general decolonizing methods, Call-Cummings et al. (2019) discuss the urgency of re-visiting CIE research methods, with an eye to de-colonializing them. They conclude that for CIE to be inclusive, researchers must "look, listen, and learn" (6).

Decolonizing our methods and looking at theories about what comes *after* colonialism, imperialism, and modernization starts by problematizing the standard research practices, looking for biased assumptions of hierarchies, silences, and exclusions built into how research is conducted. Ethical considerations are a large part of research methods (see Chapter 5), so they urge researchers to pay attention to local contexts to build trust and mutual recognition in relationships. Call-Cummings et al. suggest being cautious about seemingly harmless terminologies such as "giving voice" (2019: 8) and paternalistic goals of empowerment, which takes us further away from the very goal of bringing the inclusivity of voices, as a way to decolonize CIE that was born when countries were liberated, poor, and depleted from many years of colonization. Bilgen et al. (2021) also note that the researcher's position in their postcolonial context could interfere with personal assumptions and need to be dis-entangled from their past: "Grounding our arguments on post- and decolonial critiques and our own experiences, we contend that how, why, and by whom 'development' research is carried out must remain under constant scrutiny. We propose a reflexive and socio-politically conscious approach of 'knowledge co-construction'" (519). See the Illustration by Ross at the end of the volume. Ross's case provides methodological suggestions on methods, such as privileging local knowledge in the research process and critically examining assumptions regarding knowledge and power. Post-interview/focus group processes involved collaborations on interpretations and critically analyzing the control over the knowledge production process. Bilgen et al. (2021) focus our attention on the socio-cultural and linguistic nuances that must be taken into consideration to deeply understand participant experiences.

Whether and how to involve sharing the knowledge authority of the text with the informants is the question many CIE studies grapple with. Marcus and Cushman (1982) see such "experimental ethnography" as tending to give up the interpretive authority, such as we find in traditional authoritative ethnography, and become instead a "mix of multiple negotiated realities … of dispersed authority" (44). This is a way to recognize the authenticity of the voice of people's education and life, which comparativists set out to understand in their context and document.

Critical Ethnographic Methods

The critical ethnographic approach emphasizes the following:

    Examining power dynamics and inequalities in educational systems
    Considering both local and global contexts
    Incorporating participants' voices and perspectives

Reflexivity about the researcher's position and biases
Connecting micro-level observations to macro-level social structures
Using theory to guide interpretation while remaining open to emergent themes

The goal is to collect rich, multifaceted data that can reveal the complex relationships between educational systems and their broader social contexts, focusing on issues of power, inequality, and social change. Anthropology of education extended the research beyond schooling to include socialization and enculturation. In the past fifty years, ethnography has grown from an internationally emerging tradition in education research to a highly prolific and productive research method in the Global South, connecting to past (traditional or indigenous) ways of knowing (see more in Chapter 4). Regarding graduate students' research, a good example comes from Sweden, where the proportion of qualitatively interpreted observations has grown over the decades. In the last period, 2015–2019, more than half of all dissertations in education research used qualitatively interpreted observation, and most were fully developed ethnographies.

Case Study

Case study methods are not new to CIE. In their insightful review of the topic, Crossley and Vulliamy (1984) identify three case-study traditions in the broader field of education—the anthropological, the sociological, and the evaluative. The embrace of case study methods in comparative education is not merely methodological; instead, Crossley and Vulliamy make an epistemological "case for the case" by arguing that what can be known about one context cannot be assumed to be true in another. This issue, which they call "ecological validity" (198), highlights the importance of using methods that examine how cultural, economic, historical, and political forces within a given context play out in schooling. To explain the world expansion of Western education, Meyer et al. (1992) collected large data sets from multiple resources. Those studies used statistics from many countries over a long period to show that Western education expansion has long gone on worldwide.

Anderson-Levitt (2003) edited case studies from five continents, using ethnography and historical research to challenge the sweeping claims of the world expansion of Western education. Using case-study methods they demonstrated how national ministries of education and local schools re-invent reforms that were transferred to their nations. On a more local level, the case studies also show that teachers and local reformers operate within and against those borrowed global models. CIE research, they conclude, needs to recognize the worldwide presence of local schooling context and local transformation of global models. This research breaks away from universalistic, culture-free methods to contextual methods of contextualization at the nexus of cross-national comparative studies. This does not mean the researcher is "culturally free"; the opposite in fact: the impact of the researcher's cultural traditions and issues of equivalence of concepts and interpretation are part of the study when the researcher engages in reflexibility. This methodological practice promotes self-awareness, humility, and questioning the researchers own pre-existing assumptions.

Vertical case study

The vertical case study differs from the traditional ethnographic case study in its simultaneous commitment to micro-level understanding and to macro-level analysis. It strives to situate local action and interpretation within a broader cultural, historical, and political investigation (for examples of such research, see Vavrus and Bartlett (2006 and Vavrus (2005)). Frances Vavrus and Lesley Bartlett (2006) have entered the debates regarding methodology and training in CIE by addressing epistemological (ways of knowing) questions about what can be known and how it can be known through comparative research. The debates over qualitative versus quantitative methods or area studies versus cross-national studies miss deeper divisions over comparative knowledge. They propose a vertical case study to compare knowledge claims among actors with different social locations to situate local action and interpretation within a broader cultural, historical, and political investigation. This enables CIE students to conduct research promoting complete and thorough knowledge of multiple comparison levels within a single vertically bounded case.

The vertical case should be grounded in a principal site—e.g., a school, a community, an institution, or a government ministry—and fully attend to how historical trends, social structures, and national and international forces shape local processes at this site. In other words, local understandings and social interactions should not be considered demographic or geographically bounded. Instead, in a vertical case study, understanding the microlevel is viewed as part and parcel of larger structures, forces, and policies. The researcher using this method must develop a complete and thorough knowledge of the context of the study.

This history suggests that both globally and nationally contextualized ethnography in CIE research is a methodology that is generally in constant flux and, at the same time, exhibits relative stability in terms of the typical markers of the method, which become future criteria for the identity of participatory ethnographic work. Case Studies share a common conviction with interpretive methods regarding the centrality of contextual understanding and detailed micro-level research, even when comparing multiple locations (see next).

Interpretive Methods and Studies

In the 1980s, methodological debate in the social sciences shifted ground, moving away from "high" or "grand" metatheories such as modernization and developmentalism (reviewed in Chapter 2) to investigate the epistemological foundations of human sciences and the ontological status of social reality. In Anglo-American social theorizing, this shift is evident in the renewal of interest in hermeneutics, the study of the methodological principles of interpretation, the plea to produce open-ended, dialogic work, and a focus on education practice, co-producing research. This shift to the method level, to problems of epistemology and interpretation, and the discursive forms of representation in the social sciences has been referred to as the "interpretive turn."

Tension 3: Context, Contextualizing

Over the years of CIE practices and the many studies we mentioned, we can see that context was used in different ways; some refer to it as "local" or "culture." As noted above, extensive studies collecting data from many other countries have been short on accounting for or contextualizing their study to individual locations. Our review of transfer and borrowing studies continued the view that "improvements [were] capable of being transported from one country to another" independent from its local context (Fraser 1964). This is an important point: when you read an article about education in a country you don't know and find that you recognize the schooling structure, curriculum, policy, or teaching method, note if contextual elements have been considered when the account is given (37). This is how we should assess many of the borrowing and transfer development studies. Are they contextualized to the local context? In CIE, the regard or disregard for context has changed not just with time but also with the disciplinary background of the researcher, their worldview, and the method they are using to study education comparatively. We have already mentioned development studies that used area studies methods, where researchers study one country in depth, including the knowledge of the language, and are deeply committed to the context of that location. Jürgen Schriewer (1992) discusses the importance of "externalization" as a key concept in the field of comparative education; it emphasizes the need to consider broader social contexts and structures when comparing different educational systems across countries.

Paradigm and Major Theories	Methods Within Those paradigms	Examples of Studies
The interpretive paradigm Transcendental phenomenology Ethnomethodology Symbolic interaction	Shifted to the level of method, to problems of epistemology and interpretation, and to the discursive forms of representation Renewal interest collaborative fieldwork Production of open-ended, dialogic work, quantitative methods, observations, interviews, focus group discussions, and photography/ Photovoice Co-production of researcher & researched Analysis of collected narrative or stories	Brown et al. (2010), 'Tackling Wicked Problems & Transdisciplinary Imagination.' Campbell and Vanderhoven (2016), 'Knowledge That Matters.' Dyson, and Todd (2010), 'Dealing with Complexity: Theory of Change Evaluation.' Gottlieb et al. (2022), 'When is an Academic Degree the Best Vocational Education?'

Paradigm and Major Theories	Methods Within Those paradigms	Examples of Studies
Theorizing in the post-era Postcolonial Post-socialism	Reevaluate where CIE knowledge is produced and circulate. New knowledge on issues of race, culture, language, and curriculum and the Global South Postcolonial critiques Postcolonial CIE Critical comparative education: vertical case studies from Africa, Europe, the Middle East, and the Americas Unintended and intended academic consequences of education reforms Comparing Soviet education in East European independent nations (after the 1990s)	Mignolo (1993), 'Colonial & Postcolonial Cultural Critique or Academic Colonialism?' Connell (2007), 'Southern Theory.' Tikly (1999), 'Postcolonialism & Comparative Education.' Khavenson and Carnoy (2016), 'The Cases of Post-Soviet Estonia, Latvia and Russia.' Rediscovering socialist education in comparative education (Silova, 2010a)

The "new sociology of education" (Young 1971) and radical education schooling research (Apple 1996) moved theoretical discussion to methodological debate. In education, shifting to the level of method, to problems of epistemology and interpretation, and to the discursive forms of representation employed by social thinkers, policymakers, and donor agencies. The methods to explore such issues have been used for a long time in the study of linguistic techniques in poetry and literature; before such methods the study of rhetoric forms of a text migrated to the social sciences and CIE. Thus, the "narrative turn" of the study of the story was effectively dislodged from its original home in the humanities and became a focus of inquiry in all disciplinary formations, including social and natural sciences, media and communication studies to management, and to medicine. In all professions, including medicine and law, they noticed that if a literary scholar has the tools to analyze a story, why could they not use such methods, as a doctor hears a "story" from each patient? A prominent literary scholar of narratology, James Phelan (2023), who already teaches medical students, wrote a guide—*Narrative Medicine*—for the health professions (see also

Columbia University's MA in medical narratology). From this guide, the move to analyze CIE data collected from participants, policy records, planning documents, and college faculties in India narrating (telling stories) on a proposed curriculum and exam policy revision was made (Witenstein and Abdallah 2023). As the references of this study show, the "composite storytelling" method was adopted from the medical profession to be used for this education research published in *Higher Education Policy and Leadership Studies*.

The overall approach emphasizes:

Collaboration between researchers and participants
Open-ended, dialogic data collection
Focus on everyday practices and experiences
Attention to context and use of thick description
Reflexivity about the research process
Co-producing researcher and researched

The interpretive researcher will not study education in the sense of linkages between education and processes of economic, social, and political change since these Western categories may be non-commensurable with those observed in the local context; instead, the researcher will attempt to grasp the meanings and interpretations that the "actors" attach to phenomena which, in Western terms, might be assigned to the categories of "education," "economic change," etc. In this connection, interpretive cultural anthropology has focused on education, meaning a key to opening the methods of conducting open-ended dialogical comparative research.

Some methodologists have questioned whether a concern for research questions can be blended with comparison. Bartlett and Vavrus (2019) explain that CIE scholars do not formulate their research questions without studying the context "because it suggests a priori categories that ignore participants' ways of knowing … This is often the case when context is reduced to a set of pre-determined variables or post hoc employed for causative explanation" (188). The concerns of the skeptics cause many comparatists not to use qualitative research methods and abandon specificity for the sake of generalization. This debate is not just from the 1970's scientific CIE methods but is still ongoing. However, as we see below, there are many other methods to learn from, which assist in being attentive to context and incorporating local knowledge for comparison and contextualizing conclusions before making generalizations.

Participatory Action Research

Data collection in participatory action research (PAR) typically involves the following essential methods and approaches:

Collaborative and iterative process: Data collection and analysis are not isolated phases but occur throughout the research process iteratively, with ongoing participation from stakeholders.

Qualitative methods: PAR often employs qualitative approaches such as storytelling, interviewing, ethnography, focus groups, and participatory observation.

Participatory methods: Techniques that directly engage community members, like body mapping, problem trees, guided walks, timelines, participatory photography/video, and participatory theatre.

Visual and narrative methods include digital storytelling, participatory oral history, and participatory artmaking (collage, drawing, murals, etc.).

Quantitative data: While less common, quantitative data may be collected, especially using participatory statistics approaches.

Capacity building: Community members are often trained in research skills to participate in data collection and analysis.

Flexible approach: Methods are chosen based on community engagement, research questions, and available skills. They can be adapted throughout the process.

Ethical considerations: Agreements on data recording, storage, and ethical principles are established collaboratively.

Multiple data sources: PAR may gather spatial, time-related, social, and technical data from various sources.

Reflexivity: Researchers often keep reflexive journals to document their experiences and positionality.

The fundamental principle is that data collection methods in PAR are designed to be engaging, participatory, and aligned with the goals of generating knowledge while promoting contextual action for social change. The specific methods used vary widely depending on the project context and community needs. Kidwai et al. (2017) define PAR as a process that helps to develop "practical knowing" for meaningful "human purposes" grounded in a "participatory worldview" and bringing together "action and reflection and 'theory and practice in participation with others" (1). The authors note that PAR is a form of knowledge generated by comparativists that involves collaboration with members of an organization to inform the organization's co-learning process for its transformation (Kidwai et al. 2017). This research method is with the people for the people rather than *on* or *about* people in international development. Standard versions of PAR also include Participatory Learning Action (PLA) and Rapid Rural Appraisal (RRA).

Setty and Witenstein (2017) note that PAR research originated when researchers worked with "traditionally exploited or oppressed communities that face challenges and populations. Those communities may face challenges and seek to alter their own circumstances" (15). By adding "Participatory" to "Action Research" methodology (revised in the 1970s), researchers found a way to address the community's specific concerns and provide a new lens to examine the source of oppression. This is how PAR assists in uncovering social injustices in the context it is used. CIE researchers use PAR to amplify marginalized voices. This method is about both action and voice needed to bring about transformative change through research. PAR allows learning *from* and *with* communities and provides a space for reflection as a part of the research design. The origins of PAR have roots in upholding the rights of scheduled tribes in communities in India.

Discourse Analysis

Discourse analysis exposes and clarifies the discursive practices by which all aspects of education are carried out. Discourse analysis and knowledge generation relocate educational theory to a meta-theoretical context where issues of constructing knowledge become central. This analysis differs from other qualitative studies in that its focus is on the form of discourse and not on practice content. The knowledge that documents constructs is analyzed not from the point of view of its truth (or falsity), or its consistency (or inconsistency) with the data collected, or with reality as experienced by the actors, but from the point of view of its ability to persuade or even to coerce the actors into action (Gottlieb 1989: 131–44). The fundamental theoretical orientation of this approach is the renewal of interest in rhetoric in the social sciences. Using methods from accounts of discourse and text, sociologists such as Richard H. Brown (1987) have undertaken to read social construction through language. Anthropologists have experimented with ethnographic methods, exploring the poetics of cultural accounts. Similarly, educationist Philip Wexler (1987) has synthesized formalism, structuralism, poststructuralism, and semiotics to deconstruct concepts such as construct validity, stages of development, rate of return, and taxonomy of education objectives. These various studies have clarified that the rhetorical forms that a writer chooses (consciously or otherwise) and those that become institutionalized through the history of publishing in a given field determine what marks a contribution to knowledge. To unpack what constitutes a contribution to knowledge in the case of a reform policy such as teacher education, we need to treat form as (relatively) binding. Through discourse analysis, it will be possible to study what has happened in a teacher education national reform and identify specific items of the international teacher education repertoire used to legitimize a local reform of the country's education system (Gottlieb 1991). Our interest in the discursive practices of an event such as education reform can be seen as part of a broader exploration of the "rhetoric of inquiry." Such an inquiry takes us beneath the masks of methodology and takes seriously the form of education documents. Education planning and policies are essential expressions of social power in education, as they convey the values of authoritative actors and institutions whose forms of knowledge about the social world are reflected in these texts and have a significant influence on education actors such as administrators, students, teachers, and parents.

Critical Discourse Analysis

CIE research has undertaken discourse analysis after Gee's (1996) methodological studies examining ways in which knowledge is socially constructed in classrooms and other educational settings. Gee (1996) noted that discourse analysis approaches draw on discourse theories and methods developed in other disciplines (e.g., applied linguistics, law, literary studies, psychology, sociolinguistics, and sociology, among others), but by studying discursive activity within classrooms and other social settings, researchers have provided new insights into the complex and dynamic relationships among discourse, social practices, and learning. Rebecca Rogers, an education anthropologist, uses Gee's analysis of discourse for her 500+ hours of participant observation notes, taken at their homes and in the community, using the method of critical discourse analysis (CDA). Mainly its applicability to the field of comparative education has followed Rogers (2004), who advised that "the analyst must work from the analysis of texts to the social and political contexts in which the texts emerge" (4). In other words, a research project is also a critique of existent social and political relations of power with an intent to disrupt. CDA also tries to link micro-level textual analysis and macro-level exploration of the authoritative knowledge generated by national and international policymaking institutions. For example, Vavrus and Seghers (2010) use their analysis of contemporary partnership, international development discourse, close reading of policy texts as discursive social practices that helped them understand how the partnership is constructed in modern poverty reduction strategies and whether there are avenues for the agency, the individual, the "community," or categories of people such as "women," "the poor," or the "socially excluded" in these documents. They found the policy studies field a particularly fruitful area to explore critical discourse analysis because policies are, by definition, texts imbued with authority. In their study, they engage in an analysis to "make transparent" an opaque element in contemporary international development discourse.

Photovoice

Photovoice is one of several qualitative methods utilized in community-based participatory research. It is an established method developed initially by health promotion researchers (Wang and Burris 1997). By utilizing photographs taken and selected by participants, respondents can reflect upon and explore the reasons, emotions, and experiences that have guided their chosen images.

The Photovoice method has become a popular method that helps the researcher take a step back, rather than being the one whose assumptions and biases may prove to be a challenge to the research. Braun (2021) narrates that Photovoice could be a powerful method to amplify marginalized voices. The Photovoice method combines taking photos, conducting interviews, and writing about the image's content. Participants are co-researchers because they take photographs and interpret their meanings for the researchers. This differs fundamentally from traditional research, where the power often lies solely with the researcher. Photographs capture the lived experience of participants and give insight to and a more profound understanding of their world. Visual images can be a powerful communication tool, challenging stereotypes and providing a platform for more intense and emotionally engaging reflection. Visual images are a powerful way of enabling social relations between the researcher and the individuals/groups being researched. This method cannot be used everywhere or in every culture; even now, everyone takes pictures all the time with smartphones. Still, this method requires ethical approval and stresses the boundaries, which include no sharing of other peoples' photographs or identifiable places.

Braun (2021) mentions that Photovoice is an underutilized method in education that enables socially just and participatory engagement interactions between the researchers and the participants. Critics have cast doubt on Photovoice's methodological rigor, questioning the method's efficacy in mitigating power imbalances between researchers and participants despite these concerns, the popularity of the method continues to rise, with the number of citations increasing by 600 percent between 2010 and 2020. This popularity is likely due in part to the flexibility of Photovoice to meet the unique needs of communities, that mostly do not have a "voice" in other CIE research methods. However, the heterogeneity of Photovoice application can lead to difficulties in determining exactly what the method comprises, and how to use it (Anderson et al. 2023). Many such qualitative methods are scrutinized to assess their rigor. While being collaborative in using a method such as Photovoice, the researcher needs to be aware of their own positionality and identity, as this method is highly interactive.

Bringing in the conversational and using collaborative elements while conducting research, and co-constructing meaning during and after the fieldwork, is not an easy task, as Ross's Illustration shows. Research methods support innovative inquiries such as Photovoice, where Black Lives Matter (as a principle, not just a movement since 2014) and methodologies supporting justice, reconciliation, and awareness of the implicit biases that haunt disciplinary research, such as CIE.

Cross-Paradigms Methods

Some topics in CIE do not neatly align under one paradigm; we are reviewing those methods and example studies under this "cross-paradigms" section to outline methods and research studies

Paradigm and Major Theories	Methods Within Those Theories	Studies in CIE
Gender/feminist theorizing/ Feminist pedagogy Feminist standpoint theory Visualization theories Social cartography Transitologies as maps	Socially situated method multi-focal research Researcher embedded in social relations Co-producing research and reporting Research *with* (not on) oppressed and disempowered including disabilities Mapping charts and diagramming CIE theories mapping Mapping education transfer Network analysis	Stromquist (1995), 'Romancing the State: Gender and Power in Education.' Mayberry (1998), 'Comparative Roles of Collaborative Learning and Feminist Pedagogy.' Sriprakash et al. (2020), 'Learning With the Past: Racism.' Moreton-Robinson (2013), 'Australian Indigenous Women's Standpoint.' Educação et al. (2011), 'Diagramming Gender's Private and Public Manifestations.' Stromquist (1995), 'Use of Social Cartography in Feminist Thought.' Paulston (1994, 1999), 'Mapping Comparative Education: Paradigms and Theories.' Gorostiaga (2017), 'Perspectivism and Social Cartography.' Rappleye (2010), 'Comparing Maps, and Mirrors.' Menashy (2019), "International Aid to Education."

Data collection in socially situated methods, feminist standpoint theory, and multi-focal research embedded in social relations typically involves the following approaches:

Qualitative methods:

Observations: Researchers immerse themselves in the social context to directly observe behaviors, interactions, and dynamics.

Interviews: In-depth, semi-structured interviews are conducted with participants to gather their perspectives and experiences.

Focus group discussions: Group conversations are facilitated to explore collective views and social dynamics.

Photography: Visual methods are used to capture and analyze social realities.

Participatory approaches: Such research involves an intersectional lens:, data collection that considers multiple forms of oppression and identities, e.g., gender, race, class, citenzship, and disability.

Reflexivity: Researchers critically examine their positionality and how it influences the research process.

Contextual understanding: Data is collected with attention to broader social, cultural, and historical contexts.

Narrative and storytelling: Personal narratives and life histories are often gathered to understand lived experiences.

Document analysis: Examining texts, policies, and media representations relevant to the social issues being studied.

Ethnographic methods: Prolonged community engagement to understand social relations and cultural practices.

Action research: Combining data collection with efforts to promote social change and empower participants.

Multi-method approach: Combining methods to triangulate findings and capture complex social realities.

Power dynamics: Carefully considering how power relations influence the research process and data collected.

Embodied knowledge: Recognizing and valuing knowledge from lived experiences of marginalized people.

These approaches' fundamental principles are to center perspectives, or what researchers call "the researched group, or phenomena" on whom or what we collect data. Such methods assist in critically evaluating power relations among the researchers and the researched group, and help us understand and present social phenomena visually in addition to narratively. Data collection methods are chosen to align with these principles and produce rich, contextual understandings of education in comparative perspectives.

Gender/Feminist Studies

We take gender studies as an example of cross-paradigmatic research. At the heyday of development education practices in the newly independent states "Women in Development (WID)," WID did not so much reflect a "feminist" perspective in as much as they emphasized the integration of women in economic development strategies rather than questioning or reframing the conditions under which this integration took place. Still, this movement did not constantly advocate, as developmentalism did not recognize equal distribution of resources to women. A few telling examples are the introduction of sewing machines given to men for commercial use (not domestic), so that tailoring became men's work, not understanding that women did such work at home and in the commercial sphere. Once men were in charge of the mechanical resources, they took advantage of women and children to do the job, while the wealth produced was not equally distributed. Throughout developmentalism, gender in education worked hard to assert the rights of women and girls in education and the importance of equal schooling for all (see Marion's Illustration). As many studies show, schools—more than many other social institutions—are actively engaged in the construction of gender because of their socially sanctioned ideological role. Theories and research on gender in education acknowledge the reproductive nature of schooling, by which knowledge and everyday practice build upon traditional norms and values that position masculinity and femininity in starkly oppositional ways. Gender research in education has moved away from its initial concern with gender socialization patterns, the reproduction of gender inequality in schools, and gender equity reforms, towards engaging with social and cultural theory and analyzing the contested nature of gender identities in schools (Dillabough 2001). Social and cultural theories also consider schooling as a stage where transformation can occur through the possibilities it offers to treat boys and girls equally.

In postmodernity, which heralds the demise of meta-narratives (like modernization), knowledge is legitimized by its performative capabilities. To reach a space where research does not seek to produce truth, Lyotard argues approaching research views with reason not as a universal human faculty but as a specific and variable product of individual engagement. In this way, research combined with legitimizing knowledge by reason would satisfy both the desire for justice and the desire for the unknown (Lyotard 1984).

Despite the diversity in gender justice education practices, all of them seek to unmask the existence of the uncontested oppression of women. A prevailing understanding of gender and education systems contends that it is constructed at three levels: (1) structural, supported by the social division of labor; (2) institutional, shaped by norms and regulations that guide the distribution of resources and opportunities among men and women; and (3) symbolic, framed by conceptions, mentalities, and collective representations of femininity and masculinity (Stromquist 1995).

Gender studies in CIE is well exemplified by the work by Stromquist's major CIE feminist and gender scholarship. She analyzed institutions with greater power, e.g., international development agencies, possessing more significant political and financial resources, enabling them to convey their perspective and funding of social and educational programs across a more comprehensive network and stronger crossing borders in international gender work. Weaker institutions like domestic NGOs are dependent on international NGOs' feminist academics. Mapping out gendered spaces, she shows how affinities between international aid agencies and national governments' distinct discourse create their constellation. At the same time, NGOs, academic settings, and academicians create a second consolation of gender studies.

Stromquist (2011) examined gender-social space, acknowledging that space is not a natural cultural outcome but rather a political outcome. She diagrams gender's private and public features and how they manifest themselves in the educational field, and how it functions in public policy. The discussion of private space relies on theoretical literature and addresses concepts that apply to sociocultural contexts. For discussion of the public space, Stromquist focuses on gender and education. She relies primarily on her data from a cross-national study of public policies in education in Costa Rica, Brazil, and Peru. Stromquist found that spaces "should be seen both as effects and causes of conscious social action" (see Chapter 4).

Gender transformative education (GTE) is an approach that acknowledges the deeply ingrained gender inequalities of society and aims to address and change these disparities in and through education. GTE emphasizes conscientization, critical thinking, agency, inclusivity, and intersectionality as factors necessary to challenge traditional gender roles, stereotypes, and biases within educational systems and beyond (see Manion's Illustration on girls and women's education).

Data Visualization and Social Cartography

Maps are known for visual representations of locations, positions, distances, and relations. The most known are road, geographical, and world maps, replaced by software programs like "ARCGIS" and "Google Maps." Most younger scholars lack cartographic skills, having never used/read or touched paper maps or atlases. The use of flow charts, and network analysis including visualizing them are experiences, exploring and enhancing the possibilities of CIE visual methods in education. One other way this has increased is the use of hyperlinked information in education theory and practice. When information in papers or research findings are hyperlinked rather than organized in traditional, more linear ways, we find that research, writing/reporting, and reader experiences change.

> Applying visual analysis in research necessitates the creation of a mental space where a person is invited to derive information using a regular yet often overlooked medium—the visual. Exploring possibilities of visual analysis makes an important contribution to our knowledge because, building on an everyday activity of seeing, it propels one to question their first visual impressions, to look more intently in order to really see.
>
> (Baimukhamedova 2022: 308)

Visualization methods:

- Participatory mapping: Community members and stakeholders actively create maps representing their perspectives, experiences, and knowledge.
- Visual methods: Body mapping, participatory photography/video, and participatory artmaking visually capture spatial and social information.
- Qualitative methods: storytelling, interviews, focus groups, ethnographic observation.
- Document analysis: Examining existing maps, policy documents, and other relevant texts
- Collaborative workshops: Bringing stakeholders together to map and analyze social issues and relationships collectively.
- Layering of information: Combining different data types (e.g., demographic, land use, community knowledge) on maps to reveal relationships and patterns.
- Digitization: Incorporating Geographic Information Systems (GIS) and other digital mapping technologies to create and analyze spatial and social data.
- Reflexive journaling: Researchers document their experiences and positionality throughout before, while and after mapping.
- Interactive process: Data collection and analysis often coincide with ongoing refinement and reflection.
- Multiple data sources: Gathering spatial, temporal, social, and technical data from various sources to create comprehensive charts, graphs and maps.

Although there was resistance to images in the years CIE developed scientific research, in the 1990s and the 2000s, with the explosion of the internet and programs like YouTube followed by streaming services such as Netflix, Hulu, Peacock, Tubi, Amazon Prime Video, Disney+ Max, Kweli TV, and PBC online to just name a few; more and more film, television, advertising, and popular culture analyses are being used in many more comparative published education research.

Beech et al. (2024) investigated "stretching" spatial theorizing in comparative education, compared to how it has not been practiced before. They reviewed CIE research in the last ten years, finding studies that used "social topology," "spatial temporalities", and "beyond human spatialities." This search helped them to illustrate the potential of these approaches in studies such as shifts in governance, the impacts of globalization, and the complicated ways they are spatially related to education. They argue that comparative education research would benefit from such methods. This is similar to CIE scholars that celebrate the possibilities that information technology communications (ITCs), new imaging, and the explosion of information available at the tip of a finger, using AI, opens up research to so many unimagining possibilities, while some researchers lament it (see Chapter 5).

Social Cartography

Cartographic methods, like maps, are visual representations of locations, positions, distances, relations, and so forth as ways to produce spatial knowledge. Most CIE research and practices in many of the texts we quote in this book use narrative methods for representation and interpretation. Narrative expressions typically emphasize temporality; maps are one of the alternative or complementary discourses that visualize and help to examine the spatial character of education experiences and compare them across locations or sectors within one system. At the same time, hypertextuality enables the interconnections.

In the 2020s, such mapping by hand was replaced by cartographic computer programs that can map any social phenomenon more efficiently. Thinking of "geopolitical cartography," not metaphorical, the education program that addresses education disparities is the Geographic Information System (GIS), which is already used to educate students to map out global environmental degradation and its impact on their communities. Visually exhibiting the environment and conditions around the globe has vastly expanded with satellite imaging and photography taken from space, which has moved to incorporate the global and the local as never before (Ethridge and Rabiee 2023).

Social cartography, initially developed in geography, enables the researcher to consider territory, location, the institutional and individual actors that inhabit a particular social space, how these actors define problems and solutions, and the interrelationship between them. In the 1990s, critical cartography initiated a new shift in mapping theory, its methodologies and application. The critique showed how manipulation and oppression was inherent in the legitimized and perpetuated ways of mapping. For the education and academic studies in general, this shift enabled new perspectives addressing the disproportional influence of science and knowledge production in power relationships, contributing to advance knowledge. "Critical cartography pointed out that maps rarely stand alone, doing nothing, changing nothing. For better or worse, each new method or approach, each new map holds the potential to provoke an impact" (Reitz 2022: 350).

The fundamental principles of social cartography data collection include:

Emphasizing participatory approaches
Valuing local knowledge and perspectives
Using creative and engaging methods, not just words
Focusing on relationships and connections between different social groups or discursive communities
Using visualization, such as charts, maps, mapping, and non-narrative methods to display and convey meaning and construction knowledge.

Social cartography, used in mapping theoretical positions within CIE was developed by Rolland Paulston, who elaborated on Burrell and Morgan (see Figure 2), and, influenced by the interpretive turn in the social sciences, moved to map out theories in CIE (see Figure 3), in order "to create a social cartography able to visualize and pattern multiplicity, be it multiple perspectives, genres, arguments, or dreams" (Paulston 1999: 453).

Many scholars have followed social cartography in CIE research projects and other fields. The next generation of computer graphic technologies enables researchers to study the process of transferring from one system to another so comparison analysis can follow what was taken from where to where, transferred, and translated. What has come to be called the "Oxford models" of definitions and commonalities involved in education transfer and explicit borrowing formulated into a series of visual models following Paulston's Social Cartography which facilitates comparison. Rappleye (2010) used "mapping" to graph out and compare education transfer in Japan and Nepal (72–3), while the "two accounts that would never be comparable under current comparative episteme(s) because one is 'developing' and one is 'developed', one is East Asia and one is South Asia … Yet we unmistakably have here the making of comparable maps" (72) when looking at "pre-modern," "modern," and "late-modernity" education reforms.

Rappleye (2010) found huge potential in such development education mapping, while Japan and Nepal's realized modernity was separated by some seventy years; yet the arrival of late modernity in education occurred at nearly the same time "despite immense difference in context" (74). Such conceptual mapping might inch us toward reorienting comparative, as mentioned above, to think of changing the "unit idea" from state and nations to education transfer, from pre-modern, to modern to late modern.

Using a perspectivist approach Gorostiaga (2017) provides a form of comparison that contributes as a valuable tool to the study of education problems. He discusses methodological features of social cartography and how it falls within the debates of the field of comparative education in Latin America. He illustrates its application to education policy problems from a comparative perspective in the Latin American context, focused on analyzing the intertextual debate on globalization and education reform in the region during 1996–2008.

Contemporary graduate students also found and used Paulston's social cartography, for example, Astrid Høgmo (2018) for her thesis at Stockholm University—"Distance Education, System Thinking, Policy Comparison between South Africa and Norway." She mapped personal theoretical underpinnings of researchers, reform makers, and education developers in her interviews to see how those influenced individual views of social reality and "how conflicting theories of social and educational change work towards different assessments of educational possibilities and evaluations of developed results" (21).

Another interesting CIE finding of Høgmo's field research shows that South Africa has a clear distance education policy due to a US professor who was a World Bank consultant for South Africa following the first multi-racial elections in 1994. She wonders about this: "long-lasting, after such a long time, this still affects systemic thinking in policy development of Distance Education. Earlier governmental decisions involving international academia and global organizations still affect governmental thinking and acting in South Africa" (84). This fits our discussion in Chapter 4 about postcoloniality and how funding from international organizations, like the

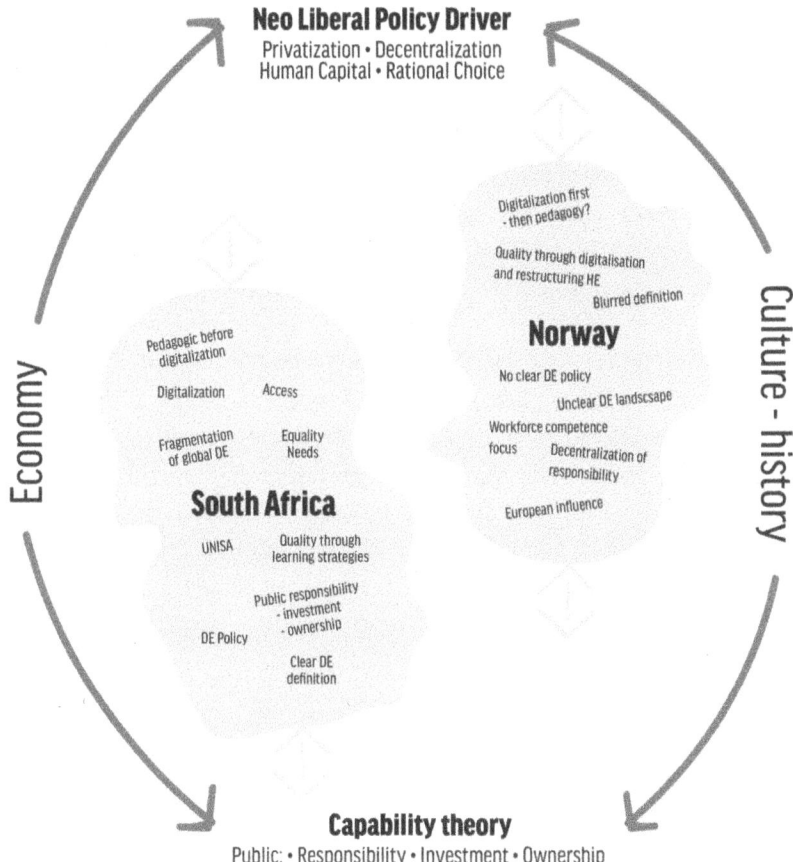

Figure 4 Astrid Høgmo (2018), Holistic system thinking Distant Education landscape, comparison between South Africa and Norway. Høgmo, A. (2018), MA thesis, Department of Education, Stockholm University, p. 84. Reproduced with permission from the author.

World Bank, and USAID funding came with US consultants in international locations like, Korea Nepal, South Africa. US professors/advisors were involved in, for instance, planning and implementation of distance education in South Africa in the 1990s after liberation from Apartheid. Høgmo's 2018 research finds that years later, policymakers are still following the transfer of imported ideas. Such contextualized approaches from the study of the locale have brought a renewed methodological interest in what is conceived of as *situated local knowledge* from international sources.

In another example Reitz (2022) was part of a group of young researchers who came together to reflect and debate the relationship between collaboration, creativity, and "co-creativity" within sustainability research. Their work (Franklin 2022) helps us better understand the potential of engaged and co-creative scholarship, if and how they can further transform sustainability agendas. Talitta Reitz was inspired by the social maps of Paulston to produce her map using an abstract representation of space to organize ideas and theories. For her "social cartography method reveals new connections about a topic and the relatedness of its elements" (334); see Figure 5.

Reitz observation that social cartography in the field of CIE, in the 1990s when Paulston applied this method, was "an entirely different way from the social reformers, illustrating its interdisciplinary diversity. With a rather loose notion of social maps which, nevertheless, fits within Vaughan's definition" (333). Paulston's mapping focused on social theoretical views rather than spatial dynamics; as you can see in Figure 6, he elaborated his CIE mapping paradigms (as seen in Figure 3), by adding the names of

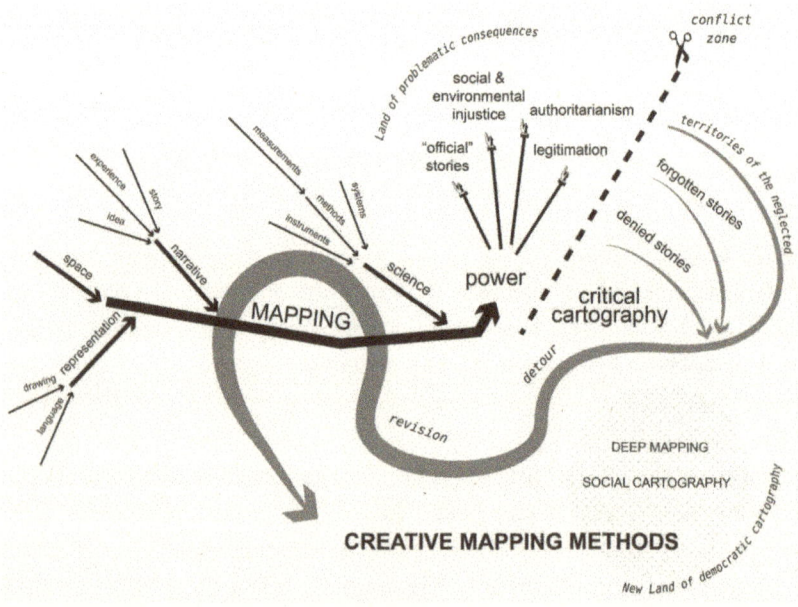

Figure 5 Phenomenographic/conceptual map of critical cartography. Reitz, T. (2022), "Back to the Drawing Board: Creative Mapping Methods for Inclusion and Connection," p. 335. Reproduced with permission from the author.

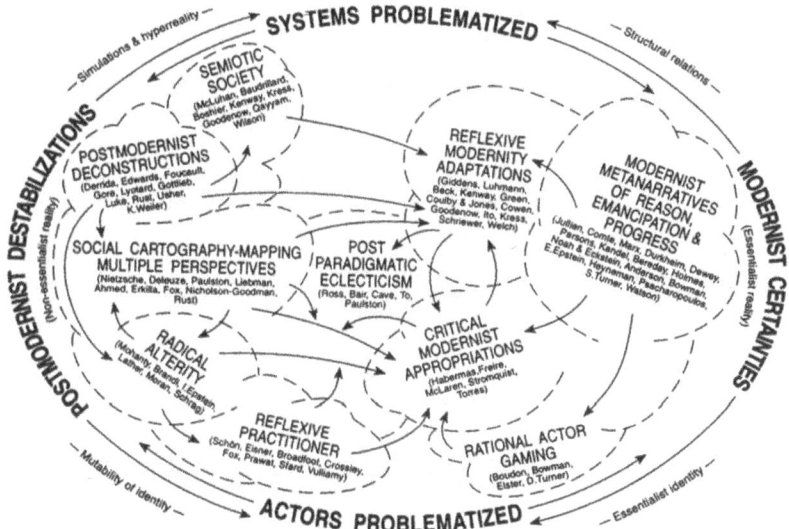

Figure 6 Paulston's mapping of knowledge positions and communities constructing and debating comparative education (and related) discourses. Reproduced from Gottlieb (2009), *"Somewhere better than this Place/nowhere better than this place" The lifemap of Rolland G. Paulston 1929–2006* **Prospects** 39 p. 97, with permission from, UNESCO IBE.

CIE and social science writers, whose published work Paulston designated within each "cloud," representing a different worldview.

In this visualization, the arrows suggest intellectual flows, and proper names refer to authors of illustrative text mapped under the worldview as Paulston appropriated them. As you look at this map, you will recognize names we mention in the chapters of this book, and in the reference list where you can read the title of the texts we used. The "clouds" and the many arrows came to visualize a more dynamic flow than the four paradigms in the squares of 2×2 (see Figure 2, Chapter 2).

Conclusion

We seek to move several issues of current debate from the more common terrain of CIE methodology and methodological training to the less familiar landscape of how methods are used in different paradigms. We contend that students and scholars of CIE are paying greater attention to what knowledge is and how it is produced (epistemes), issues related to what can be known about the world and how it can be known through comparative research before attending to the rules and procedures—the methods—used to gain such knowledge. Angela Little (2010) identifies six broad types of analysis (846):

Other' education systems, policies, practices and philosophies
Educational borrowing and lending
Contribution of education to development
Education, dependency and globalization
International education practices and organizations

This list is compact, as when she analysed the content themes of 471 articles published in *Comparative Education* between 1977 and 1998, she found a very long list "of conceptual and methodological tools that authors brought to bear on their comparative and/or international enquiry" (Little 2010: 846).

With the many methods used and such broad types of analysis, what does it mean to be a comparativist, and is there a particular method that comparativists follow? The methods have been developed in disciplines that comparative education leans on, traditionally: economics of education, sociology of education, anthropology of education, statistical analysis, computer sciences and, into the future, artificial intelligence (see Chapter 5). Studies in CIE show how these methods have been used for comparisons, both in large-scale international studies where the state-country is the unit of analysis, and case studies with a single entity at a micro level, and vertical case studies where the unit of analysis is a phenomenon, simultaneously considering the interplay between different levels of analysis, including micro, meso, and macro levels. New technologies have been introduced in comparative analysis in an international context. The most significant change in scholars' work in recent years and into the future is the internet and the information already gathered, and so much still to be gathered by local actors within their own context, which comparativists can co-produce much new knowledge.

To review methods and studies, we used the four paradigmatic worldviews we employed for the theories in Chapter 2; this allowed both for chronological organization and review, which should not be understood as steps on any linear timeline, as researchers hold different worldviews and the methods did not develop one after the other. They can be used at any time as long as you set up your research thinking about the guiding theory(ies) and method(s) that works best for you, your students, and your inquiry.

In this chapter we focused on how comparative education uses methods to research policy, social, and economic schooling planning, organization and administration, and asked how we could measure the impact of such different practices like education outcomes in various social and cultural contexts. This chapter not only listed methods but also gave examples of research studies and methods researchers employed to produce knowledge. As our experience shows, new and upcoming approaches to studying education are comparatively slow to change since, initially, CIE was (and still is) embedded in the search for scientific ways of showing the contribution of education to economic, social, cultural, and political changes. So, case studies and vertical case studies and discourse analysis and research co-producing had to prove that they are contributing to new CIE knowledge.

Academic Activities—Springboards

Springboard A

Deconstruction

A.1

In the 1980s deconstruction methods moved from literary studies to the social sciences, and anthropologists such as Arturo Escobar (1995) have applied it to study development theories and practices showing how the industrialized nations of North America and Europe come to be seen as the appropriate models for societies in Asia, Africa, and Latin America. With Colombia, his native country as an example, Escobar shows how development policies became mechanisms of control that were just as pervasive and effective as their colonial counterparts.

Comment:

- What kind of critique did Escobar's post-development ideas spark in 1995?
- He re-published his book in 2012. What kind of debate do you think it sparks today after mainstream development has begun to incorporate a softer, more human approach, more local knowledge alongside the Western-driven solutions?

A.2.
Recently there are many more examples of deconstruction of policy texts, one example being Thomas and Xu (2023), analyzing discourses of "Teach for All." Utilize critical methods to "dissect and deconstruct policy texts, discourses, and processes to analyze both the politics of education policy, and education policy as politics." Read Matthew Thomas' Illustration in this volume.

Comment:
Compare "Teach for All" across multiple programs in different countries, different language of instruction and culture, and different schooling structures. Is it possible to compare? If so, what are some considerations and assumptions? Think about comparing for what purpose? If not, explain.

    a. If you were to perform a discourse analysis of this program, what documents would you collect for such an analysis?
    b. When you read the document what would you be looking to find in them, to learn from both the form (what language they used to convince you) and from the content of the program?
    c. If you were an administrator at a school that is missing teachers, would you hire teachers that were trained in a "Teach for All" program (no college degree or teaching certification)? Explain your answer.

Springboard B
TIMSS/PISA data exercise

Choose one international data set that is relevant to your interest—civics education, math, literacy.
    How would you use this data in your own work?
    Choose two countries to compare:

- Which countries will you compare?
- What parameters were you thinking about when you choose the two countries?
- What are the characteristics you will keep in mind to compare the countries using the TIMSS or the PISA data sets.

4

Practices

Time, Spaces, Directions, Shapes

When considering how an academic field like comparative and international education (CIE) was and is practiced, we must consider how and where knowledge was/is produced, applied, and distributed and whether it is its branch of knowledge. Those questions have come up in all the chapters so far. In this chapter, we look at when, where, and what shapes knowledge, and its applications. This corpus of knowledge is published and taught at many universities around the world, in teachers' education programs, and at undergraduate and graduate levels, awarding Masters and Doctorate degrees. Chapter 1 looked at the historical roots of this production by researchers and scholars; in this chapter we will exhibit two case studies of how it was applied to plan and reform the education system of other nations, studied and published for practitioners to use. In the twentieth century and into the twenty-first, experts, consultants, foundations, and NGO members facilitate the distribution of funding, which come with advising, for education plans and reforms; learning and distributing the accumulated knowledge in many forms of publications, print, and now online; and transmitting in disciplinary studies to the next generation of comparativists via teaching, mentoring, conferences, zoom meetings, webinars, and publications. This chapter, in four parts, will explore practices and when, where, and in which global directions knowledge was/is produced and co-produced, as knowledge is shaped and produced continually. We will share some examples that occur at different times and spaces, are oriented in different global directions, and are influenced by multiple geopolitical factors. The structure of this chapter will make it easy to see how practices follow from the histories, the paradigmatic theories, and the research methods of CIE.

Time: Here, we investigate how CIE disciplinary studies developed in response to trends and geopolitical changes, including changes in world affairs, theories, research methodologies, and transformations within and across societies. While the practicing CIE can move into and across different spaces—national, international, and global—as the next section will show, when it comes to time, we cannot move backward in time and change past practices or fully predict what they will be in the future. However, we can "go" back and investigate past CIE practices to see what we can learn and change.

Space: Here we look at how CIE knowledge was produced and practiced in changing geopolitical spaces of planning, reforming, and studying education phenomena. Its earliest spaces were those of colonies and post-colonies, where national systems were invented and became education of international patterns, as reflected in studies on the spread of Western education using world cultural system theories. (Post)colonial spaces became international, which in turn became global, which turned into a dialectic relation between the global and the local. We will follow those spatial configurations to show how the spaces where CIE is practiced are socially produced spaces. As mentioned in Chapter 2, the "spatial turn" is part of the "post" theories, turning away from modernization with its orientation toward time. The theorist Fredric Jameson (1991) urged "always spatialize" as a way to contextualize. Jameson also deduces almost empirically that "space" has become a central new unit of perception and a theoretical concept, and the examples of mapping and social cartography in Chapter 3 show this. The centuries-long subordination of space to time now appears to be over. Education studies that use spatial turn show how much we need to overcome chronologies when studying education patterns and comparisons.

Directions: Chapter 1 already made it clear how significant the Cold War and the poles *West–East* were in the development and orientation of CIE practice. Right after the Second World War, comparativists had a chance to plan whole education and social systems. Soon, however, the United States was no longer the sole significant political power competing to reform the newly liberated colonies. By then, the Western education system and many CIE researchers were already in place with funding to study advice and implement comparative education research findings from the Global North to education systems in the Global South. Comparative education specialists were advising and consulting donor agencies how to implement "Northern" or "Western" research findings published in English, in nations of the Global South. They did so in the name of "never-ending economic development" (Darling, 2023:4). This section will also summarize the South-South and the South-North orientations for newer and up and coming theorizing and practicing CIE.

Shapes: Here we document shaping and re-shaping CIE knowledge production and practices. Chapter 3 has covered some relevant methods, including vertical case studies, mapping, and feminist theorizing that spans paradigms. Southern theory and its practice emphasize space and place, as do the education movements that return to indigenous ways of knowing, teaching, and learning. As well as environment and sustainability scholarship reshaping CIE practices, as they move into the central stage of comparative research.

Time

Since we cannot go back in time and practice CIE differently, time's arrow points only in one direction, from past to present to future. What we can do is value the past for the knowledge it produced and how it practiced CIE and recognize how *time*, which used to be singular and absolute, has changed into plural *times*.

We are all familiar with the timelines found in history books; the representation of *time* as a *line* appears virtually everywhere (see Rosenberg and Grafton 2010). A line is used as a visual chronology of a country or a region, or indeed of a field like CIE, and, of course, it connotes singularity (one time only) and linearity. This linearity of the timeline gives spatial form to the movement of time. As Mitchell (1980) argues, "We speak of 'long' and 'short' time, of 'intervals' of 'before' and 'after'–all implicit metaphors which depend upon the mental picture of time as a linear continuum …" (274). Under imperial regimes, a new absolute *time* was imposed on the colonies from the imperial metropolis, dating from "day one," the date of the imperial takeover. The evidence from physics that time is relative, while highly interesting, isn't as relevant to our study as the new national chronologies after decolonization, which broke up the absolute oneness of imperial time into many times—a plurality of times. Each nation has its time zones. New national times have been enacted as recently as 2022 when the Mexican government declared an end to seasonal changes of the clock between summer (daylight saving) and winter times. In addition to changing the imperial or metropolitan time (zone) in the postcolonial era, national chronology can also be altered. Nations cannot *go back* to the past; however, they can "go" back to their past, claiming their line of kings, chiefs, or national events predating colonization.

In addition to "imperial time," the liberated colonies also had to contend with the Western "educational timeline," which, starting in the eighteenth and nineteenth centuries, proliferated in atlases and textbooks and as freestanding teaching aids, combining history with geography, incorporating information about ancient time (Egypt, Persia, India, and China) but very little about Africa (Rosenberg and Grafton 2010: 130). Every historical culture has devised its mechanisms for selecting and listing (or painting, etc.) significant events since ancient times. However, "As a norm, as an ideal standard of what history *looks like,* the timeline does not appear until modernity" (15). As we already know from previous chapters, development education aims to facilitate societies and nations becoming modern. Every country, region, practice, institution, etc. was empowered to create its historical timeline.

Time travel has long been a favorite topic in science fiction, and now, when we often feel as though we are already living in science fiction, it seems more than ever like a valuable tool to think with. Nevertheless, outside of science fiction, it is impossible to go back to the past to change it. We can learn from the Cultural Resource Center education organization, "devoted to the rediscovery and application of ancient African history, culture and wisdom." They produced a poster, "Historical TimeLine Scroll document[ing] 7,000 years of world history, contrasting the relationship between African and European civilizations." It has all the traditional elements: a line in the middle, assigning dates, events, and pictures placed in chronological order. And so, long-neglected African culture is recreated on a poster for sale; it is unclear if this organization is a non-profit (ikgculturalresourcecenter.com), and we are not qualified to fact-check the events on their time point and the pictures they use. Our interest is in learning from the idea that the past can assist in better understanding the present and re-planning. A good example is a comparative study of Social Studies curriculum reforms by juxtaposing contrasting cases of the state of New York and California (Cornbleth and Waugh 1995). Focusing on the intersections of national debates and education policymaking they situate the case studies within historical and contemporary cultural contexts, with particular attention to questions of power and knowledge control and how influence is exercised in making educational changes.

Past Practices

Education Planning, Advising, and Consulting

Since the late nineteenth century, comparative education (under whatever name it might have had at the time) has built up disciplinary knowledge by researching reforms of schooling and advising governments abroad, in countries not the researcher's own, using the home country as a base of comparison for understanding other nation-states as settings for education systems. In this knowledge-building process, as Cowen (2017) reminds us, comparativists acted by seeing and reading the disconnect between what they saw and what they knew from their system or other Western systems. They used comparative education concepts, methods, and practices to translate existing local education structures and content into advising about schooling and, in some cases, planning whole national schooling systems. Kandel (1961) argued that education in new nations needed "a complete change in the spirit of education and a departure from traditional canon and practices" based on assimilation and adaptation advocated by colonial offices (Kandel 1961: 131). Educational planning, he suggested, was needed to ensure that the agriculture-based "primitive economies" of the newly independent nations would turn into "modern economies." We apologize for quoting the words used in this CER article in 1961 to show how negative and belittling CIE discourse was at that time. We reject both the words and the role this professor of Comparative Education played in what he called "underdeveloped countries." Comparative scholars worked in many newly independent nations believing that modernizing (see Chapter 2), and modern economies would lift people out of poverty.

Here, we are going to review such practices after the Second World War, where we have already seen in Chapter 1 that such "comparisons" and consulting came with funding and with a mission to make sure the newly established states benefited from the contribution of education to people's wellbeing and capitalist or socialist economic development. To begin with, we will look at two US case studies. Since the 1950s, the US State Department and what later became its US State Department AID agency funded university professors to research, plan, and advise how to spend funding to reconstruct education in countries newly liberated from colonization. The United States joined colonialization later than Europe, e.g., Spain ceded the Philippines to the United States after its defeat in the Spanish–American War of 1898. As mentioned in Chapter 1, Europe, USSR, and Japan were undergoing reconstruction after the Second World War, which left the United States as the main aid and assistance, including for education; just remember that the World Bank was established to help Europe and the UK. This assistance forms how the United States (which was once a colony) sounded and felt at the time, moving away from colonial subordinating ways. This is much like the example of Columbia University Teachers College training teachers in East Africa for forty years, as a college-to-college cooperation, funded by the non-profit Carnegie Foundation and the new US Kennedy administration. Teachers' College instructors, researchers, and students had full academic freedom to train teachers and to advise on their work in schools. Under colonialism teaching was performed mainly by missionaries, therefore teaching in schools and training African teachers was in great demand. Secular graduate students and faculty from New York were a fresh change, their ideas and methods were welcome. This tradition of education professors and their students landing their knowledge and time is still practiced, e.g., in 2015, the Teachers College launched an initiative in Kakuma Refugee Camp, Kenya (See TC, Columbia University refugee education projects). As we will see next in the two case studies, US faculty trips and consultancies were funded by the US Technical Cooperation Administration (now the US State Department AID agency), but their work was considered academically free. As you may recall from Chapter 1, the US Department of State in that era also supported Japanese Area Studies programs and their CIE faculty to research and aid Asian education systems. Without in-house technical expertise, the US State Department had to employ academic professors to assist in their development education assistance as part of a more extensive US defense program. Having discovered how few people in the diplomatic corps or military personnel spoke or read any Asian or Pacific Islands languages during the Second World War, a similar thing happened after the US invasion of Afghanistan in October 2001.

Case 1: Hugh Wood, University of Oregon

University of Oregon Professor Hugh Wood established a modern education system in Nepal in the 1950s (Rappleye 2021). Wood spent six years as the chief of the Education Division of the US Operations Mission in Nepal, funded by the US Technical Cooperation Administration, the forerunner of the US State Department AID agency. The Nepali members of the commission entrusted with reforming the Nepali system were keen to lessen dependence on foreign models of education and instructional materials, preferring instead the creation of a collective Nepali national identity as the cultural foundation for a new Nepali education system. In his report to the State Department, Wood recommended developing "patterns of education according to scientific principles and procedures rather than being guided by outmoded traditions" (111). Between 1953 and 1959, Wood's work in Nepal helped to re-design the whole education system into a Western/US model, funded by the US State Department AID agency. Thereafter, for more than a decade, young Nepalese educators came to the University of Oregon to study with Wood, graduating with PhD(s) to return to major positions in Nepal. Wood also did development education work for UNESCO in Malawi and for Westinghouse Learning Corporation in Vietnam in 1967. We can infer from the names of students in his classes that several African and Asian students had followed him to Oregon. His correspondence, archived at the University of Oregon, includes program guides from other US teachers' colleges and includes correspondence with William W. Brickman, one of the founders of the US Comparative Education Society and the co-editor of the new journal *Comparative Education Review* (*CER*). Brickman mailed Wood (a graduate of Teachers College) numerous teaching aids in 1967 and 1968.

The US State Department extended ninety contracts to fifty-three US universities across thirty-three "underdeveloped" countries worldwide (Rappleye 2021: 16). Brigham Young University worked in Iran, Indiana University in Thailand, and Stanford in Latin America and the Philippines, to mention just a few. In the 1960–70s, those contracts were the very first outside funding ever extended to colleges of education, and professors of relevant faculty departments were placed in charge of these overseas programs. Given that these programs were so new and that aid programs funded by the Communist-bloc and Europe and by the UK did not materialize until the late 1960s, US CIE faculty like Wood, and many others, were initially given a free hand to draft a whole country education system, based on comparative education research.

Case 2: Don Adams, University of Pittsburgh

Don Adams was a full-spectrum practitioner of comparative education: he did field research, consulted, taught, mentored, and helped build institutions. He practiced according to the values of his generation of comparativists. Still, later in his life, he was self-reflective and well-informed enough to express reservations about his generation's assumptions and the practice of reforming education systems with very little preparatory study of processes within the education system (e.g., teaching or administration) and little local participation or buy-in.

For decades, Adams observed first-hand the failures of externally influenced education planning in developing countries (he worked in about thirty-eight) and the remarkable tendency with which international aid agencies enlisted planning models in the face of overwhelming evidence of their inadequacy. His academic and professional reflections on this seemingly persistent anomaly led to theoretical speculations and the suggestion that there was room for extending the boundaries of the education planning debate within CIE and beyond among the donor agencies (Adams 1988). He rejected the definition widely found in the documents and publications of international aid agencies that planning included only "the examination of feasible alternatives and choosing among them according to an objective."

His scholarship was consistently based on his experiences as a consultant for international development agencies in more than thirty locations, beginning with South Korea in 1954–1955 for the United Nation, and 1957–1958 for the International Cooperation Agency, where he single-handed reconstructed the whole Korean education system. Adams was involved in Korean education research planning and policy for fifty years, from his work under remonstration after the war (which divided Korea in two) to 2010, when he published a large, edited book with scholars from the Korean Educational Development Institute (KEDI), many of whom had studied with him at the University of Pittsburgh. His career reflected a continual effort to link planning and policy formulation with research and theory.

Early in his career, Adams published a series of textbooks covering education and national development topics aimed primarily at advanced students in CIE and international aid agencies. In the 1960s, Adams served on the board of *CER*, shaping the practice of CIE with many articles: in 1960 one on Korea, and one on Japan; in 1965, on education and social development; in 1960 articles such as "Development Education" in a state-of-the-art issue from 1977; in 1990 "Analysis Without Theory Is Incomplete";

and so on. Adams published 118 research papers or book reviews—edited papers written by his PhD students from thirty-two different countries, just to emphasize his influence on the field (Adams n.d.).

Adams, in a 1966 article, coined *development education*. Not education for development, not development of education but combining the two as one (the way we are using it in this book). In the 1960s and 1970s, Don Adams was also on the board of CER. the major CIE journal, and was president of CIES. Commanding great influence, under the motto "The best way to study education is comparatively." His three early books analyzed the role of education in modernization and national development, drawing on his involvement in education planning in South Korea, Latin America, and Africa. As with Professor Wood, students followed him to Pitt, training a generation of educators from overseas that occupied leading positions in their home countries, such as Director General of Pakistan's Ministry of Education, an Indonesian Ministry of Education affiliated, and a large Pitt alumni in South Korea, holding leadership positions in government, education, and other industries.

Towards the end of his career, Adams argued that instead of forcing the messy diverse world into a "sanitary" conceptualization of planning, a diversity of knowledge claims, assumptions, and the cognitive and cultural backgrounds of education planners should be brought to bear (see Chapter 5). Competition between different planning models should be encouraged, potentially resulting in new plans that are more in tune with local knowledge. This position is a long way from his own position in the past and Hugh Wood's in the 1950s who, as we have seen, thought that the Nepalis' desire to retain the distinctively Nepali character of their education system was guided by "outmoded traditions." As we will examine below, re-shaping CIE practices with theories and practices from the Global South are about local education practices from the (far) past into the future.

Past Present

Adams' ideas, derived from experience, can help guide CIE practice in the present. Although Adams did not speak about a researcher's "positionality" or of knowledge "co-production," his long education planning experiences, and concepts like "qualities" of education rather than "quality" in his later book, are worth reflecting on. They guide the new qualitative research, where knowledge production shifts away from the researcher who analyzes and explains social phenomena and who submits reports and gives advice on planning and policy, and instead moves towards the researcher as he engages with those being researched in mutually learning from and teaching each other. Researchers, no matter how much they read and or how many videos they watch, always need to learn much more about the local context. When the linguistic, social, cultural, and knowledge gap can be reduced, there is a chance to focus on the co-production or co-creation of education planning, policy, and research. Co-production and co-creation have been proposed as a model for interdisciplinary work in CIE. Because of its democratizing potential, such co-production can transform planning and policy processes (Rubalcaba 2022).

As Adams grasped already in the 1980s, development education is better if we understand how innovations are created and implemented locally by the society we have come to advise. Many comparativists and World Bank advisors were and still are true believers in the role of education in economic, social, and political development. Aid, not only in the past but in recent practices, is expected to facilitate changes in the whole education system, for instance, in the cases of Afghanistan and Iraq in the aftermath of the United States' post-9/11 wars on terror. One sure way to know that Western education patterns have been transferred is to follow the money backing up the funding stream from the World Bank, Asia Development Bank, US State Department AID agency, UK Department for International Development (DFID), renamed, "Foreign, Commonwealth & Development Office (FCDO)" in 2020, and private foundations, among others. In the past, development education was deeply involved politically in recipient countries, and places like South Africa, Zimbabwe, and Ghana have a long history of support from international agencies and foundations, both under colonial regimes and after their collapse. For example, in the 1950s, the Rockefeller Foundation funded education in Southern Rhodesia (subsequently Zimbabwe), where they had business interests in developing commercial poultry farms, funded a new university, and awarded scholarships to excellent students to attend university in California. Those students went back to teach, or became ministers in the newly liberated colony (Musoni-Chikede 2022).

Conclusion

Time is increasingly subject to pluralization. Space and time changed at the beginning of the twentieth century with the introduction of technologies of telegraphy, telephony, railroads, and automobiles, and later flight, radio, television, etc. Current digital technologies (the internet, social media, streaming television, etc.) affect experiences of time and space even more profoundly than earlier mechanical technologies did. With digital technologies, as the cultural historian Stephen Kern writes, our thinking has expanded: we are now "thinking about the texture of time as variously arhythmic, collagist, disrupted, overlapping, layered, nested, folded, vibrating, and turbulent" (Kern 2025: 10). While we know that particle physics and genetic engineering have introduced plural times, for our study, what is more important is that the new national chronologies of decolonization have increased the number of times we can study development education. The histories of postcolonial nations are no longer just their colonial-era chronologies; instead, these nations have looked back and found other histories and education patterns at past points in time. This makes a profound difference in the way we think about CIE practices.

Spaces

Where CIE is Practiced

CIE was and is practiced in different spatial locations and configurations. However, as mentioned in the introduction, as many studies used historical approaches, time took presidence over space. The "spatial turn" in the social sciences has been explored in CIE, mostly in policy studies. National spaces, the original locus of CIE practice, have moved practices into international spaces, and the international space got woven into the global. Understanding the interactions, tensions, and contradictions among the national, the international, the global, and the local is crucial to understanding contemporary practices of CIE. Dependency and critical theories, such as Southern theory, see space as central to changing education practices. This section looks at spaces as social construct, influencing and shaping those practices. Bear in mind, however, that the spaces of CIE practice have not transformed linearly from one type of space to another successively over time; instead, the types of spaces—national, international, global, and local—have overlapped, and CIE practice has sometimes straddled multiple spaces at the same time or gone back and forth between them. Often, they are not used as binaries, global/local, or national/international.

We are not primarily concerned with learning spaces where education is taking place, as in the study by Brown and Schweisfurth (2024), who describe what they learned from two government primary schools in northwest Tanzania—adapting the vertical case study method from Vavrus and Bartlett (2006) (see Chapter 3). Brown's dissertation fieldwork used a spatial lens that "opened up opportunities to identify and investigate the bundles of trajectories producing learning spaces and the social and pedagogical effects their interaction and negotiation produced" (477). As we saw in Chapter 2, Jameson (1998) identifies our time, "late capitalism" in the political and economic and cultural sphere, insisting that the history/*time* that the nineteenth century was obsessed with lost its domination on social thought and what replaced it is *space*. Jameson extended the "spatial turn" that was already announced by Foucault in 1969; by saying that the present will be above all the era of spatial lens. In a cross-national study of public policies in education in Costa Rica, Brazil, and Peru, Stromquist (2011) found that spaces "should be seen both as effects and causes of conscious social action."

What follows is our interest in looking at CIE practice with a spatial lens, a boundless space in which objects and events occur and have relative position and direction independent of what occupies it. Spaces where education systems are planned, and policies are designed, where CIE researchers study reforms and how systems are influenced by geopolitical, spatial connotations, willing or unwillingly, as well as changes, reforms, teaching methods, and school architecture, to just name a few, move from space to space or among them, while those spaces are physically the way we use them, e.g., "globalization," "North," and "South" are social constructs concepts.

Colonial Space

Within the spaces of the colonial regimes set up by European powers worldwide, education was planned and supported by the colonial administration and missionary orders. On the receiving end, where it impacted people in the colonial space, colonial education was exclusive and not open to all. However, there was always pressure for equal access to European-style education, which only intensified after the Second World War, in which so many people under colonial masters were enlisted to fight. The same happened in the US, when the returning African American servicemen and women were unwilling to go back to segregation and would not send their children to study in separate schools under the "separate-but-equal" system of US schooling; so, too, in the colonies there was increased demand for educational access. Addressing this problem in the colonies meant new infrastructure and legal steps. For example, in the French colonies, through a series of laws, existing colonial institutions assimilated with those in France. Colonial imperatives to maintain inequality of status and rights between the colonizers and the colonized could not continue. New institutions were created quickly to satisfy the high demand for education. The immediately apparent achievements and benefits that Africans with a European education thought they had secured in articulating their demand for equality in education meant that they acted as agents of the expansion and reproduction of European education in Africa. This was referred to as the "colonization of the mind through education" (Assié-Lumumba 2016: 20). Inadvertently, expanding educational access facilitated "miseducation" and created a new generation of alienated Africans, which rejected being colonialized (Mazrui 1975).

Another immediate solution to the pressure for education access was sending African students abroad. The absence of post-secondary institutions in the colonies made it necessary to send students to France or the UK for higher education, and established local universities, not just the Rockefeller university in Rhodesia but also at University of the Cape. The British colonizer Cecil Rhodes, who extracted diamonds and gold from Africa, was the prime minister of Cape Colony from 1890 to 1896 and gave the land, the British took from the people, to establish the University of Cape Town (UCT), which has exhibited a bronze statue of Rhodes since 1934. The colonial idea to educate the colonized is one of the most profound impacts that colonial rule had. Colonial education systems were not just about teaching; they were instruments of cultural erasure and suppression. For decades there were calls to remove the statue of Rhodes but after only one month of student protests the statue was removed in April 2015. Not all colonial education can be eradicated with the removal of a statue; Rhodes also left funds to establish the Rhodes Scholarship to award students from former British territories scholarships to study at Oxford University. The competition for this prestige scholarship is held every year, and in the United States only two students from every five states are selected. Everyone including the recipients (among them President Clinton, basketball player Bill Bradley, songwriter Kris Kristofferson, and Pete Buttigieg, secretary of transportation under Biden) know that colonial conquest and natural extraction paid for their education. De Beers, founded in 1888 by Rhodes, still operates today as the world's leading diamond company. UCT students' protests resumed the following year because the "remove Rhodes' statue" was just a symbol to a university that fundamentally transformed from twenty or thirty years previously and opened to black students. Looking beyond the numbers, there is not one black, woman, full professor at UCT, the law faculty; out of 200 academics, only ten are black, and only one of those ten is a black South African (Daniel and Platzky, 2024).

The legacies of colonial education go far back and deep since higher education institutions were "created by the African political and educational leadership were modeled after European universities" (Assié-Lumumba 2016: 21). This is an example of how colonial powers continued to operate after independence as this period came to be called neo- or semi-imperialism, rule without occupation. To rebuild an exploited country, all-natural resources and people's labor were inaccessible to reconstruct a whole nation's education system. It is not just models of education that remain colonial, but all the funding still came from the colonial powers to rebuild the newly independent countries' education. To plan a whole education system, as we saw above in the case of South Korea (which was all paid for by the United States via the UN), to meet the massive demand for education is expensive and monumental; funding came with advice and "modern" Western education patterns, or the way UCT students' put it: "We want a complete shift in the thinking about curriculum. It can't be Eurocentric anymore. We need a curriculum that is about our continent, and not just the negatives, but the positives as well," as reported by Don Boroughs (2015) on NPR. The idea that the 1994 political and economic compromise worked out best for all South Africans is now less accepted by the young people that didn't fight for liberation but, like at UCT, students see discrimination with open eyes.

In many studies that retrace development education, you can find the grants and who funded them, and from where the advisor came; which is how you can tell what education transfers took place. See Chapter 3 which discusses how Høgmo (2018) found that distance education system thinking and policy followed a model that an education professor from the United States had transferred to South Africa more than fifteen years before. Such model transfers can last long after the advisor left, or funding has run out. Yet studies like those of cultural ethnographer James Clifford (2013) show that development schemas exists in all local cultures, yet like the many studies of education transfer (e.g., Lee et al. 1988) individuals, like teachers, or schooling culture on the receiving end of neo-imperialism, have powerful assimilative mechanisms to change the composition of imports, e.g., active learning, teachers education, or assessment patterns and content when it came to implementation.

National and International

The postcolonial era was the time when national educational institutions were built. The demand for education at the national level presented a monumental task. In the 1950s, the United States was one of the only sources of funding education institution-building abroad, and it undertook institution-building projects with assistance from comparative education experts who researched and had planning models and funds from agencies to modernize education and assessed its impact on economic and social change. The nation-state was assumed to be the basic focus of research of CIE until about the mid-1970s. The nation-state was treated as a unit in itself, and, often, research set out to ask how education contributed to the development of the social structures within a nation-state compared to other states in which they found similar elements.

Comparisons were made of states within a region, such as Southeast Asia, Africa, Latin America, or Europe, "focused on education in individual nation-states that presumably shared similar cultures, histories, and economic structures. Topically based studies also were situated in national frameworks, asking, for example, if one national school system was more to economic growth than another" (Kelly and Altbach 1986: 91). The category of comparative research focuses on schooling within a nation-state, working on urban/rural distinctions applied to nations as the unit of analysis (see Chapter 2).

The education economist Mary Jean Bowman (1969) showed that education variance is often as excellent, if not more significant, within a nation as between nations. Class and ethnicity may not operate similarly regarding education access and outcome throughout a single country. It points out the apparent necessity of looking at regional variation given the growing trends in the de-centralization of education and the de-concentration of educational decision-making in many countries with a few different regions. In 1975, Meyer et al. documented the effects of the contemporary world structure on nation-states, using World-Systems theory to analyze how the world political economy influences development patterns and can create disparities between core, semi-peripheral, and peripheral nations. World-Systems theory (see Chapter 2), as practiced by CIE scholars, challenged the use of the nation-state as the unit of analysis and argued that education systems are often affected by more factors outside that country than the factors inside it, urging CIE research to focus on identifying this force as an international order.

Once this consolidation of studying the world as a system was well underway, economic analyses of development education within the national context also captured the position of a country within the international system. Many studies have shown how the languages of the colonizer continued to dominate in former colonies, how textbooks, curricula, and educational technologies were borrowed from core nations, and how the types of reforms adopted and their success or failure were no longer affected just by *national* but also by the *international* flow of transfer of education planning practices and policies, as well as its globalist politics (Steiner-Khamsi 2004). International political economics determined who, where, and what would be funded and which national institutions should be reformed.

An example of how an independent state, namely Brazil, agreed to adopt an international reform funded by the World Bank (WB). Described in a 1998 plan, spelling out all the details the country (the "borrower") must follow if it accepts the grant—in this case US $62.5 million—with outcomes to be assessed by the World Bank. The national project FUNDESCOLA has been influenced by the lessons from Chile, Uruguay, and other Latin American countries in promoting school subprojects: (1) primary education for the procurement of context-appropriate materials and increasing stakeholder input; and (2) the Colombian Escuela Nueva program, which achieved practical results in the modular use of textbooks, capacity building of teachers, student-centered learning, evaluation of student attainment, and community participation for multi-grade schools (World Bank 1998: 17). *Escola Ativa*, or "Active School," had already been piloted for seven years in Northwest Brazil, one of the country's poorest regions, with a US$92 million loan from the World Bank to expand and improve primary schools. Reviews of its success were mixed; the World Bank's observed that not all the funding was used for education, but some of its politicians used it for jobs, and scholarships. State secretaries draining project resources was not a new finding, where the funds were diverted for local needs and not for implementing the World Bank's (hundreds of pages long) plan. So why did the World Bank offer Brazil another US$62 million in 1998 to implement this same Escola Ativa program that had already been piloted with mixed results?

In the 1980s, the World Bank became the most influential and powerful agency in education development. The difficulties of many low- and medium-income countries that were facing external debt due to an enormous increase in interest rates induced a change in the lending policy. Both the International Monetary Fund (IMF) and the World Bank established a new system of loan conditions based on implementing specific macroeconomic measures and institutional reforms. The conditions of such loans in education were highly dependent on priorities and strategies of international education models and limited the number of options available. "In this way, the new lending system reduced national autonomy to set educational strategies and significantly restricted the available policy options. Recipient countries were aware that they had to adopt the recommended policies to keep receiving funding from the World Bank" (Bonala et al. 2013: 481).

The proliferation of new communication systems and the latest technologies in the closing decades of the twentieth century made transferring teaching and learning models much more fluid and made copying and adapting them easier. New combinations between popular transnational culture and local or national traditional cultures were made continually, as well as the global flow of knowledge. The Organization for Economic Co-operation introduced the concept of "Knowledge Society" during the heyday of *neoliberal* education reforms in the 1990s, when decentralization and choice through privatization were promoted, including linear transition approaches to Knowledge Society. For example, in Latin America, reforms in the 1990s were based on the idea that education systems had to adapt to a "Knowledge Society" based on economic policies without considering national processes (Artopoulos 2023).

The drive for universal primary education was a world movement, and the unparalleled education reform at the secondary and tertiary levels had little to do with national education needs. Meyer et al. (1992) suggested that the changes in technology and communications and the internationalization of the labor market moved education functions to be viewed within a transnational context. They called on CIE to reorient its inquiry by looking at "the world society" rather than the national state.

International and Global

We reviewed globalization in Chapters 1 and 2 and mentioned studies of international convergence of national education systems. The national becoming international as far as education went was coupled with another directional move in the name of global economic governance. Through international structures, the United States continually assists low-income nations without direct control. This was achieved first by a significant demand for education; after that, there was a desire for primary education for all relevant groups, bringing developing countries under the global capitalist economic system. Among these global institutions were the World Bank, the IMF, the US State Department AID agency, the United Nations, and many other international development agencies, such as those of the UK and Nordic countries.

We have mentioned the World Bank (WB) in all our chapters; their education sector within "human development" evolved to the point that they influenced the definition of the global education agenda. It was the largest funder of education in the newly established states, holding an unmatched power till the 2020s, "the definition of education problems and adequate policy solutions" (Bonala et al. 2013: 485). The role of the WB in global development education goal setting is illustrative in their own document (World Bank 1998: 103). The ultimate impact of international education goals has been influenced by the WB's research showing that what a neoliberal economy needs is primary education for all. In the 1990s, all borrowing countries (as already mentioned, Brazil and India) had to prioritize primary education for development (Colletta and Sutton 1989), the same with other donors that wished to collaborate on funding with the World Bank. We will see in Chapter 5 that Sustainable Development Goal 4 (SDG4 on education) was also influenced by the World Bank, as in the mid-2000s they made a *learning turn* no longer enforcing "education for all," even if only primary schooling, but turning toward a knowledge society promoted by information communication technologies (ICT). As Francine Menashy (2019), at the OISE in Toronto, has found, "greening" education in nations in Africa is not funded, because education use to be funded by World Bank or by one donor to a single nation. This funding model is replaced by multi-smaller donors that form an International partnership within a region so a few systems collaborate, for greater impact.

Besides the International Association for the Evaluation of Educational Achievement (IEA), elaborated on in Chapter 3, another global comparison is on enrollment statistics worldwide, reported by the Education for All initiative under UNESCO (see Chapter 1). This comparison resulted in extensive "Global Monitoring Reports" since 2000, continuing from 2016 under "Global Education Monitoring Reports." The influence of these global international reports in legitimizing cross-country comparisons grew to the point that they are influencing the contents and curricula of far different systems that do not participate or score as high as others. Ramirez and Meyer (2012) called these research and curricular changes "post-national," which stressed the global cultural influence on education structure and content at the expense of nation-states' school organization, curricula, teachers' education, and students' assessment. Research literature on education transfer increasingly seeks to understand how globalization, the international community, and "best practice" discourses have informed and transformed understandings of education borrowing practices (Steiner-Khamsi 2004). This global dependency on criteria of "what works" and international "best practices," at the potential expense of local context, has been investigated by the studies of education borrowing and lending (see Chapter 3). As part of these global educational borrowing practices, several newer subjects have become more prominent in national school curricula, including environmental studies/ecology and civics or citizenship education. These two subjects continue to be linked in IEA international comparisons and the UN 2030 SDGs.

Globalization is an effective construct, to the point that some practitioners go as far as to suggest that the nation-state will have to give up its national borders when it comes to economic survival. From a historical perspective, Steiner-Khamsi (2004) writes that the current wave of globalization is reminiscent of earlier transnational education discursive practices, such as "democratization, modernization, and development, [which] each had an impact similar to that of globalization" (5). She thinks the pressure from international agencies on low-income countries, such as neoliberalism, is real, as well as determining loans (see above the collective power of the World Bank). Yet many such countries, despite economic and political pressure to comply with international standards in education, import educational policies but still use them in local contexts. Thus, convergence of education systems is not inevitable. From a historical perspective, globalization does not always have the effect of homogenizing societies across the world. Technological change encourages such homogeneity in positive ways, and at the same time, it could be said that culture seems global. Nevertheless, global culture differs significantly from location to location; see James Clifford (2013) *Becoming Indigenous in the Twenty-First Century* with indigenous variations of past education experiences coming into the future (see below).

Beyond Globalization

The question arises: did the resurgence of geopolitical conflict and competition post-9/11 (2021) spell the downfall of globalization, with implications for CIE? After 9/11 and the onset of the war on terror, publications about the end of globalization or the new phase of militarized globalization increased. They are only more pertinent with the 2000s wars, United States in Iraq and Afghanistan, Russian and Iranian interventions in Iraq and Syria (2015); Russia takeover of Karmia and invasion of Ukraine and the ensuing war in the Middle East (both still ongoing as of 2025), reviving questions about empire and whether it marks a new stage of the globalization with wars both military and economically (see the Springboards at the end of this Chapter). However, most scholars suggest that declaring globalization over is premature, as structures of world order, governance patterns and organized violence, economic and education patterns, and cultural flows, environmental degradation and inequality, exclusion and domination persist.

We have mentioned a few times the wave of internationalization of higher education and universities (not only in the US) as they portray themselves as *global universities* to attract international students, to internationalize the learning experiences of their students, support faculty research and international partnerships; see illustration by Blanco in this volume. In their research, George Mwangi and Yao (2021) found that despite the interconnectedness between internationalization and globalization, often universities' internationalization efforts are categorized as domestic priorities that are distinct from international issues, as if the local is separate from the national, which is also separate from the global. Looking at programs and plans at many different institutions, internationalization depends on a continuous flow "that extends between, around, and within the global, national, and local" (56). In the 2000s "glonacal" described multi-scalar, or levels of analysis, not only in education, where individual and institutional and nations showed open possible flows from any direction, interacting local, national and global scales; see section above. Like in other spheres the local scale in education and knowledge production is continually invented and remade. As a result, contemporary internationalization points to the interconnectedness and immediacy of how global pressures were very much present in local and regional priorities in the 2000s and 2010s, to the point of needing a "cosmopolitan turn in social and political theory" (Beck and Grande 2010). Beck and Grande (2010) discuss the dilemmas of a theory of cosmopolitan modernities, in particular problems of political agency and prospects of political realization. They address methodological cosmopolitanism key problem, we discussed in Chapter 3, namely the problem of defining the appropriate unit of analysis. At the same time (2011) Christian Moraru published a foundational study of this whole period, suggesting *"Cosmodernism"* as the cultural model for the post fall of the Berlin Wall (or end of the Cold war, as we knew it) and the period of accelerating globalization. In CIE most visibly higher education research dealt with the various scales, local, regional, national, and global, looking at the intersections between scales. Especially between national, international and global, research on student mobility.

Rizvi (2006), see also his illustration in this volume, criticizes the tendency to view globalization as a homogenizing force in education, where policies and practices from the West are simply transferred to other contexts without considering local realities and needs. He suggests that researchers should utilize "imagination" to understand the complex and dynamic ways global forces, regional cultures, and power relations shape education policies. He proposes a critical approach to education policy research that examines the power dynamics and inequalities embedded within global education policies. These are influenced by how capital and its cultural mediations are played out under globally emergent socio-economic conditions, which began to manifest themselves in the South earlier than in the North, most visibly in Africa (see below on theorizing from the South).

Network analysis of a range of global education topics (Menashy and Read 2016) confirms the dominance of knowledge production from the "global North," which, as the example from Latin America showed, is used by donor agencies to reform education in the "global South." When examining the directions of such flows of economic cooperation, education funding, and education borrowing and lending, the Global South is pulling away from the terms we have described as the "global order."

Conclusion

We started this section by claiming we can look at education changes spatially. In doing so, in this section, we provided ways of orientation and knowing spaces where education is funded and practiced. The example of the World Bank persuaded the international community of the need to prioritize primary education as the development priority in the 1990s for both donors and borrowing countries, showing how the international community acted upon the local. However, toward the end of the 2010s, the landscape of aid has changed. Menashy (2019) performed a comprehensive analysis of the global education landscape using a network analysis of hundreds of organizations engaged in education, showing the rise of multiple development ideas and crucial shifts with new pooled funds while the power of the World Bank and the IMF has been declining. In the global education arena, most notable are the *Global Partnership for Education* (GPE) and the *Education Cannot Wait*, an international fund dedicated to education in emergencies. At the end of the 2010s, what changed was a seemingly small shift from "global." It might also imply some deflation of the "global" and "planetary" overbearing discourse, not just in education but also in the Humanities, aided by ICTs, which were predicted to undermine national borders entirely.

Although we have distinguished time and space so far, we must also acknowledge their connection. Bartlett and Vavrus (2017), in Chapter 3, reminded us how time and space are inextricably interconnected. Changes in contemporary education are reshaping education policy and planning spaces, moving to international and global levels. In contrast, at the national level, as we mentioned above, due to international influences, the borrowing translates into differences in local practices in the classroom, at schools, and in networks of schools. These changes have been analyzed regarding managerialism, welfarism, privatization, and development of hierarchies, none of which were there before. Landri (2014) found that these "new spatial configurations remain relatively unexplored since most policy analysis displays a simplified description of the 'social' enacted in education policies" (596). Asking: "How does this education policy-making space materialize in practice? Is there a single, or are there multiple instantiations of education policy-making space?" (597). In conclusion, the education planning and policy-making space is fluid among national, regional, and international networks, among users of local and global knowledge, practicing CIE.

Directions

Directions and Orientations in CIE Practices

The directional orientations that frame CIE's experiences were very clear during the Cold War (see Chapter 1), when everything unfolded on the West–East or (depending on one's perspective) the East–West axis. Not only was CIE developed and funded due to this West–East conflict over what is education and why it is comparative and international, but its practices were supported by grants oriented around the spatial division at the end of the Second World War, A reorientation of the main direction and flow of education knowledge-production and transfer occurred after 9/11 and the onset of the war on terror, from *West–East* whereas before we mostly saw a *North–South* direction.

"North and South, like East and West, belong to each other. The flow of imperial representation—West *to East*, North *to South*—is not informed and predictable in reception" (Mead 2003: 169). Here, we will add that Southern academic scholarship migrates to Northern centers, and as *South–South* cooperation is critical and revisionist practices become essential, particularly when the BRICS countries (Brazil, Russia, India, China, and South Africa) are trying out or at least declaring new development models, including education funding and advising. We will engage with this emerging direction of the Global South along the South–South axis. As Connell (2007) reminds us, the North, with its domination over theories and knowledge production, needs to start paying better attention to the Global South and its critical social sciences and new knowledges.

West–East and East–West

This era of worldwide West–East conflict is basic to CIE, where comparativists were given opportunities to plan whole educational and social systems after the Second World War when, during the 1950s, Europe was reconstructing, and the United States was the only funding source (which is why the World Bank was set up). As we mentioned above, the Soviet bloc had not yet begun funding development abroad, and US academics were advising the US State Department on how to invest in reconstruction funding in the name of economic growth.

During the Cold War, the United States and the USSR dominated the West–East or East–West orientation, amassing nuclear warpower in a race, dominating world affairs, and developing different social and economic ideologies, driving different educational conceptualization. There were not only threats of war but also proxy wars, in Korea, Vietnam, and Angola. And, of course, there was the space race, which the United States initially "lost" to the Soviet Union when the artificial satellite *Sputnik* was launched into orbit; but the United States ultimately "won" by landing humans on the moon in 1969. Everyone remembers the "Iron Curtain" that divided the Soviet socialist East from the democratic capitalist West so that, for instance, East and West Germany could not easily exchange visitors or goods, and the Berlin Wall divided what had once been Germany's capital city, into West and East zones. This history helps explain the curiosity of the first cohort of CIE members about the Soviet Union and socialist education. Kent State University organized group tours, and their students did not just study about other systems but also visited them. This West–East education tours were the beginning of *study abroad* which developed into *education abroad* ("education" offering more options than "study"), which in turn has lately been renamed *global education* as part of the internationalizing students' learning experience at higher education that aspire to the status of a "global university." (Whereas "abroad" is different than your own country, "global" is anywhere, so, for instance, students can undertake study tours of the slums of Baltimore or Rocky Mountains hiking.)

This change was followed not only because the percentage of US students that cannot study abroad could not grow due to prohibited cost but because internationalization magnifies higher education equity. As George Mwangi and Yao (2021) found after 9/11, the individual institution uses internationalization to emphasize international branding and profile, income generation from international students, faculty international research, strategic alliances, and knowledge co-production with partner institutions. This shift "reflects globalizing forces, national events, and political changes that led to greater focus on nationalism, protectionism, and border control in tandem with an increasingly corporatized and neoliberal" (562). As mentioned, institutions' internationalization is one of the ranking indicators, and those different ranking tables are valuable for marketing the institution to international students (Blanco et al. 2021). See Blanco' illustration as well as that by Yao and George Mwangi.

Studying the "other" has deep roots in comparative education. Logically, the "East" includes also the Far East, and the "Silk Road" countries of Central Asia and the Middle East were already known in the ancient world, and we learned a lot about education and knowledge production in China, India, Egypt, and Greek, to name a few. This also includes the "Orient," which is a spatial correlative of otherness that, as Edward Said argued (see Chapter 2), was made up of the "Western Imagination." The images of "Oriental" otherness that still circulates in popular culture and academic discourse alike were a factor facilitating President George W. Bush's declaration of a global "war on terror," followed by regional wars in Afghanistan and Iraq—both sites of education investment paid for by the US State Department AID agency and planned by Washington, DC-based development education agencies and comparativists who worked for or with them. As we now know, those education reforms did not work as envisioned. This is used to stop or reevaluate *all* the operations of the US State Department AID agency, or like the new executive branch as of January 2025 declared the US State Department AID agency closed. A few weeks later Myanmar was rocked by a 7.7 magnitude earthquake and the United States has been unable to meaningfully respond due to the administration's decision to slash all foreign aid.

North–South

In the 1950s and 1960s, the practice of CIE entailed experts and education models being transferred from the North to South and in the 1990s to East Europe (after the collapse of the Soviet bloc). Many of the research studies in Chapter 3 also show that while the data gathered is from education systems located in the Global South, the researchers are mainly from the North or, if they are from the South, they have degrees from English language universities and publish in peer-reviewed journals in the North. The contributors to the edited *Bloomsbury Handbook of Method in Comparative and International Education* (Thomas, et al., 2025), are an interesting case. The thirty-four chapters were written by multiple contributors based in Australia, Japan, Norway, Spain, the UK and the US, but they studied mostly in the UK and North America. For that matter, our reference list at the end of this book also reflects this clearly, research publications written by and published in the North, reflecting the dominance of Northern institutions of knowledge production and dissemination even when the scholars themselves hail from the Global South. The case of the World Bank's loans to Brazil for development education is, in this respect, exemplary: "The overall narrative is the same: a system of ideas generated in the Global North gains political influence in the North and is then imposed on the Global South" (Connell and Dados 2014: 119).

We would like to believe that we are entering a time where these directions of orientation are going to be shuffled, as we exemplify below in the case of a social mapping project undertaken by a scholar from Palacky University in Olomouc, Czech Republic, in collaboration with the University of South Africa, with support from their Department of Geography and a South African foundation. The study reports on work with two communities, the Kibera slum in Nairobi, Kenya, and Koffiekraal in the Northwest province of South Africa. Published in the *South African Journal*, it can be found under "free access" on the internet; the author, Pánek (2013), whose contact information is a Gmail account, could be anywhere in the world, South or North.

The North–South and South–North axes are explored by diasporic scholars Staci Martin (in Portland, US) and Deepre Dandekar (at the Modern Orient Institute, Berlin). They co-produced a volume (2022) with thirty-four Global South scholars who share their experiences, knowledge, and their positionality of establishing themselves in academic settings in the Global North. Their stories are strikingly like that of African American intellectuals, like W.E.B. Du Bois in the nineteenth century, when highly educated men and women, diasporic in their own country due to the color of their skin, could not get access to equal education or employment commensurable with their education and skills. Drawing on critical theory, indigenous and multicultural education, and the new sociology of higher education, these Global South academics assist us in understanding what it means to practice in higher education institutes, as if in a "Third Space," co-producing knowledge on discrimination, resilience, and hope. "This third space ... does not predicate itself on fixed entities, but rather identifies politically and historically produced false binaries that discriminate against those that are trapped in the 'middle,' not necessarily because they want to but out of necessity" (Martin and Dandekar 2022: xxi).

North–South, South–North Comparativists

Being strangers in your place relates to Said's thesis in *Orientalism* (1978), which expanded the fields of anti-colonial and postcolonial studies. Said set out to answer the question of "what one really is," a pressing question for someone who was simultaneously a literary theorist, a classical pianist, a music critic, arguably New York's most famous public intellectual, and the most prominent advocate for Palestinian rights. Belonging to the East–West axis, born in the East (Jerusalem, Mandatory Palestine) and educated in the West (US), he lectured and wrote about being a diasporic scholar like those of a younger generation in Martin and Dandekar's (2022) book. His metaphor for his condition was that of a "traveler." Said's "traveling theory" refers to transmitting and adapting ideas in different directions along axes like the ones we reviewed in CIE contexts. Said's traveling theory helps us think about CIE researchers, consultants, and mentors who go across the globe to the various sites where they study, research, and teach.

"The comparative educationist as a foreigner" was, in fact, the theme of a special issue of *Comparative Education* (56 (1), 2020). Just as many of the careers of comparativists of the past involved "travel" CIE professors from one country ending up in another (including, e.g., Bereday, Brickman, Eckstein, Hans, Kandel, Kazamias, Lauwerys, Mitter, Noah, and Ulich), several of them mentioned in this book, so, too, did the seven contemporary scholars who were invited to reflect on their changing places and the field's development. Rappleye (2020), for example, reflecting on his "transnational academic mobility," tells the tale of his displacement from the West (US), where he was brought up, to the East (China), where he taught, and from the North (Oxford, UK, where he took his DPhil) to the South (Japan). He writes: "I never intended to become a 'foreign' comparativist, and I remain unsure of how long this great privilege of 'doing comparative education as a "foreigner" will last" (1). On the other hand, Takayama invites us to reflect with him on a "negative" trajectory for a comparativist. His itinerary goes from South (Japan) to North (Canada), and East (Bangalore, India and Tokyo, Japan) to North (PhD, with Michael Apple at University of Wisconsin–Madison), then back to Japan after teaching in Australia for more than ten years. This case demonstrates a sign of the researcher going through encounters or interruptions, and those encounters with "other" education have resulted in a profound transformation. Showing how the researcher has managed to turn the negative experience of disillusionment, perplexity, frustration, doubt, or discomfort into an educative form of negativity.

South–South

Connell and Dados (2014), thinkers from the Global South, show that geopolitical issues, including the formative role of the state in institutions like health, education, and the military, the expansion of world commodity trade, including minerals and agriculture, and the transformation of rural society all are being researched in the South. They suggest that Global North educationalists need to pay close attention to the "new architecture of knowledge." Adding that the "geopolitical pattern of knowledge that prioritizes the North is now recognized as a major problem in social science. It is contested in a vigorous critical literature, including work on the global economy of knowledge" (118). This critical literature includes Connell's own work on Southern Theory (see below) and her contribution to contested coloniality in CIE (Takayama et al. 2017).

While practicing what we called in Chapter 2 theories of the "post" originating in Europe and the US, corporations have morphed worldwide (e.g., Takayama [Japan], Sriprakash [UK], and Connell [Australia]). Decoloniality originated among the Global South countries. The argument for "de-Westernizing" culture and education originated in East Asia but can be found in other parts of the world, e.g., Latin America (Mignolo 2011). The return of *place* has long been a significant concern for postcolonial and decolonial scholarship. It is authors from the formerly colonized "peripheries" who have transformed space into places for working out another world-system outside the historical and geopolitical purview of colonialism and postcoloniality, as evidenced by the rise of Global South Studies (Baghiu 2019). This includes cooperation among the countries of the South. Once "South" replaced terms such as "Third World" and the so-called "underdeveloped" or low- and low–medium income countries, development education began turning to joint multi-country assistance projects among countries of the South. This came to be known as South–South cooperation, or *Sol–Sol* in Latin America.

Earlier, we gave some examples of national development agencies. To these, we can now add Japan, which, besides having developed funding programs for Africa since 2002, has promoted collaboration with other donors on a country level through their BEGIN: *Basic Education for Growth Initiative*, participating in enhancing primary education, higher education, and vocational training. Their approach to grow levels or sectors of education effectively is to utilize limited resources, therefore supporting "South–South cooperation, which promotes cooperation among neighboring countries sharing similar cultural and linguistic backgrounds" (Ministry of Foreign Affairs of Japan 2011).

Development policies and cross-national policy transfer experiences among countries of the South, exploring what South–South cooperation means in practice, is the topic of Chisholm and Steiner-Khamsi's edited volume (2008), which includes studies on bi- and multilateral development agencies such as UNESCO, and UNDP (United Nation Development Program), and covers regions such as Africa, Latin America, and the Middle East, and countries such as Brazil, China, India, Japan, Jordan, Turkey, and South Africa. To understand how such studies advance CIE practices, we observe that these studies use dependency theories (see Chapter 2) to identify possible sources of self-reliance within the countries of the South. Education borrowing and lending, and transfer among countries of the South are not new: "Development practitioners, many of them working at international agencies, have been, especially in recent years, envisioning South–South cooperation as a policy tool to help in local, regional and national development processes" (Jules and Sá e Silva 2008: 46).

South–South Cooperation

A report on the Brazilian government practicing "South–South" cooperation in providing Mozambique with half a million dollars and literacy experts to implement the Solidarity in Literacy Program-AlfaSol (de Moralis 2005). This program trained 250 literacy teachers and established 240 adult literacy classrooms over eighteen months. Brazil has expertise in teaching Portuguese. Nevertheless, by 2020, we found the reported rate of literacy in Mozambique was still only 59.78 percent (the women's rate is even lower than the men's) because most of the population speaks Bantu languages while Portuguese, the language of the colonizer, is the country's official language and the language of school instruction. Questions of South–South collaborations in education continue to be investigated, for instance, in a study by Heryadi et al. (2024) conducted between 2022 and 2024 on Indonesia's cooperation experience with South Africa. Compared to South–North cooperation, South–South cooperation, in this case, is "perceived as more economical, effective, and favorable." "Education is important in most middle-income countries," Heryadi et al. concludes, "because it aids in the formation of human capital for long-term investment and nation-building." As mentioned in Chapter 2 and 3 *human capital* discourse continues to be relevant in the 2020s, not just in human resources offices but also in education, worldwide.

BRICS: New Development Practices?

Since the heyday of the Non-Aligned Movement in the 1970s and the demand for a New Economic Order, the world has not seen such a coordinated challenge from developing countries to Western supremacy in the world economy as the one posed by the BRICS nations (Brazil, Russia, India, China, South Africa) (Desai 2013). Some analysts even expressed hope for a "new Bandung" in the twenty-first century, referring to a 1955 conference of twenty-nine African and Asian countries at Bandung, Indonesia, that created the Non-Aligned Movement of 120 nations. Regarding the global economy, the BRICS countries do not just collaborate on funding education, as in the case of China's development of higher education in Africa. Still, they are also the beneficiaries of corporate-driven globalization. Where global capital collaborated with cheap labor in export-oriented manufacturing and extraction sectors, the Chinese benefited from Africa's and Brazil's natural resources. China has lucrative contracts all over Africa, which, as we have already mentioned, is considered different from the West's neo-colonialism, since its influences on culture, including education, do not involve direct intervention. The BRICS nations are considered contender regimes, rivaling the liberal West in exporting development education. Chinese cooperation in Africa is welcome, as they fund many students to study in China, as the USSR did in the second half of the twentieth century. The Chinese scholarships are personal to individuals who want to study in China. In contrast, the Mandela Washington Fellowship for Young African Leaders (YALI), President Obama's flagship program for Africa, has, for the last fifteen years, brought 500–1,000 future African leaders to the United States each year to advance their professional and civic training for six weeks, at US universities and their home communities.

Investigating the significance of the changing geopolitical dynamics for education, Chisholm and Chissale (2024) explore whether BRICS educational programs can be considered a form of "sub-imperialism." They followed Bond (2023), who looked at BRICS own foreign direct investment trade, especially in Africa, Latin America, and the Caribbean, in the name of reversing historical, unequal trade and investment relations between the "core" and "peripheries." He found that BRICS countries are in an uncomfortable middle ground where "sub-imperialism" fits best, as they fail to promote new development practices. BRICS countries appear to be reinforcing old patterns of the so-called underdevelopment, amplifying natural resource extraction, reinforcing elite education, and adversely impacting local communities, workers, and nature.

Focusing on connections between the BRICS countries and education in South Africa and Mozambique, Chisholm and Chissale (2024) outline how scholarship programs and student flows between individual BRICS countries and Mozambique broaden existing relationships as well as constituting sites where sub-imperialist relationships can be observed. Other interventions in the education system in Mozambique fall short of local administrators setting policies, so the donors kept their superior know-how, as in the cases in this Chapter, with US experts advising/planning Western style education systems. The other interesting sub-imperialism conditions governing practices in education appear in what we hear so often in Africa and Latin America about China's economic assistance, as if dependency relations do not exist in aid relationships with China. They do not impose education models but they require political loyalties, in international forms like the UN. Is this a new, *different* development practice? Not really, conclude Chisholm and

Chissale (2024): this "no-strings-attached" approach and interest-free loans are coupled with expectations of political loyalty on critical international matters, such as the "One China policy," as well as preference for Chinese and Indian companies' workers and imported equipment, or ninety-nine years operation right at ports built by China (e.g., Port of Doraleh in Djibouti). Rather than a *new* development model, the aid coming from China has increased the leverage that African governments extract from the traditional aid organizations, to grant them loan forgiveness from IMF and World Bank(s). BRICSs has opened a "policy space" for African elites without challenging neo-liberal modes of engagement, resulting in a "diversified dependence" rather than structural change in African economies (Chisholm and Chissale 2024: 9).

Shapes

Shaping the Global Order

The most advanced first-generation liberation movement leaders across Africa agreed that economic neocolonial ties needed to be broken. The Egyptian political economist Samir Amin, already in the 1980s, wrote about a strategic program of "delinking" from the colonial past. Amin (1990) weaves together an analysis of the polarizing effects of capitalism while it's concrete political projects has been forgotten; however, CIE scholars, like the contributors to the special *CER* issue 61 (S1) 2017 on "decolonizing" are more likely to quote Mignolo (2007) on delinking: "De-linking then shall be understood as a de-colonial epistemic shift leading to other universality, such as pluriversality as a universal project" (453). Mignolo, in the United States, works with his Latin American students, making much the same point as the Southern theorist Connell, who writes about social thinkers from sub-Saharan Africa, Latin America, Iran, India, and Australia.

Southern Theory

Southern theory highlights the global politics of knowledge, where the Global South has been historically treated as a data mine for CIE research. At the same time, the Global North has been associated with generating theory, methods, and research publications. Connell's book (2007) highly acknowledges theorizing in the South and developing Global South awareness and power dynamics in generating practical useful knowledge for education planning and policy. Evoking critics of "cosmopolitanism" and "internationalism" in education discourse characterize the use of those concepts as North Global discourse (Popkewitz 2008). New studies following theorizing from the Global South document resistance to using such education constructs (Perrotta 2016), complicating the international landscape of CIE discourse of power and (re)framing the condition of postcoloniality societies.

In *Theory From the South*, Comaroff and Comaroff (2012) explored the implications of this reorientation for the social sciences, one of them being that Africa, the "ground-zero" of the Global South, has become the South–South axis from which to theorize the emerging world order of the twenty-first century, and new CIE way of practicing. Of course, we in the North are unused to hearing that our hemisphere may *not* be the front of all education knowledge and related theory work. As we have seen from Connell's point of view, the South has been ruled by elites flowing the North capitalist, modernity, and development education. As the historical review in Chapter 1 has shown, the imperial expansion of modernization into colonies across the world laid the basis for the exploitation of human labor and local ecologies, of raw materials and real estate, without the legal, moral, or political constraints that governed such extractions in the North. A civil society mission of progress and development, including the social, economic, and education infrastructures of a liberal nation-state, was never securely put in place in the de-colonized States. As a result, a "Southern" mode of capitalist modernity took hold in many of the new nations: with no liberal individual freedom, citizenship rights, equality before the law, or even allocation of resources to education (see illustration by BenDavid-Hadar). Postcolonial populations were left open to exploitation through globalization and structural adjustments imposed by highly strong corporate capital. We saw above how funding for education from the North to the South worked, it came with prescriptions. While the new South-to-South model proposed by the BRICS nations seemed to be hopefully a new development education model. On the ground as we saw from the example of Mozambique the introduction of private schooling and the hollowing out civil society's duty to educate caused the young to no longer recognizing education as a "common good." Mozambique has meanwhile opened up their markets for many more consumer goods.

The cultural theorist James Clifford (2013) agrees with Connell (2007). Theory, a product long associated with Western discursive spaces status permitted to speak confidently of *human, history, culture, education*, etc., is marked by specific historical centers with *non-Western theorists* who have encroached regularly on the territories of Western theory, working appositionally with and against (both inside and outside) dominant terms and experiences. As we have shown, diverse Global South and feminist writers have challenged the status of traditional CIE practices, particularly its trend to provide a potent overview and its suppression of location context and contextuality. We are left with the question of what "the South" *is*, given that it is not, as some would have it, simply the antithesis of "the North." What is left of global modernity cannot return to some mythical geography with untouched indigenous worlds. However, as we will see next, some constructs from the past are being rescued and may offer some educative redemptions.

Re-Shaping

James Clifford devoted three volumes to investigates cultures; in his 2013 research, he turned to study how people in California, Alaska, and Oceania experience becoming indigenous in the twenty-first century. In it, he describes indigenous histories of survival and transformation, influenced by globalization but not homogenizing. "Traditional futures," as Clifford calls them, or "past future," as we mentioned above, are prolonged processes of "returns" to the past, including ambivalent struggle within and against dominant forms of cultural, identities, and economic powers. We have summarized a few examples of aboriginal groups who persist in complicating familiar discursive practices of modernization and development education. Those "returns" are essential to CIE as one of the contested institutions *are* Western education systems, which were introduced and implemented in the name of modernization and the quest for "never-ending economic development" (Dhara and Singh 2021). Insights from localized educational interventions argues for alternative knowledge systems that continuously negotiate with the all-encompassing influence of modern education paradigms and broader social and economic modernity. As data on non-monetary "returns" to investment in education are not part of public transcript, it is important to access memories of untapped potential that offer a fresh perspective on learning, schooling, teaching, and transfer from generation to generation.

Buen Vivir, Ubuntu, Vā, and Tā-vā

A recent movement encompassing both academics and activists aims to abandon modernizing ambitions in favor of different, non-Western education principles, such as the *Buen Vivir* (Living Well) concept articulated by several indigenous South American worldviews, including *Sumak Kawsay* (plentiful life) the Quechua idea, and the Aymara notion of *Suma Qamaña* (living well together). Although it constitutes a plural movement with different branches, this development critique has gained momentum in the past two decades, mainly due to the attention given to resistance by local communities against infrastructure mega-projects threatening their livelihoods and the surrounding environments (Escobar 1992). Development had become a "ghost" haunting many Latin American capitals, which have been unable to escape its Eurocentric roots. Understanding the developments in Ecuador and Bolivia shows how both countries draw upon the indigenous tradition of the Andes, emphasizing the indigenous, non-colonial origins of the *Buen Vivir* concept (Albó 2018). The attempt to overcome the colonial past that has shaped South America's history is also taking shape in the search for new guiding principles for education. *Buen Vivir* appears to complement other efforts to seek new ideas of the *right to life* and preserving their environment. It reflects a general unease with entrenched concepts of "limitless exponential economic growth" (Dhara and Singh 2021: 121).

The same is true in many African societies, where some advocate a return to *Ubuntu* mutual aid systems and societal reintegration within local ecologies. Within CIE, *Ubuntu* was the theme of the 2016 CIES annual conference. The *Ubuntu* philosophy facilitates the critique of education in formerly colonized societies. Its pedagogy emphasizes interactive learning, where students learn best by sharing their ideas, thoughts, and experiences. The *Ubuntu* worldview differs from epistemologies, which value objective observations (data collection) by emphasizing that knowledge is generated through communal discourse. Enslin and Horsthemke (2004) show how *Ubuntu* provides a model for citizenship education in African societies, arguing that citizenship principles and tenets are fundamental and universal. *Ubuntu* is a model that works well with the 2030 Sustainable Development

Goals (SDGs) and the idea that global citizenship principles reintegrate local ecologies with developing suitability. An *Ubuntu* feminist lens is used in South Africa to address interpersonal and gender violence, showing that an individualized, human-rights, Western-based approach is inadequate as a frame to find sustainable solutions to intractable gendered human insecurity. Du Plessis (2019) uses *Ubuntu* to analyze the issues and suggest adequate local responses.

In Oceania there is a movement to use local Samoan knowledge concepts of *vā* and *vā fealoaloa'i* (social space) and *va tapua'i* (worship space) to improve education and social services. Such concepts developed in the Samoan village are essential to the Samoan view of reality. *Vā* has also been applied to the New Zealand social environment and secondary education. The concept of *vā* (*Wa* in Māori) points to betweenness or the space between—not space, but space that relates, holding separate entities and things together in unity; it is space as context, giving meaning to things. The meanings change as the relationships and contexts change. In communal cultures such as those of Oceania, the group and its unity are valued above individualism. The person is perceived in terms of the group and its relationships to the group. *Tā*, time and action, can be linked to *vā*, the space between, in a system of actions and behaviors that produces subjects and objects in the Samoan social-cultural schema. Traditional Pacific concepts of *tā-vā* have been recharged and extended to create a new and comprehensive branch in theory, derived from indigenous worldviews, that can change institutions like education (Refiti 2017: 268) understood to be participants in a still-unfolding process of transformation.

Indigenous Culture and Education

Indigenous peoples in Canada, the United States, Australia, and New Zealand, and many other postcolonial locations, struggled for many years with Euro-Western education experiences so much so that comparing the four groups provides a particularly appropriate focus for Michael Cottrell's (2010) comparative inquiry. These modern states have all tried to incorporate (including removal of kids from home) state-wide education which ignored or marginalized indigenous peoples' ways of knowing (including removal of children from homes). Currently members of indigenous groups are still among the most disadvantaged in terms of education and outcomes, using standardized evaluation tools. Cottrell (2010) noticed that closing the education achievement gap between indigenous and non-indigenous learners is a shared and urgent education policy priority, in all four countries. Demographics have witnessed a reversal of previous population decline, "indigenous peoples now constitute the youngest and fastest growing segments of populations in many regions across these four countries. Indigenous demographic recovery has been accompanied by a decolonization project based on a discourse of indigeneity" (224). This discourse is a result of postcolonial struggle by indigenous peoples to reassert control over their children's education and to see their cultures and ways of knowing, reflected in public education institutions, curriculum, and learning assessments. Indigenous peoples in Canada, the US, Australia, and New Zealand, similarly to the Pacific people we reviewed above, are bringing back concepts, long forgotten, to improve their education and social services.

For indigenous communities, schools are where their culture interfaces with Euro-Western educational systems. Schools, school divisions/districts, and provincial education authorities in Canada are collaborating with indigenous communities to develop new opportunities to improve students' participation and success in high school. These initiatives, Deer and Heringer (2023) found, are supplanting and replacing outdated and, in some instances, assimilationist education programs that, however intended, adversely affected indigenous language use, indigenous moral values, and sharing and survival of culture of indigenous people across Canada. Deer and Heringer (2023) interviewed teachers, education assistants, and administrators, and heard about the ways they created a space where community—especially parents and elderly—can come together and exchange knowledge and create relationships with schools, teachers, and administrators. Empowerment of the parental community inside and outside of the school was found to be fundamental to students' success. One teacher observed: "The use of indigenous cultural pieces such as star blanket creation and use, land-based education, smudging, and others have come to be a part of all students' knowledge and have become visible in classrooms" (47).

Conclusion

Spirit of the One Hundred Sacks of Rice, derived from a play by Yuzo Yamamoto, is the motto of Japan's project BEGIN (Basic Education for Growth Initiative). It refers to a historical event when the samurai Torasaburo Kobayashi (1828–1877), one of the chief executives of Nagaoka, diverted rice intended for hunger relief to pay instead for education. He observed in 1870:

> The prosperity of a country and the growth of cities depend on people. Build schools and develop people of ability.

As we have seen in this chapter, research, knowledge production, and other CIE practices reflect a commitment to Kobayashi's view from over 250 years ago. Ultimately, CIE is a discipline that studies and seeks to shape and reshape education's capacity to develop peoples' abilities and contribute to their countries' prosperity and sustainability. Its past practices of research, consulting, and knowledge production and dissemination have persisted, albeit transformed, into the present, on all continents and in various spaces. CIE is practiced at governmental and non-government agencies and at universities where graduate and undergraduate degrees in our discipline are offered by scholars who come and go in space, moving along all the axes of the directions we have explored. They *travel* in the sense of Said's (2000) metaphor for the modes of intellectual work that he most valued—not literal travel, necessarily, though many of the comparativists we have mentioned did travel for study and work, including short engagements for consultation on education building or teaching abroad. It was intriguing to take Said literally by looking into the biographies of highly mobile academics, comparativists who work on and mostly write about systems other than their own and who do travel. Many of us are diasporic academicians who, like Said himself, are "travelers" in the country we now teach, research, write, and mentor CIE students.

We want to conclude this chapter with a note about teaching CIE at universities worldwide. Wolhuter et al. (2008) edited reports from forty-two nations and regions, collecting chapters written by eighty authors about teaching CIE. The authors could write their chapters in one of the widely used world languages. The national/regional chapters ended up with thirty-four written in English, four in Spanish, and four in French. A refreshing idea, their conclusions are:

> If we, the comparativists, carry out comparative studies that create tangible benefits for educational sciences, educational practice, and educational policy, if we illuminate how culture and context matter, then we will construct our future building on the infrastructures established, the knowledge created, and the enthusiasm of new scholars … If we, the comparativists, illuminate

better than others how culture and context matter, then we will exceed the goals of those who had gone before us to leave a fertile terrain for those who will come after.

(416)

We believe we can claim to "come after" these eighty authors in the sense of their conclusion. Writing in 2024–2025, we are still capitalizing on the knowledge produced and co-produced by those whom we have quoted in this book, and we do think about the future users of this knowledge—the students, teachers, CIE researchers, and other scholars who are with us now, and the new ones who will come after us.

We cannot change our discipline's past, as we hope this chapter has made clear. However, we can learn from it and shape new knowledge, bringing back lost indigenous ways of knowing that were buried under colonialism and neo-imperialism when education was shifted drastically from traditional to modern. Environmental and sustainability education is rising, changing education's content and training environmentally responsible world citizens. While we who believe in the power of education cannot change the past, while our professors practiced development education in the twentieth century, we are committed to the importance of present practices, especially now, when Earth and its environments are under threat. We are committed to education that serves humans and non-humans in sustaining life on Earth. We hope this chapter on practices gives a good overview and a clear idea of when (time), where (spaces), and in which directions the discipline of CIE has shaped and is reshaping itself and education around the world.

Academic Activities—Springboards

Springboard A

Textbooks in Comparative Education

- Find (free online): Wolhuter, C., Popov, N., Leutwyler, B., and Skubic Ermenc, K., eds (2008), *Comparative Education at Universities Worldwide*, Sofia: Bureau for Educational Services.

- Read the titles of the list of Comparative Education University Textbooks in Comparative Education, pp. 399–415
- Write a short list of books you would like to find and know more. What about their topic/s has triggered your interest?

Springboard B

BRICS-Growing

The core is a formal intergovernmental grouping known as the BRICS (Brazil, Russia, India, China, and South Africa), which we mentioned above has become BRICS+ as five have been invited: Egypt, Ethiopia, Iran, Saudi Arabia, and the UAE. These ten nations account for around 40 percent of crude oil production and exports. They also account for one-quarter of global GDP, two-fifths of international trade in goods, and nearly half of the world's population. Adding another dozen nations that have applied for membership, including dynamic emerging markets such as Thailand, Vietnam, and Bangladesh, would raise the group's share to one-third of global GDP.

On October 24, 2024, Russia hosted the 16th BRICS Summit with a plenary session, chaired by Vladimir Putin, in the BRICS Plus/Outreach format, bringing together leaders, delegations from Asian, African, Middle Eastern, and Latin American countries, and the heads of several international organizations. This is while the war in Ukraine has just recruited North Korean soldiers, and the wars in the Middle East includes Iran. There is mounting tensions between the world's great powers.

Think and Comment:

- Do you think a structural shift in the global order has been quietly underway?
- Do you think those large developing nations can exert more significant influence in world economic affairs? If so, how?
- How are they beginning to build alternatives to Western-led geopolitical institutions?
- What are the possible results for Western-type schooling and credentialing?

Springboard C
Buen Vivir & SDGs

New programs incorporate human relations with nature, aiming for harmony with nature and condemning the excessive exploitation of natural resources. As announced in Bolivia, excessive industrialization resulting from Western accumulation models does not offer humanity a solution. *Buen Vivir* is a culture of life based on the ancestral knowledge of indigenous peoples that aims to balance between humans and nature alike and investigates ways of life that had been suppressed by colonization. "We must return to being because colonization has made us into 'wanting to be.'" The Plurinational State of Bolivia sets out ten critical elements for *Buen Vivir* as part of "Saving Planet Earth to Save Humanity."

Comment and Write:

How do the elements of *Buen Vivir* or any other "back to tradition" knowledge system, fit (or not) with UN 2030 Sustainable Development Goals (https://sdgs.un.org/goals/)?

5

Building Blocks

Introduction

This last chapter is devoted to the building blocks, which contributed to comparative and international education (CIE) becoming and being a discipline taught at universities, awarding graduate and PhD degrees, introducing CIE to teachers (Hayhoe and Mundy 2008), to undergraduate students, as part of the foundations of education, mentoring them by educationalists and comparativists that are organized and contribute to their professional organizations. Looking forward, we would like to summarize the building blocks that have established this field of study, and those that are sustaining CIE as a professional practice. While theories and methods have not been layered linearly, Chapter 4 has helped us contextualize how knowledge production has been built both in time and space, looking critically at the past and the present being shaped and re-shaped, by new building blocks, and contested some of the social theories that have defined CIE. As we have pointed out numerous times and demonstrated with examples, CIE practitioners are studying and practicing worldwide, in a variety of ways and contexts. We name a few blocks, helping to think on building a career, and ethics to observe when doing research.

For future building blocks we draw on current movements such as sustainability, a movement that education and comparativists are already involved with and will see into the future. Together with just transition and green skilling, which might replace development education or become a part of it, in education for work skills to meet an unknown future. The same with artificial intelligence (AI), it is going to build CIE in the future and we are unsure to what extent and how it will change our teaching, learning, and research.

We start with an example, the organization of a CIE resource library in the 1950s as organized by a librarian that has some advice for us when it comes to building a knowledge base: *try to observe things as they are and then look ahead and calculate what they may be and so act and prepare accordingly.*

Building a Research Library for Comparative Education

A 1965 article by Thelma Bristow details how the University of London Research Library for Comparative Education came to be organized. In 1945, the Chair of Comparative Education in the Institute acquired books and pamphlets on his travels. He made personal contacts so that other faculty could follow those visits and acquire education literature from elsewhere. A room, separate from the Central Institute Library, containing the quickly accumulating material in numerous languages was getting too full. The critical point was to move away from citing the comparative collection of education reference material by country. Bristow, who took over the management of the collection in 1954, noted that Comparative Education is not a straightforward discipline: "Books and articles must be acquired and arranged about comparative education so that they may become part of comparative education" (213). In other words, there was no list of CIE books a librarian could buy, to build up a collection useful to researchers, teachers, and students; books and articles needed to be classified as part of "comparative education."

Bristow's cataloguing, and her listed subdivision, are not only the past disciplinary building blocks, but also long-lasting ones, given their disciplinary ability to fuse multiple theoretical perspectives, as we saw in Chapter 2, with topics to research like national problems and education reconstruction, as we saw in Chapter 3. Bristow's 1950s catalog of comparative education shows its long history as a field of inquiry and one that is particularly suited to exploring systems of education and their components, primary, secondary, higher education and adult and women's (girls') education, and their administration and curriculum. "Education of the personality" is just another name for what we call critical thinking, social and leadership skills, and civic education. How education contributes to the development of personality is still a research topic. The disciplinary subdivisions are *all* still part of CIE; Bristow's advice is that we need both to

Disciplinary subdivisions	Subject numbers
F0 History of education	0 Theory of Education
F01 Comparative Education	1 General aspects of education
F02 International Affairs	
F02.1 International understanding	2 Primary education
F03 Nationality problems	3 Secondary education
F04 Sociology, economics, etc., subdivided	4 Adult education
F05 methodology of educational research	5 Curriculum
F06 Political aspects	6 Women's education
F07 Educational experiments	7 Education of the personality
F08 Educational reconstruction (underdeveloped areas etc.)	8 Higher education
F09 Administration	9 Administration

Figure 7 Information redrawn from Bristow, T. (1965), "The University of London Research Library for Comparative Education in the Institute of Education," *Comparative Education Review*, 9 (2): 213–18.

catalog what we know and to look ahead and prepare for what we need to learn and practice in the future.

Organizational Building Blocks

In addition to organizing the topic and the materials to study from, like in the case of a CIE library, establishing a discipline entails organizing the researchers, teachers, and students. To organize the people so they are recognized as belonging, this building block is a professional organization or association. To organize within associations or professional societies are building blocks, as it organizes a profession or a field of study. By opening it up to those who belong and close it to those that do not. By doing so they legitimize the profession and build up its knowledge, with annual conference(s) and journal(s), which act as gatekeepers to what is legitimate knowledge and what is not. The American Educational Research Association (AERA) was founded in 1916 to encourage and improve scholarly inquiry related to education and evaluation and to promote the dissemination and practical application of research results. The Comparative Education Society of the US was formally launched at the third annual conference of

Comparative Education at New York University in 1956. At that time, the field was led by men, university professors who filled the Society's leadership roles, including the editorship of the new journal *Comparative Education Review*. The Society's first secretary, Gerald Reed (Kent State), organized the Society's first trips to study schools abroad in Europe and Russia. After that, societies around the world established conferences and publications, newsletters, and journals that assist in building CIE as worldwide disciplinary studies to support and build local or regional capacity to grow and exchange knowledge and support researchers, students, and teachers.

Professional Associations

The Comparative Education Society in Europe (CESE) was founded in 1961 during a meeting at the University of London School of Education. The British Comparative and International Education Society became independent of European society in the 1970s. The Japan Comparative Education Society (JCES) was established in March 1965 with ninety-four members, and the first president was Masunori Hiratsuka, Director of the National Institute for Educational Research. The CIE association in China was established in 1978, sustaining both a conference and publication, as well as attending CIES the US conference. The World Council of Comparative Education Societies (WCCES) was conceived in conjunction with the International Education Year in 1970, in collaboration with UNESCO. WCCES comprised twenty-eight national Comparative Societies from every continent, eventually growing to forty-seven member societies. The 1980 World Congress of Comparative Education Societies was hosted by JCES in Tokyo and a congress in South Africa in 1998 and in 2022 in China. Moving this triennial conference to different locales helps local associations to be recognized by hosting and showcasing their CIE work. CIES' past President serves as the WCCES President helping support WCCES which is not a fee membership organization and is in need of support from CIES (which is by far the largest association, among all around the world). This outline of CIE's institutional building blocks helps clarify the structure within which practitioners can join an organization, attend a conference, and receive the association newsletters and journal, which amounts to their being part of the CIE professoriate.

Latin American education reform and revitalization of academic debates in education and other areas of social sciences in the late 1980s has resulted in the (re)emergence of several national societies of comparative education, including the Argentinean, Brazilian, and Mexican societies, and in the establishment in 2010 of the *Revista Latinoamericana de Educación Comparada* (*Latin American Journal of Comparative Education*) and the creation of an *Iberoamerican Society* in 2014 (Gorostiaga 2017).

Oceania Comparative and International Education Society (OCIES) is the new name of a combined CIE association that originally started as the Australia Comparative Education Society, founded in 1973. In subsequent years, the Australia-based society changed its name to include the key term *International*, becoming the A*I*CES in 1975. In 1983, when New Zealand hosted the comparative education conference, ACIES became ANZCIES, the Australia New Zealand Comparative and International Education Society. These name changes reflected organization and reorganization of the broader CIE during these years, when smaller societies found that their members were sometimes more active at CIES in the US than their home-country organization (see below about CIES). This in turn revived and refocused in some quarters the ongoing debate about the Global North's continued domination of Global South with respect to CIE knowledge-production and consumption (Spratt and Coxon 2020).

While associations do build up professional belonging among members and their conferences facilitate exchange and learning from one another, the cornerstone of a discipline is published work. Members of CIE professional organizations, know which journal is a stronger building block within the academic profession.

Professional Journals

Professional associations worldwide, and their professional journals and regional and international conferences, continue to make up the building blocks of disciplinary studies. The editors of the refereed journals and edited volumes are the gatekeepers of the discipline. Their policies of inclusion and exclusion shape what knowledge circulates and whether it has influence. These journals also play a part in determining tenure and promotions, which depend not only on publishing, but doing so in journals that are ranked higher than others; all journals are ranked on a few different ranking systems, and some have a higher citations index. Influential knowledge circulation is achieved by quoting studies, assigning them to CIE courses. Publications, conference papers, and symposia construct disciplinary thinking and shape and reshape CIE's knowledge circulation, as Chapters 2, 3, and 4 showed, theories and methods are shaped by and are shaping CIE discursive practices.

Journals that publish peer-reviewed articles in English and are considered international in scope (i.e., not exclusively regional) include the following:

- *Compare: A Journal of Comparative and International Education*
- *Comparative Education*
- *Comparative Education Review*
- *Globalization, Education, and Societies*
- *International Educational Journal: Comparative Perspectives*
- *International Journal of Educational Development*
- *Pedagogy, Culture and Society*
- *Prospects*
- *Research in Comparative and International Education*

Besides the above, regional and CIE associations around the world publish their own CIE journals. The Japan Comparative Education Society published its first journal in 1975 titled *Nihon Hikaku-kyoiku Gakkai Kiyo* (The Bulletin of Japan Comparative Education Society). In 1990 the name was changed to *Hikaku Kyoikugaku Kenkyu* (Comparative Education). China's *Foreign Education Journal* was established in 1980. Several other journals first appeared in the 1990s, including *Tertium Comparationis: Journal of International and Intercultural Comparative Education*, sponsored by the German Society (1997) and the Mediterranean Society of Comparative Education's *Mediterranean Journal of Educational Studies* (1996). The University of Hong Kong's Comparative Education Research Center (CERC) was established in 1994, supporting comparative education research and disseminating information through newsletters, research activities, seminars, symposiums, and conferences. While for years their studies in comparative education were co-published with Springer (a German multinational publishing company), in 2024 they moved to co-publish with Routledge, a brand of the humanities and social-sciences publisher Taylor & Francis (an international publisher based in the UK and New York), which publishes no fewer than 226 journals in the field of education, as well as many of the books we have mentioned in the present book, as you can see from our reference list.

Several journals in our field were and are sponsored directly by development organizations—notably, the UNESCO journals the *International Review of Education* and *Prospects*. Within the broader field of international development, several non-governmental organizations (NGOs) have also contributed to comparative educational debate by supporting academic journals, including Oxfam's *Development in Practice* (established in 1991) and *Gender and Development* (from 1993).

Organizations and Foundations

The Carnegie, Ford, Rockefeller, and other major US foundations were among the first non-religious organizations to be involved in spreading Western schooling to nations of Africa, Asia, and Latin America well before the twentieth century. Foundation officers viewed the extension of Western-grounded education as crucial to these nations' stability, prosperity, and orderly development (Arnove 1980). The Ford Foundation continues to fund educational projects in conflict-ridden regions worldwide, including a few large education programs in South Africa, and teacher training and education reconstruction in Bosnia. Although programs have changed in the past 100 years, the direction of Foundation funding has shared comparative education's faith in the ability of national education systems in Africa, Asia, and Latin America, among others, to eradicate poverty and contribute to endless striving for economic development, supported by theories of modernization and developmentalism (see Chapter 2).

UN Organizations

The role of foundations, agencies, and organizations, and their officers, many of them holding degrees in CIE, point to the involvement of both national and multinational aid agencies, which have increasingly advocated policies while simultaneously underwriting research studies to show the relationships among education, economic, and social development. International institutions have played a crucial role in promoting comparative approaches to education and its relation to economic development, and political stability. The United Nations and their Educational, Scientific and Cultural Organization (UNESCO), as early as 1949 and as recently as 2004, adopted the concept of development, education for all, and the 2030 Sustainable Development Goals, including lifelong education. UNESCO is involved in developing international educational indicators, and its Statistical Yearbook and Global Education Report are widely distributed. Its data are used as a basis for comparison in many research studies and decision-making on international aid and loans. As early as the 1963 meeting they "focused on the identification and classification of contextual data in comparative education, an indication that the field was striving to become more systematic in approach" to serve agencies and foundation funding decisions (Kobayashi 1973: 1).

US Comparative International Education Society (CIES)

Within comparative education societies "a hierarchical structure exists in the field of knowledge production, wherein some countries occupy a central paradigmatic position for other countries located at the periphery" (Manzon 2018: 45). The sociocultural structures, ways of knowing, values, and practices in which CIE research is embedded, reflect the values and priorities of the largest CIE society. CIES was established in 1956 with a handful of academics from New York, of which Halls (1977) provides an early historical analysis. It now has 4,788 members in 2023, 2,293 members from the US, and the rest from other countries, making it effectively a *world* rather than an American society. The same goes for its board; members from many countries serve on it, including the presidents. Between 1961 and 2023, eight were from Canadian universities, two from non-academic agencies, and one from Hong Kong. The next three are from the University of Cambridge (2024), Oslo Metropolitan University (2025), and Waseda University in Japan (2026). Conferences were held mostly in the US but also in Canada (twice), Mexico, Puerto-Rico, and Cuba, once. With about 3,000 members attending the annual conference, it serves as an event with diverse presentations and establishes what new scholarship is circulated. CIES's journal, *Comparative Education Review* (*CER*), is distributed to all members and all libraries at universities worldwide that subscribe, including differential fees for low-income countries. The same with students—all associations have a reduced fee for students. Students do not have to wait to get their first post to join one of the many CIE associations as they typically have reduced membership fees and conference fee rates. Many have mentoring programs for new scholars and grants for travel to the conference. It is a great mechanism for networking, learning about the field, and maybe even hearing about a teaching position that will open soon. Becoming a member in an association while still a student serves as a building block both personally, to belong and start professional relationships, but also for the association that must build its future membership, connect intergenerationally, and pass on its accumulated knowledge to establish a disciplinary continuity.

Academic Careers in CIE

We have mentioned many scholars from around the world, and their national origins, backgrounds, and career trajectories are no secret in our era of internet searches. Moreover, journal articles usually include a short biographical note, which gives you a flavor of their career trajectories in CIE. The examples of career trajectories that we mentioned demonstrate how the Global North/South division is being blurred. Academics raised in the South have often studied in the North; some return home to practice, while others stay in the North and practice there, influencing the disciplinary practices of the Global North with their "Southern" sensibilities. If we just look at the contributors to the Illustrations (which follow Chapter 6), we can understand CIE's worldwide reach. The life stories in the special issue of *Comparative Education* (5 (1), 2020), from which we drew two examples of "comparative educationists as a foreigner," are all contemporary scholars writing about "doing comparative education," attesting to how study, life, and work send them in many different directions, letting the experience of transcultural and transnational relocation serve as confirmation of their capacity to think creatively, be proficient in other languages, and be grounded for practicing CIE.

CIE scholars nowadays are part, not of "brain drain," but of "brain circulation," studying and working in many locations and countries. CIE is not just multidisciplinary in its scholarship but also in its practice, occurring across and blurring all the historical divides in education development—North/South, West/East, national/international, etc. Graduates in CIE also join the World Bank, UNICEF, UNESCO, and development NGOs like FHI 360 and IREX, and are placed in country offices where national and international agencies and NGOs implement education projects. Many came to do their graduate and PhD degrees after extensive years of field experience in the Global South, including programs such as ASER (which means "impact" in Hindi), generating and disseminating evidence, and linking development ideas and action by building the capacity of individuals and institutions to design, conduct, and understand education assessments. Pratham ("first" in Sanskrit), one of the largest and most successful NGOs in India, with an office in the US, focuses on innovative interventions to address gaps in the education system. Teach for All in different countries (see Thomas' Illustration) and BRAC, an international development organization started in Bangladesh, now with nearly 100,000 staff across four continents, are just a couple of the many NGOs in this divide-straddling category.

CIE practitioners might major in other disciplines and may not necessarily even study in a college of education. Many CIE scholars come from disciplines like economics, social work, international relations, curriculum and instruction, policy studies, and so on. CIE graduates tend to join international organizations, as each country has development agencies. The UN agencies operate in many different countries, and the same with the World Bank as they have country offices on continents and in countries to which they are loaning funds for development education. Local colleges and universities not only have large colleges or schools of education but in the US they also have Area Studies regional offices funded (every four years) by the US department of education. At any given time, there are about fourteen such centers of each region such as Latin American, Middle Eastern, East Asian, Southern Asian, and Russian centers (now more typically called Eastern European and Slavic centers, or even Euro-Asian centers); and of course, many universities also offer majors in international studies. CIE degree holders work at offices of international affairs, with units such as global education, international students and scholars, and international partnerships. Now there are both for-profit and non-profit organizations that provide the same functions for universities, such as recruiting students from other countries, offering education abroad to university students, and so on. Most higher education institutions worldwide have such units or offices, with their location within the higher education structure varying. To be a comparativist can mean working at a university, national or international agency, or NGO, doing research on societies and international education topics, publishing (in English) in a peer-reviewed CIE society journal, presenting work at CIES or the conferences of European CIE associations, or WCCE, and mentoring students and new scholars, writing comparative international education theses, dissertations and papers, and editing books.

Ethics in CIE Research

As we have named "research" as a building block of CIE we need to add to it ethically conducted research. Ethics in research builds the integrity of scientific findings, and ensures that research is conducted responsibly, preventing exploitation and upholding the principles of informed consent, thus safeguarding the wellbeing of research participants, and protecting the researcher as well. CIE has even more challenges than some other disciplines as at many points the research is fieldwork in other countries where there was (is) a gap between the Western high ethical guidelines that are not enforced in the country. As we mentioned in Chapter 4, we observe that the Global South was "data mining" for the Global North researchers.

McMahon and Milligan (2021) found that more ethical guidance is needed to support CIE researchers. They suggest five building blocks as core ethical values:

- transparency and honesty
- respect and care
- conscious freedom
- experiential and tacit awareness and
- reflexive practice

As we mentioned in Chapter 3, scholars are concerned about who is left out and why, whose voices are being reflected in your study, and how the research highlights the voices of the neglected. Bilgen and Schöneberg (2021) did research with college students about why positionalities matter. They found each person's history and cultural experiences create their positionality. As with all perspectives, positionality is also bounded by a range of intrinsic and extrinsic elements. Researchers that know their cultural autobiography can walk through the process of understanding their own positionality so that they can identify the "filters" they use when evaluating research situations and assessing what they bring with them to the research task. See illustration by Karen Ross in this book.

The study of education comparatively in international contexts is so profoundly embedded in development's endless search for ever-greater economic achievements that, only systemic, cultural, and ideological acquired Western academic education has affected the future of individuals and whole groups. In Ghana, already in the 1960's, students and their parents were against vocational education offered by national education placements. Foster (1965) found out that parents knew: "an academic degree is the best vocational education." A newer study Gottlieb et al., (2022) with Israeli Bedouin women and men, who studied in Jewish, Hebrew high school, shared their education stories of a minority in a majority society. The education with the majority, (different language, and religion), rather than in their own segregated schools, secured their entry to higher education and future as professionals. Race, politics, and other social institutions that intersect with Western schooling spread worldwide excludes people in many places including the US, Canada, New Zealand, and South Africa, as exemplified by Rudolph's (2019) case of Aboriginal education in Australia. While CIE researchers and practitioners show how education contributes to peacebuilding (see Ross's Illustration), education has also played a role in internal armed conflicts and civil wars. Education, whether the lack of it or its poor quality, can and does create a strong sense of injustice over group/caste or ethnic exclusion, as examples from Cambodia, Rwanda, Guatemala, and Somalia were documented by Colletta and Cullen, 2000.

Menashy and Zakharia (2022) found "the near-absent attention paid to racism and white supremacy in the global education arena." Therefore, they set out to understand "the perpetuation of racial power hierarchies in global education governance—spaces of global-level policy making, financing, and advocacy in international education development" (461–2). The authors performed a broad content analysis (discussed in Chapter 3) of the electronic versions of each of the 227 documents for any mention of race, using keywords like race, racism, and racial (racialization/racialization) in both the main document text and in any footnotes or endnotes,

What they found was a discourse that identified inequities between rich donor countries in the Global North and Global South countries that received educational financing (see Chapter 4). Key terms in this discourse were the need for "recipient ownership," "localization," and "participation of beneficiaries," or "community participation." Organizational websites commonly made broad references to "discrimination" and "marginalization" when describing educational issues, but language that specified "race" or "racism" was notably rare. This finding is guiding the ethics of CIE research to establish race or racialized vocabulary and contextualize their use of all such categorizations with the place, culture, and people you are working with.

Bhattacharjea and Byker (2017) help address how the CIE field can destabilize and transform knowledge hierarchies through research and practice. While asking how CIE research practice can create socially just interactions anchored in ethics, they take us on a journey with citizen-led volunteers from an India-based non-profit center (ASER). They document the interactions between the ASER volunteers and the survey respondents, raising issues of respect, responsibility, and openness in dialogue. This analysis presents research in a new light, its ethics depend on contextualized evidence-based action that is grassroots and introduces meaningful change. Working from an equity-driven conceptual and theoretical perspective. George Mwangi and Yao's (2021) lens includes a guiding principle on how scholars theoretically and conceptually ground their studies. For George

Mwangi and Yao it is essential to interpret how conceptual/theoretical frameworks in CIE research acknowledge, reinforce, or challenge unbalanced power dynamics and global (in)equities among the researchers and the researched. See also their Illustration in this volume.

Additionally, Ross's illustration regarding her positionality when working on education for peace among two groups at war further exemplifies ethically centered research practices. For graduate students and seasoned researchers alike, positionality can be complex to express and write; see the paper by seven emerging researchers from the University of Waikato in New Zealand (Chin et al. 2022). Through short case stories, they draw attention to the different conceptualizations of researcher positionality and uncover challenges and dilemmas you can learn from. Finally, Shukla's illustration highlights his research team's goal of empowering heads of schools in Indian primary/secondary schools through a leadership program where they learn how to utilize tools that can lead to school transformation. Part of the ethical dimension lies in the empowerment of heads of schools to ensure that the decision-making onus lies on them and not with the researchers since they know their context best and can contextualize what is needed to implement transformation processes.

Future Building Blocks

Now we turn from the building-blocks of the present-day to speculating about future building-blocks, which are already emerging, beginning with education for sustainable development. The 2030 agenda of the United Nations initiatives on sustainable development include 17 Sustainable Development Goals (SDGs). Examining the goals of education for sustainable development, researchers have observed that they mainly address implications for curriculum and curriculum theory, as well as addressing the democratic impasse involved in global education policy to save the earth. Ole Andreas Kvamme (2023) includes in his analysis a UNESCO report and finds it specifically necessary as it suggests to think of *education* as a global common good. In an increasingly divided world, according to the UN 2030 SDGs, "education and knowledge should … be considered global common goods. This means the creation of knowledge, its control, acquisition, validation, and use, are common to all people as a collective social endeavor" (Kvamme 2023: 410). As such, the SDGs can be considered as a future building block of CIE, given also that UNESCO is involved in CIE associations around the world and is at CIES' annual meeting. In 2025, due to the new political constraints from the US about cutting all aid to international organizations, few UNESCO officers have attended. This is related to the United States' administration stated intention (May 2025) to dissolve the US Agency for International Development (USAID), circumscribe foreign assistance, and terminate at least 5,341 international aid projects. Many directly or indirectly involve education, including an estimated 211 awards to various UN agencies. As we have indicated, so many education projects—affected by such cuts and aid—will have to be followed by the users of this book.

Sustainable Development Goals and Education

The broadening scope of environmental education is reflected in the transition from the organizing concept "Environmental Education" to that of "Education for Sustainable Development." Little and Green (2009) describe sustainable development as encompassing three spheres: environment (including water and waste), society (including employment, human rights, gender equity, peace, and human security), and economy (including poverty reduction, corporate responsibility, and accountability) (172). Sustainable development has economic, social, environmental, and governance dimensions. Those who see the environment as enveloping human systems would see this as a dilution of the ecological dimension, while others noted that sustainable development subsumed environmental concerns, transforming environmental education into education for sustainability.

"Ecological scientific literacy," a branch of science, seeks to provide objective factual knowledge. In contrast, "environmental/sustainability citizenry literacy" is an area of education that deals mainly with ethical, social, cultural, and value-laden considerations. Even today, many comparativists continue to assume that the nation-state is a relevant unit of comparison in that national cultural traits can explain education practices in each country, as in the International Education Assessments (IEA). This assumption still underpins much comparative research but is increasingly questioned in the context of globalization, cross-border migration, cross-national systems of education, educational organizations that operate across borders, and transnational education-borrowing (Zuzovsky 2021).

As education services are increasingly corporatized and commercialized internationally, scholars have argued they have become more vulnerable to neoliberal consumerism (Robertson 2012). For example, as we already mentioned, Higher Education internationalizes students' learning experiences in the direction of global citizenship in order to satisfy the interests of universities, which are ranked on league tables for which "international" is one of the parameters (Blanco et al. 2021). The *Times Higher Education* (THE) has started to rank universities on Sustainable Development Goals. Western Sydney University topped the ranking in 2024 for the third year running, scoring exceptionally high for SDG 5 (gender equality), SDG 15 (life on land), and SDG 12 (responsible consumption and production). The university has prioritized research in areas relating to SDG 4 (quality education), SDGs 13, 14, and 15 (relating to environment and sustainability), SDG 3 (good health and wellbeing), and SDGs 11 and 12 (sustainable cities and communities, and responsible consumption and production). A series of critical initiatives have also been introduced to increase its sustainability, including implementing solar power, offsetting the carbon footprint of international travel, and installing more electric vehicle charging stations on campus. Many universities have centers for sustainability research and degree studies in environmental sciences sustainability.

For CIE, the most interesting is SDG 4, "obtaining a quality education for all," as well as SDG indicator 4.7.4, "the percentage of students by age group (or education level) showing adequate understanding of issues relating to global citizenship and sustainability" (https://sdgs.un.org/goals). This has already touched universities' worldwide internationalization programs, which, as we have already mentioned, aim to internationalize the learning experiences (i.e., education abroad) and to grow global citizens, including gender equality, with skills appropriate for tomorrow's economy (UN Women, 2024). The SDG era suggests rethinking education for sustainable development and global citizenship education (GCE), with far-reaching implications for CIE research, policy, and practices (Iyengar and Caman 2022). CIES already has a particular interest group in sustainability, and some comparativists have included youth climate activists' voices in academic spaces such as CIES, UN conferences, and through organizations like the Sustainable Development Solutions Network USA (SDSN USA). In fact, emerging insights among youth voices using ICT to share their experiences and projects and accelerate actions on the SDGs (Iyengar et al. 2017).

The ambition of SDG 4 to achieve inclusive and quality education for all reaffirms the belief that education is one of the most powerful and proven ways forward for sustainable development. This goal aims to ensure that all girls and boys complete free primary and secondary schooling by 2030. It seeks to provide equal access to affordable vocational training, eliminate gender and wealth disparities, and achieve universal access to quality higher education.

Just Transition and Green Skilling

When we reflect on current and future distributions of labor around the world, all-too-familiar divides—North vs. South, male vs. female etc.—can be seen in labor force participation rates. The percentage of the working-age population has declined over the last decade in the Global North. In contrast, Africa has the youngest-growing population on the globe. The differences between male and female employment rates across the globe still reveal a significant gender divide between males' and females' education (see the Illustration by Manion). Many more men are gainfully employed than women, although the size of this gap varies across regions and countries. The SDGs' International Labor Market Indicators review and gender equity studies found much wider gender divides in labor force participation rates in certain regions, favoring men in South Asia, the Middle East, and some parts of Northern Africa. The International Labor Organization defines *just transition* as "greening the economy in a way that is as fair and inclusive as possible to everyone concerned, creating decent work opportunities and leaving no one behind" (UNDP 2022). The transition should address past harms and propose ways to create new relationships that undo past power hierarchies. The philosophy of just transition amounts to an education that is alien to studies and practices reviewed in this book. It requires shifts in the principles, processes, and practices underpinning the political economy of an extractive economy and moves toward an evolving green economy. This calls for an entirely different education and extensive re-skilling.

The mismatch between supply and demand regarding Technical Vocational Education Training, part of SDG 4, cannot be resolved with only education policy changes in the TVET system. In their study, Witenstein and Iyengar (2023), in collaboration with an India-based non-profit, found that the demand-driven factors, the psycho-social aspect biased against women, must change before girls/women can avail themselves of vocational education. Women are not allowed to work outside their homes or enhance their skills due to safety concerns, or the males in the families do not permit them to do so. Male dominance and female dependency may not provide a conducive environment for accessing skill development opportunities through TVETs, which are needed to transition to "green skilling"—preparing students with knowledge, abilities, values and attitudes needed to work and live in, develop and support a sustainable and resource-efficient society.

Comparative analysis of TVETs across countries on the deterrents to accessing Technical and Vocational Programs, especially for women in South Asia, would help to understand the macro issues along with the gendered nuances that Witenstein and Iyengar (2023) have been able to highlight. For instance, essential policy suggestions based on gender issues that have emerged from this study are: TVETs that are only for women, with flexible hours, yet linked to local jobs, may stand a chance; counseling the males in families is highly important for female participation and ensuring the utility of the courses in their daily lives. Therefore, revamping the existing courses, which include retail sales, hospitality, security, welding, etc., to match skills with the needs of local employers might be a good strategy, resulting in more job opportunities for women. The courses could include computer basics, typing, cyber security, wellbeing, gender studies, public health, etc.

The move to "green skilling," as the United Nations Industrial Development Organization proposes, and work on a more just division of world labor hold new collaborative research for CIE. This is made possible, like never before, without the travel of researchers from the North to the Global South and with the reduction of carbon footprint by using many communications technologies and platforms such as Zoom and WhatsApp. The other CIE collaborative research possibilities lay in the unprecedented increase of international students studying in English-speaking universities from China, Korea, India, and other Global South countries. They have always been a CIE research building block it is just that now global education issues have extended to a broader audience including political actors. In the May 2025 election in Australia, for instance, there were calls to limit the number of international students in the country due to housing shortages, even though this would be detrimental to the economy at large, as international students generate economic activity and bring much-needed income to the universities (especially given recent cuts in higher-education support).

Digital Learning and AI Prospects

Digital technologies have influenced CIE knowledge-production and sharing more profoundly than any other previous technology. As the cultural historian Stephen Kern (2015: 2) notes, the most conspicuous single technology of our time is the internet:

> It was conceived as an open network ... users just had to follow its technical protocols that were transparent and public ... The Internet, augmented by the World Wide Web, enabled users to access knowledge from myriad sources with results worldwide instantaneously, as well as copy and recall it at the same speed, with the results that this technology transformed the world in unprecedented ways.

The internet has impacted many disciplines, but especially a field like CIE, which is internationally defined and practiced in so many countries, with consequences for the building, re-building, and researching of education systems and the transfer and borrowing of educational goods and ideas. Once communication technologies developed, together with the enhanced movement of people around the world, the exchange of material and cultural goods and ideas sped up, affecting how education is planned and reformed. One can look up and learn from plans, programs, curricula, lesson plans, and teaching and learning videos on and in many different locations and school systems, comparing and learning from them, quoting them to policymakers and changing one's own practices in response to them. ICT has advanced learning in one giant step (Iyengar 2015). Where previously access was dependent on networks and computers, now smartphones have given access to anyone acquiring a phone with connectivity. ICT as increased the scale of not just communication but long-range and rapid exchange of data about friends and acquaintances, about books consulted, about papers to be archived and read later, etc., as well as connecting us internationally to those we know (or don't know) and from whom we can learn, both in the immediate present and from the past. The same applies to, e.g., visual representations, maps, charts, diagrams, and moving images, which we can view, learn from, and make our own. ICT is not limited to the experience of looking up facts about the past and present (time) but also introduces us to new experiences of distance and proximity (space). What was once far and expensive to access is now near and for free (with apps like WhatsApp, FaceTime, WeChat, and Weixin). Interactive social media sites now accompany many kinds of online publication, including academic publications. The use of ICT has profoundly influenced teaching and learning, as Iyengar et al. (2017) have shown in their study of its accelerated action on Sustainable Development Goals.

Payal Arora's research on introducing digital technology to working people in the Global South found that what divides social classes in this new Industrial Revolution is leisure—some have it and while others do not. Her book on the "next billion users" brings to light the divide in access to digital leisure and "challenges the sacred tenet on which the global digital project has been built upon over decades—the belief that a good digital life for the poor would be based in work and inherently utilitarian" (Arora 2019). Instead, what she found when she researched communities and their actual preferences and uses of technologies was that it overwhelmingly included leisure activities, such as one-to-one and group messaging, the sharing of photos, videos and music, the accessing of social media, online gaming, the consumption of audiovisual content, dating and romance and shopping.

Arora et al. (2022) have considered the digital leisure divide an essential aspect of existing digital gaps experienced by forcibly displaced communities, focusing on communities and their actual preferences and uses of technologies. Their study covers the main infrastructural, cultural, economic, legal, and political limitations that hinder the connectivity of forcibly displaced people. They emphasize the various forms of connectivity and specific contextual limitations and opportunities in different locations. In terms of digital media use, their fieldwork supports refugees' and migrants' preference for mainstream platforms such as WhatsApp, Facebook, and YouTube in this context. This report proposes a typology of digital leisure activities, including entertainment, gaming, sex/sexuality/intimacy, content creation, social capital, community voice, and contemporary livelihoods.

The current progress of AI research might transform education, compelling institutions to rethink future jobs and workforce training. Zawacki-Richter et al. (2019) reviewed higher education spaces and suggested many personalized learning models that could emerge based on individual students' needs, abilities, and learning styles with AI. This could help identify practical pedagogical approaches for diverse student populations across different cultural and socio-economic backgrounds, where and how comparative education studies are conducted, as well as CIE teaching. There are high expectations that AI-driven tutoring systems will become intelligent and can provide personalized instruction and support diverse students, potentially complementing or supplementing human teachers. The great hope is that these systems could be designed and adapted for different educational contexts based on comparative research. The authors note that equity, fairness, professional training, and data privacy issues remain challenging. Overall, much speculation exists about AI's potential to enhance comparative education research and practice (Grassini 2023). Still, its responsible and ethical development and deployment requires careful consideration of the challenges and the context of implementation, so we do not end up with another "Western education" transfer from a few Global North centers to the rest of the world.

We can learn more about the challenges of switching to digital learning from the chaos that the worldwide coronavirus pandemic (2020–2023) wreaked on education, teaching, and learning, and classroom life as we once knew it. The Covid years lent an urgency to the development of new approaches to accommodating a wider variety of students. New realities of the kind that higher education faced during the pandemic and potentially faces now again with the introduction of AI calls for something like an imaginative "world-building" exercise by CIE scholars. Since the release of ChatGPT, one of the most surprising aspects regarding generative AI has been that it threatens to automate the intellectual and creative tasks of teaching and learning. It might still take reflection and time for CIE to account for the full influence on theory building, methods, doing research, and practicing teaching and learning. See more at the CIES 2025 annual meeting topics that was devoted to "Envisioning Education in a Digital Society." What is becoming clear is that higher education is only following private companies, which are leading the way in discovering what AI can do and will do with education structures, content, and work. Job training with AI might take over soon.

AI research, writing, and translation will automate and adapt how we transact work in education spaces, including CIE research into other education systems. In his final, *CER* journal editorial Nordtveit (2023), who was the chief editor for ten years, is optimistic about AI, anticipating a "gradual transition from a knowledge economy to an artificial intelligence–supported economy." AI is the first among five transformative dimensions of CIE he observed over his decade as editor (701). While some of us engage more directly with AI, for example, as teachers, in individualizing learning capabilities, we endorse the idea that the field ought to take stock of and study the implications of the rise of AI for CIE teaching, learning, and practices as a critical measure of the field's future. Emerging speculations on AI and CIE have recently been published in a text by Curtis et al. (2024). Their chapter, entitled "The Emergence and Progression of AI in Comparative and International Education," offers resources and explores implications, with a nod to the role that CIE can play in critiquing the place of AI in education, especially with respect to how the field comes to terms with its colonial history.

Many universities have labs and teams working to discover ways to use AI in education for sustainable development. It is hard to imagine how AI will influence research teaching and learning CIE, as it is not an IT or ICT network, even though sometimes it is used with such computer assistance programs. The input in AI is Large Language Models (LLMs); the output cannot be anticipated, but the hope is that artificial "intelligence" will in due course produce knowledge, not just information. For the time being, it is generating language. The language it produces arises from surfacing patterns of vast quantities of text that have been scanned; consequently, all AI models are biased by their training data. Inevitably, many leading models show a strong bias toward Western values. They can also exhibit new biases created by the attempt to align their outputs using human feedback of one kind or another. As Curtis et al. (2024) set out to address the impact of colonization and modern technological innovation on AI and digital technologies.

We argue that these technologies are exacerbating existing inequalities and perpetuating colonial power dynamics in the form of coloniality. We advocate for the decolonization of AI to address these issues and ensure that AI benefits all individuals and communities (Simone, et al. 2024).

As we are on the verge of giving AI many more responsibilities in the educational sphere, as in other spheres of our culture, Ted Chiang (2010), a contemporary science-fiction writer, reminds us, "Not so fast." There are no shortcuts in education, Chiang tells us: just as we need decades, or maybe a lifetime, to "grow humans," so we will need just as much time and care to "grow" AI before it ever in the position to help us educate our own young. Chiang has observed that "meta-cognition," or thinking about one's thinking, is something that most humans can do but that neither animals nor current AI are capable of.

Conclusion

In this chapter we revered the building blocks of CIE and its knowledge when it comes to how to catalog it to better use by teachers and learners. Organizations, such as CIES, are the building block of CIE as a profession, in which members take part in annual and regional conferences and contribute to the professional journals, such as *Compare* and *Comparative Education* (both from the UK) CIES the US association that took over as the organization to belong to, has become the international forum to meet and present work. To present your paper at CIES is presenting at an international CIE association, to the point that smaller associations, i.e., New Zealand had to be combined with Australia and the Island nations to form one association that can sustain professional building block: annual conferences and a publication, CER, associated with the society. In the nineteenth century, the education "discipline" was not only a division of knowledge but also an idea that produced personal discipline in individuals. CIE is a discipline, but not all knowledge production in our field is disciplinary, as we see when CIE researchers observe people engaged in their educational endeavors, such as street children, gang collectives, or quilting parties. Information technology, direct mail, and texting play a role in formal and non-formal education and in organizing parents to protest education reforms that do not align with their personal and community values. Such vast networks of communications, reaching geographically and demographically disparate populations, represent a new building block for CIE research. The field is tied to more significant changes, not least to the complex relationship between international relations and education policy and practice (see the Illustration by Fazal) as the example of research on International students shows.

Education sciences have a long history, dating to the rise of scientific, positivist approaches to gathering knowledge. These building blocks enabled the advances of the social and successive technological revolutions, establishing and eroding education as a common good. During the 2020–23 pandemic, these advances were sorely tested when teaching and learning adopted online technologies to replace face-to-face, in-person instruction. Education, public, and private organizations continue to use these technologies intensively. The next building block might be new developments in the capabilities of AI and its implications for teaching and information distribution, which will continue to affect all levels of education. As we can recall from Chapter 2, Donna Haraway (1991) predicted that because of the organically human and technologically artificial nature of AI, our "authorization of interpretation is lost," and with it "the ontology grounding [what is being] and 'Western' epistemology" (what or whose knowledge it is):

> But the alternative is not cynicism or faithlessness, that is, some version of abstract existence, like the accounts of technological determinism destroying "man" by the "machine" or "meaningful political action" by the "text." Who cyborgs will be is a radical question; the answers are a matter of survival.
>
> (153)

Those AI capabilities and implications are still in the process of being digested at the time of writing this book, yet they do already offer many new avenues for CIE to consider.

The relevant different theories, as Chapter 2 shows, the employment of methods, as Chapter 3 illustrates, and the production and dissemination of knowledge, as reviewed in Chapter 4, keep CIE at the forefront of the study of education. A field like CIE, so aware of its meaning-making, with so many blocks to build its growth and changes—as the reference list of this book shows—is continually striving to stay at the forefront of the broader disciplinary studies and advances of education as a whole.

Academic Activity—Springboards

Springboard A

SDG indicator 4.7.4: "the percentage of students by age group (or education level) showing adequate understanding of issues relating to global citizenship and sustainability" (https://uis.unesco.org/sites/default/files/documents/sdg4-data-digest-2019-en_0.pdf)

Connect SDG 4.7 to what you read or know about global citizenship and what you read in Chapter 4 about *Ubuntu*.

What do you think about the Enslin and Horsthemke (2004) question: If and how can *Ubuntu* provide a model for citizenship education in African democracies? List the pros and cons for each of the options.

Springboard B

Seekers v. Experts: Blanco, G. L., and Witenstein, M. A. (2024), "Conversations: Matthew Witenstein with Gerardo Blanco." *Diaspora, Indigenous, and Minority Education*, 18 (2), 83–91. https://doi.org/10.1080/15595692.2024.2325299

    Gerardo Blanco: For me, there are two crucial issues, and I see them as being interconnected. On the one hand, we have the issue of backsliding of democratic systems and structures around the world. Of course, some places have not been democratic for a long time. I think that is a significant issue. This is particularly important when diasporic communities displaced, communities, and migrant communities are often the object of arguments against democracy or to justify the backsliding of democratic structures. So, I think that is one issue. But we see this across Europe as well, sort of saying the State needs to have these special powers because we are responding to these, not to mention, of course, countries that are in active conflict; as you can see, the connection with diaspora, migration, and displaced communities is evident. The second issue is also similar and connected with this, which is increased social polarization. I think, in many ways, technologies are accelerating the divide regarding how we are in these echo chambers, not only in intellectual institutions but across society.

Comment and write:

What do you see as the major issues CIE can research and learn in relation to diaspora, indigenous, and minority *education* in your own community, city or town, or academic program?

6

Conclusion

"We Are All Comparativists Now *and* Internationalists"

"We are all comparativists now **and** Internationalists" is what Phillips and Schweisfurth (2014) write at their conclusion to comparative and international education textbook, making the case that there is no comparative education without international study of education comparatively. Agreeing with Don Adams that "the best way to study education is to study it comparatively."

This volume aims to create more space in academic teaching and learning to explore histories, theories, and methods, both quantitative and qualitative studies that consciously consider local contexts and especially scholarly discourse while leveraging some version of the comparative method to generate distinctive theoretical and practical insights into contextualizing educational phenomena. Publishing or presenting such work at local and international conferences facilitates the circulation of findings and insights, so we debate, learn, borrow, and transfer knowledge of our practices, as well as mentoring the next generation of comparativists.

Rereading the histories in Chapter 1, the theories in Chapter 2, and methods and practices in Chapters 3 and 4 suggests thinking about comparative and international education as a discipline across disciplinary boundaries—whether between area studies specialists or between economic or social experts or education generalists. The methods of comparing have involved and are still evolving with digital technologies to transform research in CIE to ensure that research is at the forefront of tackling crucial issues of the have and have-not access, when it comes to elementary or lifelong education, cultural memory, and identity, and creativity, communications in a digital age.

The illustrations, following this chapter, by contributors with outstanding backgrounds, show the array of their subject matter and how CIE has branched out—generating new insights and deeper understandings by focusing on the need to study similarities/differences across education phenomena, using comparative methods in context.

> **Chapter 1** showed that history is the default setting for understanding CIE today, entailing several more or less unexamined assumptions about what comparative education means and how it should be comprehended—historically. As we attempted to *historicize* CIE teaching, research, and practice, that is, when we seek to restore it to the interpretative horizon of its time—and this even includes research of our historical moment (see Chapter 3), when we seek to learn and generate how to "do" and become an education comparativist—we operate on the assumption that the examples we shared can only show what we know at this historical moment, and what we foresee into the future. We do not assume this text has covered all the histories, theories, methods, and practices. Instead, we offered this text to be read and studied as a reflection of CIE in the 2020s. To use it otherwise would be to read it a historically.
>
> **Chapter 2** covered theories in four major paradigms and theorizing across and after "post" theories. A field like CIE, which sought to align itself with the social sciences, could not escape the debates and contradicting worldviews and theories regarding what "being" and "knowing" are. Those "paradigm wars" that erupted in sociology, economics, and later in anthropology in the 1980s impacted how to compare educational phenomena and what working in international settings means. Social systems were not as simple and homogeneous as the functionalist theories suggested. Theorists highlighted the persistence of traditional values and indigenous ways of knowing despite economic and political changes. Sociologists, anthropologists, and historians have often commented on the tendency of economists to pay inadequate attention to culture when investigating the operations of societies. Such studies led CIE to re-think that convergence toward modern society replacing completely traditional values was unlikely as theorized by functionalists' economics of education.
>
> **Chapter 3** showed how different methods have been employed to produce knowledge in various paradigms, with examples of research in many rich arenas where CIE has spread its wings. The use of such a rich repertoire of methods over time and over the "turns" in social sciences. The development of sophisticated statistics to collect and analyze, and compare education practices and outcomes in many countries, amount of data that we could not imagine how easy it will be for new computers and

new programs to execute. At the same time anthropology and qualitative methods have made long strides at the researcher/researched nexus, how positionality of the researcher makes a difference, and the Global South is no longer the place of *data mining*. While the Global North and English are the major place and language for publication. The fact that comparative and international education have time and again looked inward, imagined, and re-imagined its theoretical underpinning, adopted innovative methodologies, and multi-disciplinary approaches keeps CIE at the forefront of the study of education, worldwide. This is why many teacher education and education foundation programs offer CIE courses, as well as so many universities around the globe (Wolhuter et al. 2008).

Chapter 4 studies the range of practices in time and space as they move in different directions, helping us to see both new directions, such as South-South, and South-North, challenging the strong North-South hegemony on funded research projects and publishing them in English. Over the past two decades, young scholars have developed a new understanding of the critical social, economic, and environmental challenges that the globe is facing. CIE is now influenced by scholars from the sustainable sciences, the newly established environmental humanities, and the Global South, demanding that CIE, in and out of the academy, rises to the occasion with less conventional scholarship, new, more creative, and more concerned forms of research and engagement. Practices such as green skilling, just transition, global citizenship, and Sustainable Development Goals, to just name a few examples of how a disciplinary field like CIE can help build a more sustainable way education, can and should contribute to knowledge about education's contribution to environmental well-being.

Chapter 5 rethinks how the field has established itself as a professional organization that both exhibits knowledge (conferences and journals) but is also a gatekeeper to what CIE is and can be in the future of contemporary practices, with or without artificial intelligence (AI). This calls upon us to re-think the very ways in which we create CIE knowledge, communicate it across different disciplines, and engage with students, learners, education planners, policymakers, donor agencies, and their consultants. To that effect, we must navigate the multiple venues educators are involved in, like peace education, sustainable development practices, and social challenges such as refugee education or students coming hungry to school (research shows that if parents only had $1, they would rather pay for education than food). Those examples mean that a multi-disciplinary field like CIE can negotiate politics at Ministries of Education, social services, planners, social scientists, social justice activists, and others. CIE research and practices negotiate through language, research methods, and practices, theorizing in different paradigms, and spanning different discursive practices.

It would be simplistic to conclude that CIE's lack of one firm academic institutional structure led to the field's fragmentation, with competing goals, theories, methodologies, claims, and role ambiguity inherent in its practices (e.g., scholar versus policymaker, practitioner versus social scientist). The question is whether this fragmentation made it impossible for comparative educators to work collaboratively or exchange information with one another, given the different worldviews they embraced as an initial point of dialogue, or whether this fragmentation indicated a commitment to diversity and openness, to competing framing, pragmatic differences, and research methodologies. It is an open question. Angela Little (2010) proposed that we think about our challenge less in terms of definitions of the field(s) and more in terms of what we might do together in the future. Our identities, she suggests, should derive more from what we do than from surface definitions of who we say we are. She offers our field a six-point challenge (850):

1. Share a mission
2. Recognize and seek out diversity
3. Build bridges
4. Search for context-specificity and universals
5. Present our research more clearly
6. Allow methods to serve, not dominate

The basics of the historical context of studies and practices are wedged deep in post-Second World War reconstructing world order. Chapter 3 showed how research is building bridges across qualitative and quantitative methods, and how theories and practices bridge across North and South CIE knowledge productions. By leaning on and quoting scholars from both the South and the North we recognized diversity and were seeking out context specific examples to help us build more generatable ideas.

This volume's chapters, clearly, we hope, expand our analytic understanding of how CIE was built historically, how we continue to practice it, and why its future is very important to us. As we demonstrated and stated in the introduction, this book is a textbook of the fundamentals for learners, instructors, and scholars that would like to know more about comparative and international education, in a comprehensive and systematic way. From the basics of the historical context of studies and practices wedged deep in post-Second World War reconstructing world order. Including the principles and considerations in past and present comparative international education, studies, methods and theories. For this multidisciplinary field, we should recall what the librarian Thelma Bristow wrote in 1965: Books and articles of theories, methods, plans and policies, and curriculum borrowed or designed, and of course, what knowledge AI will put together for all learners to use, "must be acquired and arranged about comparative education so that they *may become* part of comparative education."

Illustrations/Reflections

Introduction

During the writing process for this text, we chose to include research and practice areas while leveraging these insights among experts who are contributing to the field of comparative and international education. This led us to connect with a diverse set of colleagues who have spent years working in the field on various research and practice dimensions of comparative and international education (CIE). We hope this gives you a flavor of some of the angles and perspectives on how contemporary topics and themes are researched and practiced within CIE. These topics include internationalization and global education, education finance, school climate, educational equity, international student experiences, and teacher education, among others. As you will see, the scholars included here use diverse methods to investigate these research dilemmas, such as defining collaborative research, quantitative research methods, and qualitative research methods.

There are multifaceted ways these Illustrations can be used; this is why we mention each in different chapters and sections of the book. First, we have intentionally referred to the different Illustrations throughout the book, which as you turn to them at that point, they both highlight and provide deeper understanding of topics across the book's chapters. As the book provides an overview of the field, each reflection provides an opportunity to deepen knowledge and insights into diverse, relevant themes. We are excited to offer you a sense of some current CIE debates and discussions, as well as introduce you to several active comparativists in the field. They enrich relevant topics and assist in better understanding of the field's current ways of knowing. To build on that, since the illustrative topics are short readings that summarize important dimensions of each author's work/research, we encourage you to examine the respective reference sections of each and turn to them if this is a topic that interests you, and look up and delve deeper into more of the author's work, as some do quote their work but not all of it.

The goal of the book as a comprehensive overview is to integrate the Illustrations across the chapters, so they serve and are used to further your understanding of topics and their place within CIE. They can relate to research methods and theories as you will notice each used a different way to frame the topic/issue. They facilitate more detailed coverage, which is why we call them Illustrations, while some are case studies, an in-depth, detailed examination of a particular case within its context. You may consider asking yourself the following questions as you read the Illustrations:

- Within which paradigm is the topic more aligned?
- Which research method is more relevant to continue to explore the topic/issue?
- What are some practices to explore the topic?
- Whose voices are reflected and whose are missing? What can we learn from noticing this?
- What are some ethical considerations of the research topic that you think the author has had to take into account?

The contributors, as you can see from the list following the contributions, are at different institutions, and work and write on very different topics. While all the contributions are relevant to learning and knowing comparative and international education, some might be relevant to other classes and topics, or to a research project, or a class you teach. Finally, we hope each Illustration helps broaden your perspectives, introduces new topics to add to this textbook, while familiarizing you with some of the current work/writings of practicing comparativists.

Iris BenDavid-Hadar

Education Finance, Equality, and Equity

Keywords: education finance, equity and adequacy, educational policy-making, equitable resource allocation

The domain of education finance is swiftly evolving, exerting a substantial impact on policymaking across many countries. As its name suggests, this field delves into the interconnectivity between finance and education, examining how resources are distributed within the education system and its subsequent impact on education outcomes. Notably, research in this field has played a pivotal role in shaping education policies and advocating for educational reforms. Policy reforms pave the way for new research inquiries, and the insights gleaned from research efforts contribute to developing more effective policies and practices. Education finance primarily addresses the complexities of enhancing education through the conceptualization, design, and reform of methods by which resources are allocated within the education system. This includes the re-evaluation and creation of allocation mechanisms and funding formulas (BenDavid-Hadar 2018a, 2018b, 2023; Kolbe et al. 2020). Furthermore, it entails prioritizing education within national budgets and securing international financial support for educational endeavors (BenDavid-Hadar 2018b).

The ongoing discourse defines what constitutes an effective, efficient, fair, and just allocation, and explores the inherent trade-offs between these objectives. This discussion has relevance within the theoretical frameworks of education finance, situated within the intricate web of conflicting and competing values. Among these values, prominent within the Western world, are liberty and equality/equity. The tension between these values intensifies the policymaking process, as highlighted by Brighouse et al. (2018), arguing that explicit and careful consideration of these tensions can lead to more effective policy decisions and performance.

Liberty, defined as the capacity for individuals and groups to select and optimize personal preferences, is often esteemed as a paramount value, particularly within the US context. However, political theory literature posits a discernible trade-off between liberty and equality. Levin (2001) contended the extension of liberties tends to exacerbate societal inequalities and divisions, whereas a preference for equality helps mitigate such disparities. Abrams (2016) scrutinized the experiences of Sweden and Chile, both of which embraced school privatization under conservative leadership, resulting in increased social inequity through school choice. Elaborating on this, Baker (2016) asserted that for expanded liberty to contribute to greater equality, the available choices must be substantively equal, aligning with a common set of societal standards. He raised a crucial question: if the available choices are substantially equal, what justifies choosing one over another? Consequently, systems of choice and competition inherently rely on differentiation and perpetuate inequality.

The exploration of avenues to enhance educational outcomes, including the distribution of educational achievement (EAD), spans a diverse array of considerations. This involves tackling the right to education from a funding perspective, narrowing the achievement gap, and elevating the overall academic performance. Central to this pursuit is analyzing the interplay between funding distribution and the EAD. Various measurements and concepts have been devised to delve into this issue, encompassing aspects such as horizontal equity, vertical equity, wealth neutrality, the equality of educational opportunities, and adequacy (BenDavid-Hadar 2018b).

Equity in education finance

The literature underscores the pivotal role of equitable education in fostering a more just society (Baker 2021; BenDavid-Hadar 2016, 2023). It posits that aligning education finance policies directly with equity enhances their effectiveness in advancing equitable education. In recent years, a growing literature body has underscored the causal relationship between equitably allocated resources and enhanced academic, economic, and social outcomes, particularly among disadvantaged students (Jackson and Mackevicius 2023; Johnson 2015; Lafortune et al. 2016). Nevertheless, a critical factor influencing outcomes lies in the efficient utilization of these allocated resources (Handel and Hanushek 2022).

When education finance policies explicitly align with the principles of equity, they gain an enhanced capacity to nurture equitable educational opportunities (Baker et al. 2020; BenDavid-Hadar 2018b, 2023). Equitable education finance policies play a pivotal role in addressing disparities and advancing social justice. By allocating resources based on students' needs and ensuring equitable access to quality education, these policies empower marginalized students to excel academically and professionally (Allier-Gagneur and Gruijters 2023; Heyneman 2015; Heyneman and Loxley 1983), particularly in low-income countries where educational inequalities are pronounced.

The importance of equity in education outcomes is further emphasized in the Sustainable Development Goals 2030, as a means for achieving a country's sustainable development. Furthermore, it has an impact on human capital development thereby contributing to enhancements in economic prosperity (Hanushek and Woessmann 2020), labor productivity, and the growth rate of GDP (Arnold et al. 2007; Lucas 2002). Additionally, fostering equitable education is integral for cultivating a just society and ensuring equal opportunities (BenDavid-Hadar 2016; Drew 2020).

This discourse pertains to political philosophy, since it delves into how a state perceives its responsibility to ensure the right to education. Democracies, in particular, are bound by the commitment to establish a just and equitable education system, necessitating corresponding fair and equitable education finance policies. Nevertheless, policies also need to navigate to compete on a global scale and address the financial demands of education with stringent fiscal constraints.

Future directions

Demographic changes, exemplified by the contemporary waves of massive immigration, contribute to the intricacy of allocating resources fairly and equitably. Within fiscal constraints, a state might opt to invest more in gifted and talented students, aligning with Plato's philosophy, or allocate additional resources to the less advantaged students, in line with Rawls's (1971) Theory of Justice. The literature extensively explores the tension between the goal of global competitiveness and the goal of maintaining social cohesion (e.g., Stiglitz 2012). A potential breakthrough could emerge by adopting Sen's (2009) concept of comparative justice. Accordingly, an allocation method can strive to enhance the relative position of students from their initial starting point on the EAD (BenDavid-Hadar 2016, 2018a).

Countries adhering to the existing paradigm of equity and adequacy in shaping their education finance policies, emphasizing the connections between funding and outcomes, could encounter challenges in elevating their competitiveness, a crucial requirement in our increasingly globalized knowledge-based economy (Mazarr 2022). Additionally, it is posited that centering school finance within the framework of equity and adequacy may potentially intensify difficulties in sustaining social cohesion.

Furthermore, according to Stiglitz (2012) in "The Price of Inequality," global competitiveness hinges on fostering cohesion. A school finance policy relying solely on the government's responsibility for meeting minimum or standards-based performance may miss the mark in the current era of rapid knowledge breakthroughs. Therefore, contemporary school finance policies might find utility in rethinking their framework, and embracing a dynamic, improvement-oriented equity notion (BenDavid-Hadar 2018b) that supports creating a learning society (Stiglitz and Greenwald 2014).

References

Abrams, E. S. (2016), *Education and the Commercial Mindset*, Cambridge: Harvard University Press.

Allier-Gagneur, Z. C., and R. J. Gruijters (2023), 'Beyond Heyneman & Loxley: The Relative Importance of Families and Schools for Learning Outcomes in Francophone Africa', *Compare: A Journal of Comparative and International Education*, 53 (4): 654–73.

Arnold, J. M., A. Bassanini, and S. Scarpetta (2007), 'Solow or Lucas?: Testing Growth Models Using Panel Data From OECD Countries', *OECD Economics Department Working Paper 592*.

Baker, B. D. (2016), 'Exploring the Consequences of Charter School Expansion in US Cities', *Economic Policy Institute*, Washington, DC. Available online: https://files.epi.org/pdf/109218.pdf (accessed September 9, 2023).

Baker, B. D. (2021), *Educational Inequality and School Finance: Why Money Matters for America's Students*, Cambridge: Harvard Education Press.

Baker, B. D., A. Srikanth, R. Cotto Jr and P. C. Green III (2020), 'School Funding Disparities and the Plight of Latinx Children', *Education Policy Analysis Archives*, 28 (135).

BenDavid-Hadar, I. (2016), 'School Finance Policy and Social Justice', *International Journal of Educational Development*, 46: 166–74.

BenDavid-Hadar, I. (2018a), 'Funding Education: Developing a Method of Allocation for Improvement', *International Journal of Educational Management*, 32 (1): 2–26.

BenDavid-Hadar, I., ed. (2018b), *Education Finance, Equality, and Equity*, vol. 5, Basel: Springer.

BenDavid-Hadar, I. (2023), 'Resource Allocation and Funding Formulae: A Review', *Prepared for the Israeli Ministry of Education Chief of Scientist* (in Hebrew).

Brighouse, H. (2008), 'Education for a Flourishing Life', *Yearbook of the National Society for the Study of Education*, 107 (1): 58–71.

Brighouse, H., H. F. Ladd, S. Loeb, and A. Swift (2018), *Educational Goods*, Chicago: University of Chicago Press.

Drew, D. E. (2020), 'STEM Education, Economic Productivity, and Social Justice', *Oxford Research Encyclopedia of Education*, Oxford: Oxford University Press.

Handel, D. V., and E. A. Hanushek (2022), 'US School Finance: Resources and Outcomes (No. w30769)', *National Bureau of Economic Research Working Paper Series*, Cambridge: National Bureau of Economic Research.

Hanushek, E. A., and L. Woessmann (2020), 'Education, Knowledge Capital, and Economic Growth', in B. Green (ed.), *The Economics of Education*, 171–82, Cambridge: Academic Press.

Heyneman, S. P. (2015), 'The Heyneman/Loxley Effect: Three Decades of Debate', in M. Siman and G. Qing (eds), *Routledge Handbook of International Education and Development*, 150–67, Abingdon: Routledge.

Heyneman, S. P., and W. A. Loxley (1983), 'The Effect of Primary-School Quality on Academic Achievement Across Twenty-Nine High- and Low-Income Countries', *American Journal of Sociology*, 88 (6): 1162–94.

Jackson, C. K., and C. L. Mackevicius (2023), 'What Impacts Can We Expect From School Spending Policy? Evidence From Evaluations in the US', *American Economic Journal: Applied Economics*, 16 (1): 412–46.

Johnson, R. C. (2015), 'Follow the Money: School Spending from Title I to Adult Earnings', *RSF: The Russell Sage Foundation Journal of the Social Sciences*, 1 (3): 50–76.

Kolbe, T., D. Atchinson, C. Kearns, and J. Levin (2020), *State Funding Formulas: A National Review*, Washington: American Institutes for Research.

Lafortune, J., J. Rothstein, and D. W. Schanzenbach (2016), 'School Finance Reform and the Distribution of Student Achievement (No. w22011)', *National Bureau of Economic Research Working Paper Series*, Cambridge: National Bureau of Economic Research.

Levin, H., ed. (2001), *Privatizing Education: Can the School Marketplace Deliver Freedom of Choice, Efficiency, Equity, and Social Cohesion?*, Boulder: Westview Press.

Lucas, R. E. (2002), *Lectures on Economic Growth*, Cambridge: Harvard University Press.

Mazarr, M. J. (2022), *The Societal Foundations of National Competitiveness*, Santa Monica: Rand Corporation.

Oberfield, Z. W., and B. D. Baker (2022), 'The Politics of Progressivity: Court-Ordered Reforms, Racial Difference, and School Finance Fairness', *American Educational Research Journal*, 59 (6): 1229–64.

Rawls, J. (1971), *A Theory of Justice*, Cambridge: The Belknap Press of Harvard University Press.

Sen, A. K. (2009), *The Idea of Justice*, Cambridge: The Belknap Press of Harvard University Press.

Stiglitz, E. J. (2012), *The Price of Inequality: How Today's Divided Society Endangers Our Future*, New York: Norton.

Stiglitz, E. J., and C. B. Greenwald (2014), *Creating a Learning Society: A New Approach to Growth, Development, and Social Progress*, New York: Columbia University Press.

Gerardo L. Blanco

Internationalization and Global Education

Keywords: internationalization discourse, higher education, pedagogical strategies, neoliberalism, globalization

Conceptualizations of comparative and international education, as academic and professional fields, often start at the global level, by the identification of key features across educational systems and their mutual influences or through shared practices or approaches. At the same time, many grassroots initiatives take place, seeking to make schools, universities, and other educational organizations more internationally focused and engaged. Such development of an international orientation is at the core of internationalization. However, and despite the presence of descriptive and normative definitions of internationalization, the most effective strategies and purposes for internationalization remain contested, their purposes are still fluctuating, and above all, the locus or action and agency (individual, institutional, national, supra-national) is heatedly debated. These tensions are the main focus of this short entry.

While internationalization of education may involve all educational levels and contexts (Tarc 2019), tertiary or postsecondary education has seen a significant concentration of actions and debates and therefore provides a significant space for analysis. In this sense, it is clear that internationalization, in the most traditional sense, is the product of the assumption—stemming from the neoliberal globalization processes of the 1990s—that education constitutes a commodity to be traded across countries, placing student mobility as its main manifestation, and

Europe—along with key White-settler contexts like Australia, Canada, the UK, US, and New Zealand, as its epicenter (see de Wit and Altbach 2020). The process of internationalization has diffused across the world, introducing internationalization ambitions in every national context. Definitions of internationalization have proliferated, co-existing with, rather than replacing, each other. Notwithstanding the existence of multiple definitions, the origin and history of the concept are crucially tied to neoliberal modernity in the Global North.

Even though in-person mobility paused and then became digitized during the Covid-19 pandemic (Onanda et al. 2022), mobility has remained an almost exclusive focus of attention for internationalization. However, digital approaches, such as collaborative online educational learning, or COIL (Gelashvili and Blanco 2023), have emerged, along with the understanding that internationalization at home is important, but very challenging to achieve (Blanco 2021). In this sense, technology-mediated strategies to make curriculum and pedagogy more international and focusing on the intentional contact between domestic and international students with a focused-on dialogue constitute some of the most promising approaches. Even when that is the case, as I have experienced and documented by leading a living-learning community that brought international and US students together, the limits and opportunities for erring are abundant (Blanco 2021; Blanco et al. 2022). These efforts made clear, for example, that creating psychologically safe environments that promote dialogues across national identities is difficult while the world at large has normalized racist and xenophobic attacks. Moreover, fear among students and faculty to offend others is significant and therefore retreating into safe and superficial topics can become the default in interactions both inside and beyond the classroom. Whether the classroom is physical or digital makes little difference.

The locus of internationalization in current debates has been frequently reified. It is now normalized, for example, to speak of countries developing internationalization strategies, or universities internationalizing themselves. The most widely utilized definitions of internationalization (Knight 2003; de Wit 2013) refer to the concept as process, rendering its subject invisible. These approaches fit with the neoliberal globalization context in which the concept was developed and align with the desire to interact with decision makers at the national (ministries) and supranational level (UNESCO, World Bank, etc.), which has emerged as the dominant aspiration of researchers of Comparative Education and a core justification for the field's existence. For practitioners of internationalization and international education, the same desire to legitimize their practice by interfacing with policymakers can be equally observed.

In contrast, we can imagine internationalization as primarily about emotion and longing (Metcalfe and Blanco 2021). If internationalization is about anything at all, it is about people longing for an encounter. People longing to connect and teaching learners to long for people and places they have yet to encounter. Even if the encounter is fraught or even potentially fatal. As Amy Scott Metcalfe and I have argued: "If comparative and international studies of the university live to see the future, we must shed the dead weight of stiff performances and understand that the approaches that have shaped and sustained our field so far are unlikely to move it forward" (Oleksiyenko et al. 2021: 622–3). Therefore, my closing invitation is to push the mimics of the field and venture into activities and inquiries not yet legitimized.

References

Blanco, G. L. (2021), 'Global Citizenship Education as a Pedagogy of Dwelling: Re-Tracing (Mis)steps in Practice during Challenging Times', *Globalisation, Societies and Education*, 19 (4): 432–42.

Blanco, G. L., B. Zhao, and B. Ji (2022), 'The Promise and Limits of Engaging International Students Through Living-Learning Communities in US Research Universities', in M. Mohamad and J. Boyd (eds), *International Student Support and Engagement in Higher Education*, 133–45, New York: Routledge.

de Wit, H., and Altbach, P. G. (2020), 'Higher Education as a Global Reality', in *The International Encyclopedia of Higher Education Systems and Institutions*, 643–650, Dordrecht: Springer.

de Wit, H., and P. G. Altbach (2021), 'Internationalization in Higher Education: Global Trends and Recommendations for its Future', *Policy Reviews in Higher Education*, 5 (1): 28–46.

de Wit, H. (2013), 'Reconsidering the Concept of Internationalization', *International Higher Education*, 70: 6–7.

Gelashvili, M., and G. Blanco (2023), 'COIL as a Way to Enhance Internationalization: Balancing Evidence and Proliferation', *International Higher Education*, 116: 28–30.

Knight, J. (2003), 'Updating the Definition of Internationalization', *International Higher Education*, 33: 2–3.

Metcalfe, A. S., and G. L. Blanco (2021), '"Love Is Calling": Academic Friendship and International Research Collaboration Amid a Global Pandemic', *Emotion, Space and Society*, 38: 1–4.

Oleksiyenko, A., G. Blanco, R. Hayhoe, L. Jackson, J. Lee, A. Metcalfe, M. Sivasubramaniam, and Q. Zha (2021), 'Comparative and International Higher Education in a New Key? Thoughts on the Post-Pandemic Prospects of Scholarship', *Compare: A Journal of Comparative and International Education*, 51 (4): 612–28.

Onanda, I., J. E. Jon, and G. Blanco (2022), 'Mobility for Academic Collaboration Post-COVID 19', *International Journal of African Higher Education*, 9 (3): 83–104.

Tarc, P. (2019), 'Internationalization of Education as an Emerging Field? A Framing of International Education for Cross-Domain Analyses', *Policy Futures in Education*, 17 (6): 732–44.

Irving Epstein

Affect Theory and its Contribution to Comparative Education

Keywords: affect theory, corrective theorizing, assemblage, meaning making, interconnection

Affect theory is an umbrella term for a number of theories that have highlighted the importance of conceiving of consciousness, emotion, and action in holistic and interrelated terms. It has become a prominent force in shaping cultural studies discourse and its tenets are increasingly being applied to social science questions. For many, it is viewed as a corrective to mainstreamed modernist assumptions that view human beings as autonomous individuals, distinct from other living objects by virtue of their ability to exercise consciousness and rationality. Instead, its proponents view knowledge as embodied within all life experiences. Gilles Deleuze and Felix Guattari, in their seminal work *A Thousand Plateaus, Capitalism and Schizophrenia* (1987), formulated several key concepts that have become associated with affect theory. Of primary importance is the notion of intensity of encounter, pre-conscious, undefinable, elastic dimensions of movement and potentiality that universally connect living and non-living entities to one another. A key characteristic of intensities of encounter is their rhizomatic nature: the interconnection they create occurs horizontally, as entities engage with one another in a non-hierarchical fashion.

A second concept embraced by affect theorists is assemblage. Assemblage assumes that entities come together and form relationships that are flexible and dynamic as opposed to being bounded and fixed. Within the realm of social theory, Bruno Latour (2007) has viewed assemblage as an explanatory device that elucidates how ideas are interconnected and how through rigorous examination, one can discover linkages that are less readily visible. Within the realm of political action, authors such as Judith Butler (2015) have noted the ways in which social movement followers assemble and disassemble while engaging in advocacy and protest.

Notions of assemblage and intensities of encounter both embrace the concept of contingency, another key component of affect theory. In spatial and temporal terms, contingency implies deterritorialization as well as impermanence. It rejects efforts to categorize, position, and separate phenomena into discrete forms. Indeed, insofar as indeterminacy is a key characteristic of twenty-first century life, contrary assertions that promote permanence as a defining attribute of lived experience are summarily rejected.

A final concept associated with affect theory is that of meaning-making, most forcefully argued by Margaret Wetherell. Wetherell (2012) contests the view that a clear distinction between conscious and pre-conscious intensity can be chronicled. In her view, what brings all of these theoretical components together is a desire for meaning making, an aim whose power lies in its reassertion of the importance of interconnection. For affect theorists, an embodied view of life experience emphasizes in varying degrees, all of these components: intensity of encounter, assemblage, contingency, and meaning making, although they may emphasize some of these concepts over others.

Given its interpersonal and polymorphous nature, it makes sense that educational scholars would find affect theory principles appealing, and in recent years, they have increasingly affirmed the importance of these principles to their work. Affect theory has thus been applied to analyses of pedagogy (Albrecht-Crane and Slack 2003), teacher education (Colmenares 2018), sex education (Lesko 2010), and youth studies (Lesko and Talburt 2012). Within the comparative and international education field, affect theory has been applied to studies of educational provision in conflict and trauma producing areas (Zembylas 2015), human rights concerns involving the memorialization of mass atrocity, aesthetics and music education, sports, school violence, student protest (Epstein 2019), global university rankings (Epstein 2019; Shahjahan et al. 2020; Shahjahan et al. 2021), Latin American media (Colmenares 2017), international film (Epstein 2023), Covid-19 (Epstein 2021), and scholar/researcher challenges implicit in conducting international development work (Vavrus 2021). The appeal of affect theory for comparative and international education scholars is easily discernible. First, it offers a flexible, holistic perspective in contrast to a field that has been characterized by fragmentation and rigid categorization. Second, it encourages inquiry in areas that have been under-researched within a field that has too often relied upon derivative intellectual frames and organizing perspectives. Finally, affect theory acknowledges the precarity that has increasingly defined twenty-first century human experience, but whose effects are often ignored by contemporary educational planners and evaluators.

Critics of affect theory point to the ill-defined relationship between consciousness and pre-consciousness as being particularly problematic and in need of further clarification. Additionally, the ways in which non-living entities express affect, influence humans, and are themselves influenced by humans need further investigation as do the connections between living non-human and human entities. Finally, as a set of concepts very much embedded within Western philosophical and cultural traditions, it is incumbent upon affect theorists to ensure that their terms of reference reflect a multiplicity of knowledge traditions. This being said, there is a growing recognition of its significance among comparative and international education scholars as its relevance to post-foundational inquiry is widely appreciated.

References

Albrecht-Crane, C., and Stack, J.D. (2003), 'Toward a Pedagogy of Affect," in J.D. Stack (ed.), *Animations [of Deleuze and Guattari]*, 191–216, New York: Peter Lang.

Butler, J. (2015), *Notes Toward a Performative Theory of Assembly*, Cambridge: Harvard University Press.

Colmenares, E. (2017), 'El Chavo de 8 as an "Intimate Public" in Venezuela: What Happened to the Good Life?', in D. Friedrich and E. Colmenares (eds), *Resonances of El Chavo del Ocho in Latin American Childhood, Schooling and Societies*, 111–27, London: Bloomsbury Academic.

Colmenares, E. (2018), 'Affecting the Theory Practice Gap in Social Justice Teacher Education: Exploring Student Teachers' Stuck Moments', Unpublished PhD diss., Teachers College, Columbia University.

Deleuze, G., and F. Guattari (1987), *A Thousand Plateaus, Capitalism and Schizophrenia*, Minneapolis: University of Minnesota Press.

Epstein, I. (2019), *Affect Theory and Comparative Education Discourse: Essays on Fear and Loathing in Response to Global Educational Policy and Practice*, London: Bloomsbury Academic.

Epstein, I. (2021), 'Education and COVID-19 Through the Lens of Affect', in W. Brehm, E. Unterhalter and M. Oketch (eds), *States of Emergency: Education in the Time of COVID-19*, NORRAG Special Issue, No. 6.

Epstein, I. (2023), *Education, Affect, and Film: Visual Imaginings, Global Explorations*, London: Bloomsbury Academic.

Latour, B. (2007), *Reassembling the Social: An Introduction to Actor Network Theory*, Oxford: Oxford University Press.

Lesko, N. (2010), 'Feeling Abstinent? Feeling Comprehensive? Touching the Affects of Sexuality Curricula', *Sex Education, Sexuality, Society and Learning*, 10 (3): 281–97.

Lesko, N., and S. Talburt, eds (2012), *Keywords in Youth studies. Tracing Affects, Movements, Knowledges*, New York: Routledge.

Shahjahan, R.A., P. E. Bylsma, and C. Singai (2021), 'Global University Rankings as "Sticky" Objects and "Refrains": Affect and Mediatisation in India', *Comparative Education*, 58 (2): 224–41.

Shahjahan, R. A., E. L. Sonneveldt, A. L. Estera, and S. Bae (2020), 'Emoscapes and Commercial University Rankers: The Role of Affect in Global Higher Education Policy', *Critical Studies in Education*, 63 (3): 275–90.

Vavrus, F. (2021), *Schooling as Uncertainty: An Ethnographic Memoir in Comparative Education*, London: Bloomsbury Academic.

Wetherell, M. (2012), *Affect and Emotion: A New Social Science Understanding*, Beverly Hills: Sage Publications.

Zembylas, M. (2015), *Emotion and Traumatic Conflict: Reclaiming Healing in Education*, Oxford: Oxford University Press.

Caroline "Carly" Manion

Sharpening Girls' and Women's Education Agenda: Gender Responsive and Gender Transformative Approaches

Keywords: gender responsive education, gender transformative education, broad-based school change, pedagogy, practice

For decades now girls' and women's education has been promoted by actors operating at global, regional, national, and local levels, with strategies dominantly informed by economic instrumentalist and/or human rights logics, and with education often framed as a key pathway to "empowerment" (Murphy-Graham and Lloyd 2016; Unterhalter 2007). A wide range of interventions are represented in the history of international education to achieve gender equality in and through education, with the earliest policies focused largely on increasing girls' and women's access to education. As gender parity (understood as equal boy/girl numbers) was achieved in terms of access/enrollment (largely in the primary and basic education sub-sectors), research and advocacy has highlighted gender-based problems and inequalities in the schooling *experiences* of differently positioned learners (see for example, Baily and Holmarsdottir 2015; Parkes et al. 2016).

In this short essay, I discuss and offer a summary overview of two interrelated approaches at the leading edge of efforts to advance change-oriented agendas for gender equality in and through education: gender responsive education (GSE) and gender transformative education (GTE). Reflections concerning the opportunities and challenges for GRE and GTE conclude the discussion.

Gender Responsive Education

GRE entails "Addressing the different situations, roles, needs, and interests of women, men, girls, and boys in the design and implementation of activities, policies, and programs" (Inter-agency Network for Education in Emergencies (INEE) 2019: 102). The Forum for African Women Educationalists (FAWE) has been a leader in developing gender responsive pedagogy training materials and curriculum for educators and educational leaders. And, while FAWE represents the first generation of gender responsiveness teacher training, other organizations, for example, Plan International and UNICEF, are also contributing in meaningful ways to this area of policy and practice.

In their toolkit for teachers and schools, the authors of the FAWE toolkit, led by Dowde et al. (FAWE 2005, 2018), frames the learning of gender responsiveness as a journey that begins with gender sensitivity: the ability to recognize gender issues and acknowledge gender norms, roles, and inequalities. Gender sensitivity is understood as the starting point for building gender awareness, described as, "The ability to identify problems arising from gender inequality and discrimination, even if these are not apparent on the surface" (Dowde et al. 2018: 12), Yet, neither gender sensitivity or gender awareness necessarily involve action to challenge and change the balance of power associated with dominant gender roles and norms; instead, the focus is on developing new understandings and new knowledge.

For FAWE, gender responsiveness refers to this next level, where action is taken to correct gender bias to help ensure and facilitate gender equity and gender equality (Dowde et al. 2018: 12). Gender responsive pedagogy is an approach to teaching and learning that recognizes boys, girls, trans, and gender diverse learners often have unique learning needs with these also relating to their different social locations (i.e., intersectionality considerations). Gender responsive pedagogy seeks to make teachers aware of gender and gendered expectations in schools but importantly does not end with awareness; instead, it calls on teachers to use their gender awareness to promote gender equality across all schooling dimensions, including, class organization and management, lesson planning, pedagogy, teaching and learning materials, and assessment.

Gender Transformative Education

GTE is an approach acknowledging the deeply ingrained gender inequalities of society and aims to address and change these disparities in and through education. GTE emphasizes conscientization, critical thinking, agency, inclusivity, and intersectionality as factors necessary to challenge traditional gender roles, stereotypes, and biases within educational systems and beyond. GTE "seeks to utilize all parts of an education system—from policies to pedagogies to community engagement—to transform stereotypes, attitudes, norms and practices by challenging power relations, rethinking gender norms and binaries, and raising critical consciousness about the root causes of inequality and systems of oppression" (UNICEF 2021: 6). Connecting with research and advocacy concerning the need to move beyond goals relating to girls' and women's *access* to education (Baily and Holmarsdottir 2015; Donville 2022), GTE calls for "equipping and empowering stakeholders—students, teachers, communities, and policymakers—to examine, challenge, and change harmful gender norms and imbalances of power that advantage boys and men over girls, women and persons of other genders" (UNICEF 2021: 6). Engagement of boys and men is critically important in gender transformative approaches as well, not only as framed as being "part of the problem" but also based on the idea that dominant and stereotypical gender norms hurt all people and constrain possibilities, including for boys and men. Hence, GTE stands to benefit not only girls and women, but also boys, men, and gender diverse people.

Together with Plan International, Transform Education, the United Nations Girls' Education Initiative (UNGEI), UNICEF published guidance on "how to do" GTE (UNICEF 2021). The theory of change is that transformations across seven focal areas are required to support the achievement of GTE goals: (1) policies and political engagement; (2) pedagogy; (3) school environment; (4) participation of children and young people (5) community leadership; (6) stakeholder engagement; and (7) evidence generation. This multi-prong roadmap for implementing GTE helps illustrate the ambitiousness of the project and its emphasis on holistic action (including multi-sector) and synergies across actors, sites, and activities. For example, applying a transformative intentionality in the participatory creation and adequate funding of relevant and sustainable policies across sectors, including education; training and support for effective adoption of gender responsive pedagogical approaches and teaching and learning materials; school infrastructure development; as well as changes to the organization and management of schools and classrooms; mobilizing communities, families, and learners in support of school and society-wide gender transformations; and the strengthening of participatory systems for ongoing monitoring and evaluation of transformative policy agendas and related knowledge production to inform policy development.

Conclusion: Challenges/Opportunities for Gender Transformative Education

The other side of most policy challenges are opportunities, and the case of GRE and GTE is no different—what may be seen as a challenge represents at the same time an opportunity for reasoned action toward the desired change. First, resistance from education system actors, learners, parents, and communities can affect implementation and sustainability of GRE and GTE policy and practice (UNFPA 2023; UNICEF 2021). Change-oriented and transformative approaches, be they related to gender or otherwise, aim to alter the status quo and the power dynamics and relations therein, thereby raising the risk of push-back against related goals, principles and practices (UNFPA 2023). For example, there may be resistance on the grounds that these new approaches represent the imposition of foreign ideas/ideals. Beyond building acceptance, understanding, and commitment to gender transformation in and through education, is the need for capacity-building and ongoing support for front-line actors such as teachers and school leaders responsible for implementing gender responsive and gender transformative policies and practices (Dowde et al. 2018; UNICEF 2021). Lastly, monitoring and evaluation of GRE and GTE policy and practice poses challenges related to measurement (e.g., what indicators to use, why and how) and the difficulties accompanying measuring social and cultural transformations, particularly given the slow speed of such changes as well as their unevenness (i.e., gender transformation may be more observable and advance more quickly in schools than in wider society).

Ultimately, GRE and GTE are marked by an intentionality to spur and facilitate broad-based change in gender norms and relations both inside and outside of school environments. It is such an intentionality that distinguishes these leading-edge approaches from earlier orientations that emphasized girls' and women's access to education, with little attention being given to what happens in schools. As change and action-oriented approaches, GRE and GTE hold much potential for addressing the root causes of gender-based inequalities, in and beyond schools.

References

Baily, S., and H. Holmarsdottir (2015), 'The Quality of Equity: Reframing Gender, Development, and Education in the Post-2020 Landscape', *Gender and Education*, 27 (7): 828–45.

Donville, J. (2022), 'Guidance Note: Gender Transformative Education and Programming', Plan International. Available online: https://plan-international.org/uploads/sites/28/2022/03/GLO-AOGD-IQE_Gender-Transformative-Education-and-Programming_ENG_2020-08.pdf

Dowde, C., A. Shell, V. Thamaini, and L. Trackman (2018), 'FAWE Gender Responsive Pedagogy: A Toolkit for Teachers and Schools', 2nd edn., *Forum for African Women Educationalists*. Available online: https://fawe.org/ (accessed August 14, 2023).

FAWE. (2005), *Gender Responsive School: The FAWE COE Model: A Handbook for Education Practitioners*, Nairobi: Forum for African Women Educationalists.

Inter-agency Network for Education in Emergencies (INEE) (2019), *Guidance Note: Gender Equality in and Through Education*, New York: INEE.

Murphy-Graham, E., and Lloyd, C. (2016), 'Empowering Adolescent Girls in Developing Countries: The Potential Role of Education', *Policy Futures in Education*, 14 (5): 556–77.

Parkes, J., J. Heslop, F. J. Ross, R. Westerveld, and E. Unterhalter (2016), *A Rigorous Review of Global Research Evidence on Policy and Practice on School-Related Gender-Based Violence*, New York: UNICEF.

UNFPA (2023), *Gender Transformative Approaches to Achieve Gender Equality and Sexual and Reproductive Health Rights. Technical Note*. UNFPA Mexico, Available online: https://www.unfpa.org/sites/default/files/pub-pdf/UNFPA_GTA-2023.pdf (accessed August 17, 2023).

UNICEF (2021), *Gender Transformative Education: Reimagining Education for a Just and Inclusive World*, New York: UNICEF. Available online: https://plan-international.org/uploads/2022/01/unicef_plan_ungei_te_gender_transformative_education_web_copy_10dec21.pdf (accessed August 16, 2023).

Unterhalter, E. (2007), 'Gender Equality, Education, and the Capability Approach', in Wiebke Kuklys (ed.), *Amartya Sen's Capability Approach and Social Justice in Education*, 87–107, New York: Palgrave Macmillan US.

Unterhalter, E. (2008), *Gender, Schooling and Global Social Justice*, New York: Routledge.

Fazal Rizvi

Geopolitical Shifts and Comparative Education

Keywords: geopolitical in education, marketization of education, (de)colonization, educational systems change, educational development

In this short paper, I want to argue that approaches to comparative education are inevitably shaped by geopolitical shifts, but in ways that are historically contingent and politically contested. Educational policies and practices are deeply affected by the ways we believe the world to be ordered, and the ways we would like it to be ordered. In this way, I point to the complex relationship between international relations and comparative education—of the need to understand to how geopolitical shifts influence our educational thinking, and how we describe systems of education around the world.

Geopolitics is a slippery and highly contested concept: it refers both to a set of practices and institutional arrangements as well as various discursive constructions. At its core however is the premise that geography plays an important role not only in determining the great power politics of international relations but also in shaping the conduct of citizens, corporations, international bodies, social movements, governments, as well as institutions including education.

The discourses of geopolitics thus involve attempts to understand how connections between place, the state and politics are affected by geographical arrangements, such as boundaries, coalitions, spatial networks, natural resources, and mobilities. These arrangements have the potential to redefine the ways in which political power is exercised, enforced, or undermined at both global and local levels. According to Dodds (2019), geopolitics involves three basic concerns: how questions of influence and power are shaped by spatial considerations; how geographical frames are helpful in making sense of global changes; and how this understanding can provide insights into the future behaviors of states, and their likely impact on individuals and institutions.

Traditionally, these concerns have been addressed through a realist lens (Dalby 2013). The realist approach to geopolitics assumes that the relations between nation-states are largely anarchical since there is no world government capable of restricting their actions. Hence, self-interest often drives the exercise of power in international relations, with nation-states as primary actors. The core function of nation-states is to provide security and protect the domestic space and its citizens from the threat of the chaotic international.

In this way, realism presupposes a binary between the *inside* (domestic, state) and the *outside* (chaotic, international). It assumes the relationship between nation-states to be inherently asymmetrical. It characterizes a stable global political space to be one in which chaos and anarchy is brought under a degree of control, either through various forms of strategic agreements between nations or through the dominance of some nations over others.

The critics of this approach (for example, Sharp 2009) argue that this realist view, states the extent of conflict and competition, and that the interstate system displays equally a capacity to collaborate, negotiate international law and work through intergovernmental bodies such as the European Union. Without denying the importance of nation-states, they insist moreover that nation-states are not the only actors in the configuration of geopolitics. The critical reading of geopolitics moreover refuses to see the world *as it supposedly is* but highlights instead the need to examine the relationship between geography and politics as ideologically constructed, "imbued with social and cultural meaning" (Dodds 2019: 34). It regards the relationship between place and politics as always contingent, complex, and contextually determined—and always ideologically framed.

From this critical perspective, we might ask how geopolitical shifts have historically affected the ways in which systems of education have been organized and how they have changed. We might note for example how before the Second World War, the spatial politics of colonialism largely created and fashioned the modern systems of education, as well as the relationship between them. Education systems operated within the registers of the geopolitical imagination of the colonizers. The colonial curriculum and pedagogic approaches were designed mostly to serve the empires, producing subjects that were loyal to their interests.

As various colonies began to gain political independence after the Second World War, the geopolitics of the world shifted markedly. Yet most of the colonial arrangements remained persistent, despite attempts to cultivate new nationalist forms (Fanon 1967). This persistence was due partly to the failure of the decolonized states to imagine new ways of thinking about the nature of knowledge and the role of their own education played in creating and transmitting it. Global inequalities resulting in the lack of resources also led them to turn to the economically developed countries, their former colonizers, for aid and development assistance to expand their systems of higher education, to create a knowledge and skills base necessary to realize their nationalist aspirations.

The developed nations in turn often portrayed foreign aid as their moral responsibility, even as it was strategically always a way of extending their political influence and commercial interests internationally. Additionally, this ideology of "developmentalism" (Escobar 1995) played an important role in the machinations of the Cold War, with higher education becoming aligned to the competing geopolitical interests. Both the Soviet Union and the United States, for example, sought to extend their geopolitical influence through scholarship programs offered to students in the developing countries, supposedly to prepare them to meet the requirements of national economic development (De Wit and Merkx 2012).

Since the end of the Cold War, this understanding of development persists to an extent, but is now tied to a view of geopolitics that has increasingly been shaped by modes of thinking associated with ideologies of free markets and liberal democracy. The neoliberal understanding of globalization has encouraged a new kind of political imagination that does not quite abandon the ideas of international cooperation and development assistance but augments them with perceptions of inter-state relations couched in commercial terms (Steger 2017).

These imaginaries highlight the benefits that can be derived from a global interconnected market economy. It is underpinned by organizational reforms such as globally stretched production, outsourcing, intercompany business, strategic alliances, clustering and diversification and technological innovations especially in the areas of information, communication, and transport. It promotes the formation of transnational networks to boost the production and distribution of goods and services, leading to the expansion of the movement of capital, goods, services and people, and the rapid development of high information technologies, telecommunication networks and intellectual capital (Rizvi and Lingard 2010).

These market ideologies have arguably become hegemonic, influencing almost all areas of human activity, including education. With the crisis of socialism on a global scale, there has been little competition to these ideologies. At the same time, intergovernmental organizations, global corporations, and other non-state actors have become highly influential. Around the turn of the century, the World Trade Organization, for example, negotiated rules to govern patterns of international trade, in goods and services alike to embed competition in most spheres of life. The work of intergovernmental agencies, such as the OECD and the World Bank and non-state actors such as foundations and think tanks are now major global carriers of neoliberal sentiments.

These shifts have clearly reconstituted the geopolitical space within which the nation-states now relate to each other, contributing to massive changes in almost all areas of social and economic relations in every region of the world. However, over the past two decades neoliberal imaginary has come under sustained attack for its failure to deliver on its promises of equity within and across nations. The global rise of Asia has transformed debates about geopolitics, leading to tensions that have had major implications for the possibilities of international collaboration in education (UNICEF 2019).

At the same time, geopolitics of the world is increasing shaped by the growing recognition of environmental crises and climate change; the changing forms of governance based on developments in datafication and artificial intelligence; the shifting modes of communication linked to the popular uses of the social media; the changing nature of work and labor relations; the growing awareness of geopolitical shifts; the increasing recognition of expanding social and economic inequalities; the revival of nationalism, populism and anti-globalization sentiments; and the growing levels of distrust in most of our key institutions, including higher education.

These developments of historic significance are transforming geopolitical relations, even if the neoliberal imaginary and institutions remain powerful. The geopolitical shifts they represent clearly demand rethinking the nature and scope of comparative and international education. The view of comparative education most aligned with this dynamic understanding of geopolitical shifts was proposed some two decades ago by Robert Cowen (2000), who underlined the importance of "reading the global" to describe its local expressions and challenges. He stressed the need to explore "moments of educational metamorphosis, rather than assuming that the equilibrium conditions and the dynamic linearities of development of educational systems can be predicted."

Further Reading

Cowen, R. (2000), 'Comparing Futures or Comparing Pasts?', *Comparative Education*, 36 (3): 333–42.

Dalby, S. (2013), 'Realism and Geopolitics', in K. Dodds, M. Kuus and J. Sharp, *The Ashgate Research Companion to Critical Geopolitics*, 33–47, Farnham: Ashgate Publishing.

De Wit, H. and G. Merkx (2012), 'The History of Internationalization of Higher Education', in D. Deardorff, H. de Wit, J. Heyl, and T. Adams (eds), *The SAGE Handbook of International Higher Education*, 43–59, Thousand Oaks: Sage.

Dicken, P. (2007), *Global Shift: Mapping the Changing Contours of the World Economy*, 5th edn, London: Sage.

Dodds, K. (2019), *Geopolitics: A Very Short Introduction*, Oxford: Oxford University Press.

Escobar, A. (1995), *Encountering Development: The Making and Unmaking of the Third World*, Princeton: Princeton University Press.

Fanon, F. (1967), *Black Skins, White Masks*, New York: Grove Press.

Rizvi, F. and B. Lingard (2010), *Globalizing Education Policy*, Routledge: New York.

Sharp, J. P. (2009), 'Critical Geopolitics', in A. Kobayashi, *International Encyclopedia of Human Geography*, 2nd edn, Oxford: ScienceDirect.

Steger, M. (2017), *Globalization: A Very Short Introduction*, 4th edn, 45–9, Oxford: Oxford University Press.

Karen Ross

The Implications of Commitments for Research Practice
Reflecting on a decade of research collaboration

Keywords: identity, positionality, relationship, Jewish, Palestinian

In this Illustration, I discuss my work of over a decade with *Sadaka Reut: Arab Jewish Youth Partnership*, a Jewish-Palestinian binational educational organization in Israel whose name means "friendship" in both Arabic and Hebrew. I focus on a few key questions that my partnership with Sadaka Reut has raised about research practice in comparative and international education scholarship, specifically as these relate to *identity* in research, and *relationships* in the scholarship we undertake.

Before moving into this discussion, it is important to give some context for the kind of educational organizations bringing together Israeli, Jewish, and Palestinian youth (both those who are citizens of Israel and those who are not). These organizations proliferated in the years following the signing of the Oslo Accords in 1993; by 2000 (following the outbreak of the Al-Aqsa Intifada or 2nd Intifada), many disappeared. Currently, in 2004, binational organizations in Israel, and all organizations bringing together Jews and Palestinians, face enormous difficulties in their work due to the political context.

That being said, the questions I emphasize here arose in the context of the scholarship I conducted with Sadaka Reut starting in 2010, during my doctoral studies, and continuing through 2020. As a Jewish-Israeli-American with a practitioner background in peacebuilding, I was interested in exploring, and wrote my dissertation (and first book) about, the long-term impact of programs in Israel bringing together Jewish and Palestinian citizens, with a comparative focus on Sadaka Reut and a second organization, Peace Child Israel (no longer active). I was particularly interested in organizations working within the State of Israel, where there are significant divisions between Jewish and Palestinian citizens that parallel but also differ from the divisions between Israelis and Palestinians in the West Bank and Gaza Strip. Sadaka Reut came into existence in the 1980s; this made it ideal for exploring the long-term impact of programming on alumni as well as changes in its own organizational approach over the years. Following my dissertation research, I continued collaborating with Sadaka Reut on several projects until Covid-19 made international travel impossible and led to a rethinking of my work with the organization.

Identity and positionality in research

Throughout my years of research with Sadaka Reut, I grappled with questions relating to *who I am in this work*, both in terms of how I am centered (or not) in the research I do, and in terms of how my identity claims show up in my scholarship. An important point here is that much of the research about dialogue and peace education in conflict has focused on short-term individual change (attitudinal and behavioral). However, given that they are meant to be fundamentally transformative, these kinds of programs cannot be understood solely based on pre-determined, researcher-created constructs. Thus, my research utilizes methodological approaches that center the *voices, experiences, and understandings* of those who work with and participate in Sadaka Reut programs. This comes from a desire to center the voices of those who take the time and make the effort to be part of research I undertook and is a way to focus on what matters to those who are *engaged in this work* rather than primarily what I, a researcher on the outside, decide might be important.

A second question my work with Sadaka Reut has raised relates to my positionality. I am a Jewish-Israeli-American, a tenured faculty member living in the United States, and a scholar doing research in a context where ethno-religious-national identity *really matters*. How I choose to present myself differs depending on who I am speaking with and can have significant implications for connections I form and the data co-generated with research participants. Before any meeting with a new research participant, I consider: does it make more sense to introduce myself as an American academic? As an Israeli living in the United States? Should I use Hebrew, or English, or halting Arabic as the basis for this interaction? I ask these questions because I realize that how I present myself shapes the kind of rapport I might build. Similarly, the importance of being transparent about identity in the context of interactions with others is something that I regularly reflect upon. How I present myself to my research participants shapes what they are willing to share, and thus the inferences I make about the meaning of their experiences. This has been true of all my research experiences, but none more so than when doing research in the context of intractable conflict.

Emphasizing relationships

Finally, my work with Sadaka Reut, since the start, has been characterized by a commitment to the relationships between myself and Sadaka Reut staff and to the organization. It is precisely because of the importance of these relationships, however, that in the last few years I have shifted away from continued scholarship with Sadaka Reut. At this stage of my life and career, I can only "fly in and fly out" of the region and am not able to keep up or deepen research-focused connections with the organization's staff, even as I maintain personal connections with them. This means the kind of work we did together—for instance, based on me having an ongoing presence in the organization's offices and the capacity to help meet organizational needs on a regular basis through my research—is no longer feasible. Of course, not every project requires this kind or level of ongoing relationships. But for me, relationships are central to enabling the kind of scholarship I feel is important: if maintaining them is not feasible, I question the potential value of the research I might do.

Ultimately, as a researcher doing work in contexts other than my own community, I think about the methodological implications for comparative and international research as situated in how I frame my dual commitments: to amplifying others and decentering myself, and to strong relationships with those at the focus of my scholarship. These commitments guide me in making choices both about *what* research I do, and about *how* I do it.

Further Reading

Razon, N., and Ross, K. (2012), 'Negotiating Fluid Identities: Alliance-Building in Qualitative Interviews', *Qualitative Inquiry*, 18 (6): 494–503.

Ross, K. (2013), 'Promoting Change Within the Constraints of Conflict: Case Study of Sadaka Reut in Israel', *Current Issues in Comparative Education*, 15 (2): 35–52.

Ross, K. (2014), 'Narratives of Belonging (and Not): Intergroup Contact in Israel and the Formation of Ethno-National Identity Claims', *International Journal of Intercultural Relations*, 42 (September): 38–52.

Ross, K. (2015), 'Quality as Critique: Promoting Critical Reflection Among Youth in Structured Encounter Programs', *Journal of Peace Education*, 12 (2): 117–37.

Ross, K. (2016), 'Peace-Building through Inter-Group Encounters: Rethinking the Contributions of "Mainstream" and "Politicized" Approaches', *Peacebuilding*, 4 (3): 317–30.
Ross, K. (2017), 'Making Empowering Choices: How Methodology Matters for Empowering Research Participants', *Forum: Qualitative Social Research*, 18 (3).
Ross, K. (2017), 'Untangling the Intervention-Context Dyad through Horizontal Comparison: Examples from Israeli Peacebuilding Organizations', *Comparative Education Review*, 61 (2): 327–53.
Ross, K. (2017), *Youth Encounter Programs in Israel: Pedagogy, Identity, and Social Change*, Syracuse: Syracuse University Press.
Ross, K. (2019), 'Becoming Activists: Jewish-Palestinian Encounters and the Mechanisms of Social Change Engagement', *Peace & Change: A Journal of Peace Research*, 44 (1): 33–67.
Ross, K. (2019), 'Navigating "Red Lines" and Transcending the Binary: Tensions in the Pedagogical and Political Goals of Peace Education Work', *Peace & Conflict Studies*, 26 (2).
Ross, K. (2020), 'Interrogating Impact: Whose Knowledge Counts in Assessment of Comparative & International Education Interventions?', in E. Anderson, S. Baily, M. Call-Cummings, R. Iyengar, C. Manion, P. Shah, and M. A. Witenstein (eds), *Interrogating and Innovating Comparative and International Education: Decolonizing Practices for Inclusive, Safe Spaces*, 49–63, Leiden: Brill Publishers.
Ross, K. (2022), 'Aspiring to Transformation: Solidarity and Prefiguration in Educational Social Movement Organizations', *In Factis Pax: Journal of Peace Education and Social Justice*, 16 (1): 1–25.

Kathan Shukla

Driving Educational Change Through Capacity-Building of Government School Leaders: A Case of India

Keywords: school leaders, capacity-building, educational quality, school climate, educational innovation

The last few decades have been transformational for India's school system. Rapid student enrollment expansion occurred, increasing from 22.3

million in 1990 (Govinda and Josephine 2004) to over 265.2 million in about 1.4 million schools in 2020-21 (UDISE data 2022). However, this formal school system expansion has not kept pace with improved quality of student educational experiences. There is a well-recognized concern of low student learning outcomes from primary to higher secondary levels across states. A recent educational outcomes survey indicates only 43 percent in grade eight can solve basic numerical division problems, and 25 percent leave without basic reading skills (ASER 2023). Although the poor learning dilemma is known to various stakeholders, most state governments seem to lack clear roadmaps for improving learning levels. At Ravi J. Matthai Centre for Educational Innovation (RJMCEI), Indian Institute of Management Ahmedabad (IIMA), we are working with several states (Andhra Pradesh, Delhi, Gujarat, Madhya Pradesh, Punjab, and Uttar Pradesh) primarily on school leaders' capacity-building in recent years. In this case study, I discuss our processes for our practice-cum-research for driving educational change in school systems. First, we share systemic contextual factors reinforcing lower levels of learning.

Learning Context in Government School System

As per the Constitution's 42nd amendment, education is on the concurrent list, indicating central and state governments' critical sectoral roles. Nonetheless, the public school system is mostly run by states, with the center providing regulatory mechanisms, intervening with centrally sponsored schemes per strategic requirements. With its limited capacity and resource constraints, the school system is highly centralized at the state level.

As shown in Figure KS1, state administrators are responsible for various school-level decisions. For making all these decisions, state officers often rely on data which could include enrollment rates, dropout rates, pass rates, absenteeism, number of beneficiaries in various state-schemes, and all these data by various socio-economic groups. To successfully make state-level decisions, their implementation and ensuring compliance are important. They rely on district and block level administrators, who in turn, bank on the heads of schools (HoS, i.e., principals, head teachers). In this context, the HoS is a teacher with all school administrative responsibilities. However, they have limited autonomy since many school-level decisions are taken by higher authorities. Often, HoS' conceptualization of a "good" school gets operationalized by outcomes higher authorities pay attention to.

Hence, educational quality is reduced to what gets measured at the school level because it is common to find HoS and teachers targeting only outcomes their authorities measure.

In total, numerous well-intentioned initiatives aimed at holistic education across various states face tremendous systemic resistance, with tunnel-view orientations on what gets measured (e.g., pass rates, enrollment and dropout rates). The overarching learning ecosystem is not immune to this reductionist educational practice. Students' educational assessment often consists of textbook-listed questions. A key to achieving high scores is

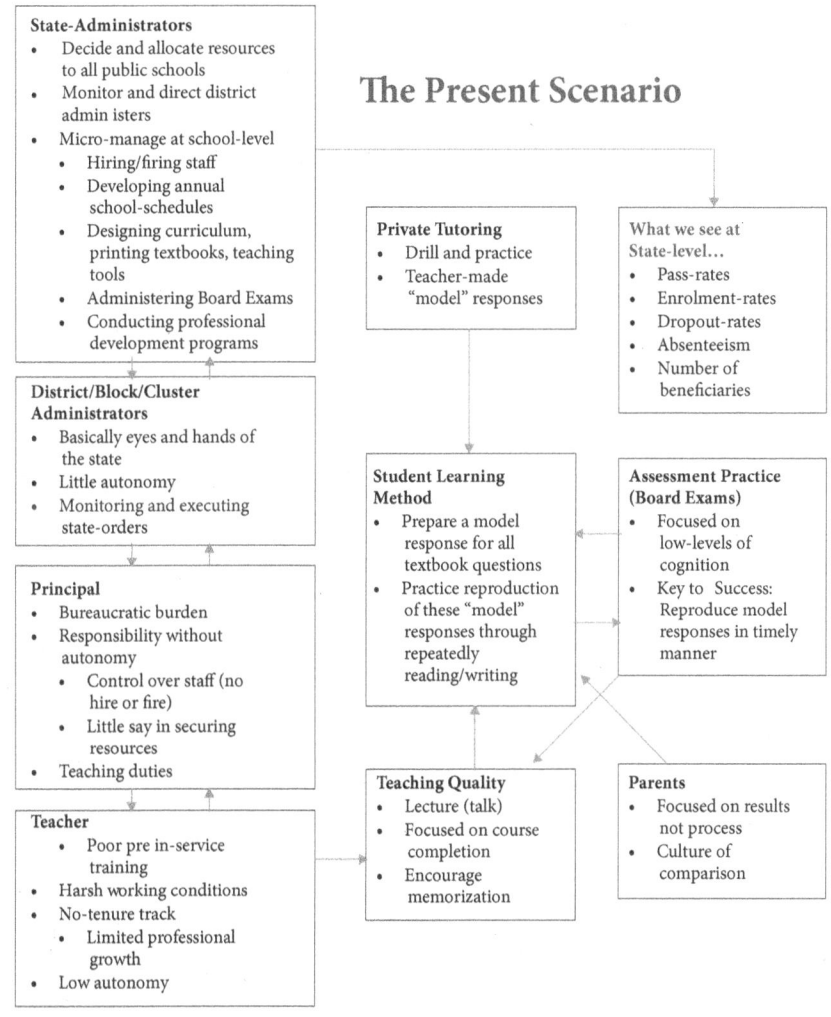

Figure KS1 Educational Ecosystem in Government Schools.

reproducing responses matching textbook wording. It is possible a student has understood the learning concepts well and reproduced a model response yet, they might reproduce the model response through memorization without understanding. Thus, higher test scores do not necessarily reflect deeper learning. In this learning context, teachers predominantly practice lecturing methods employing dictation exercises for helping students prepare model responses. Unfortunately, learning experiences continue to be dominated by rote/repetition practices, well-documented in the comparative educational literature (e.g., Chand et al. 2020; Clarke 2003).

Driving Educational Change Through School Leadership Capacity-Building

The above section helps understand the systemic inertia of teaching-learning practices in the government school system. Despite their control and decision-making powers, external stakeholders' influences are limited on what happens in classrooms. Therefore, educators within schools remain better positioned for improving students' learning experiences. Our research at RJMCEI suggests many public-school teachers continuously attempt to address poor-quality education challenges through practice-based innovations (Chand 2014; see http://www.inshodh.org/, a repository of thousands of teacher innovations in Indian public schools). Our assumption is for any positive deviance in the school system, educators within schools are more likely to develop mechanisms that could drive educational change. With this conviction, we have supported government school leaders' capacity-building in various states (e.g., Andhra Pradesh, Arunachal Pradesh, Delhi, Gujarat, Madhya Pradesh, and Punjab).

Our five-day face-to-face intervention focuses on these questions: (1) What should the definition of student success be, and what role can HoS play? (2) How do we scale-up educational innovations at the individual level by teachers and students? (3) How do we work with all school stakeholders to establish and maintain a positive social-emotional-academic climate? Employing the school climate theoretical framework we developed within RJMCEI (based on Cornell et al. 2015, 2016; Shukla et al. 2016; Shukla et al. 2020; Figure SK2), we designed sessions primarily on four dimensions (in the red boxes): (1) school leadership and management; (2) teaching-learning practices; (3) disciplinary practice; and (4) student support systems.

Improving Schooling Experience

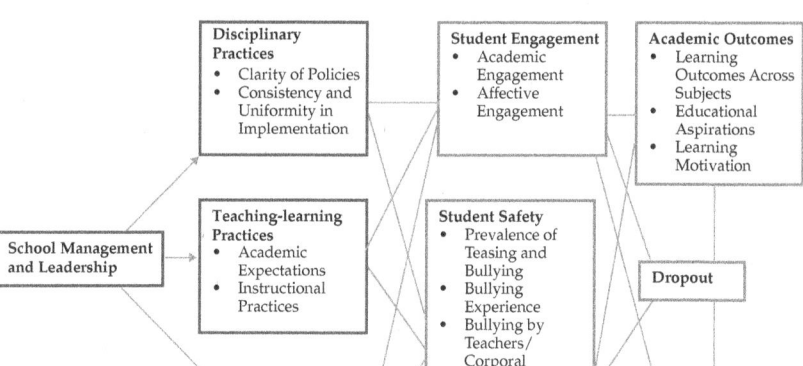

Figure KS2 School Climate Framework for Improving Holistic Schooling Experience.

HoS have control over all four dimensions, which can help improve a variety of student outcomes presented in green boxes (Figure KS2).

We explicitly state our expectation this is a leadership program without tailor-made solutions for their schools. They need to take the ownership for driving school transformation since they understand their school context. Accordingly, we equip them with student measures: (1) academic outcomes (e.g., academic engagement in school, educational aspirations, learning motivation and meta-cognitive strategies); and (2) psycho-social outcomes (e.g., academic stress, prevalence of teasing and bullying in school, emotional engagement with the school, perception of safety in schools, delinquent behaviors, depressive symptoms). The face-to-face intervention is followed by bi-monthly online meetings (1.5 hours) where typically four or five participants from a cohort of fifty are invited to present their school improvement initiatives.

The bigger challenge is scaling from individual school improvement to systemwide improvement. For this, we follow these steps: (1) documenting and studying the context-specific educational innovations executed by educators; (2) developing learning materials using educational innovation cases to be used for capacity-building throughout the state and across various levels (e.g., teachers, Head of Schools, block resource persons, and district officers); and (3) deploying the learning material in a structured, professional development program offered purely online or hybrid. One form of this model was implemented with over 160,000 educators from more than 33,000 schools in Gujarat between 2017 and 2020 (Chand et al. 2022).

For meaningful bottom-up systemwide turnaround, highly skilled specialists could be required at district-levels to cater to schools' needs. These specialists may include leadership developers, school psychologists/counselors, educational and psychological measurement specialists, policy evaluators, data managers, and infrastructure managers. In conclusion, India's school system is undergoing rapid transformations and there remains various bottlenecks. However, many champion educators make students' educational experiences meaningful within their school context. The school system can benefit from these individual-level educational innovations, but it needs: (1) measurement of operational definition of "high quality education" across levels; (2) gradual decentralization of decision-making at lower-levels of administration with serious capacity-building; and (3) effective balancing of capacity-building and accountability through data-driven decision-making.

References

ASER (2023), 'Annual Status of Education Report 2023: Beyond Basics', *Pratham, India*. Available online: https://asercentre.org/aser-2023-beyond-basics/ (accessed December 12, 2023).

Chand, V. S. (2014), 'Socio-educational Entrepreneurship Within the Public Sector: Leveraging Teacher-driven Innovations for Improvement', in A. W. Wiseman, *International Perspectives on Education*, vol. 23, 59–82, Leeds: Emerald Group Publishing Limited.

Chand, V. S., K. S. Deshmukh, and A. Shukla (2020), 'Why Does Technology Integration Fail? Teacher Beliefs and Content Developer Assumptions in an Indian Initiative', *Educational Technology Research and Development*, 68 (5): 2753–74.

Chand, V. S., S. Kuril, and K. S. Deshmukh (2022), *Teacher Development in India: Building on Grassroots Innovations and Technology*, New Delhi: Routledge.

Chand, V. S., S. Kuril, and A. Shukla (2020), 'Dialoguing with Teacher-educators, Valorizing Teacher Innovations', *London Review of Education*, 18 (3): 451–66.

Clarke, P. (2003), 'Culture and Classroom Reform: The Case of the District Primary Education Project, India', *Comparative Education*, 39 (1): 27–44.

Cornell, D., K. Shukla, and T. Konold (2015), 'Peer Victimization and Authoritative School Climate: A Multilevel Approach', *Journal of Educational Psychology*, 107 (4): 1186–201.

Cornell, D., K. Shukla, and T. R. Konold (2016), 'Authoritative School Climate and Student Academic Engagement, Grades, and Aspirations in Middle and High Schools', *AERA Open*, 2 (2): 1–18.

Govinda, R., and Y. Josephine (2004), *Para Teachers in India*, New Delhi: NIEPA.

Maun, D., V. S. Chand, and K. D. Shukla (2023), 'Influence of Teacher Innovative Behaviour on Students' Academic Self-Efficacy and Intrinsic Goal Orientation', *Educational Psychology*, 43 (6): 679–97.

Shukla, K., T. Konold, and D. Cornell (2016), 'Profiles of Student Perceptions of School Climate: Relations with Risk Behaviors and Academic Outcomes', *American Journal of Community Psychology*, 57 (3–4): 291–307.

Shukla, K. D., S. Kuril, and V. S. Chand (2020), 'Does Negative Teacher Behavior Influence Student Self-Efficacy and Mastery Goal Orientation?', *Learning and Motivation*, 71.

Sriprakash, A. (2010), 'Child-Centered Education and the Promise of Democratic Learning: Pedagogic Messages in Rural Indian Primary Schools', *International Journal of Educational Development*, 30 (3): 297–304.

UDISE Data (2022), 'Report on Unified District Information System for Education Plus 2021–22', *Government of India: Ministry of Education*. Available online: https://www.education.gov.in/sites/upload_files/mhrd/files/statistics-new/udise_21_22.pdf (accessed November 21, 2023).

Matthew A. M. Thomas

New Approaches in Teacher Education, and New Ways to Research Them

Keywords: teacher education, alternative teacher education, comparative teacher education, empirical decision-making, Teach for All

Researchers have been concerned with the education and preparation of teachers for decades. Yet, the emergence of new approaches to teacher education has raised critical questions about how to study them. Historically, most teachers were prepared in university-based "traditional" teacher education programs, wherein graduates completed several years of coursework in educational foundations, curricular content, and teaching methods, and engaged in practice teaching through prolonged and supported practicum experiences in schools. In recent decades, however, teachers entering the profession are increasingly completing so-called alternative teacher education programs, which vary widely but often have distinguishing features such condensed periods of preparation, partnerships beyond universities, or emphases on particular types of teachers, such military veterans (see Thomas and Baxendale 2022; Thomas and Boivin 2023).

Programs associated with the Teach For All (TFAll) organization serve as a prime but not the only example of alternative teacher education. These programs are based largely on Teach for America, which since 1990 has sought to recruit the best and brightest individuals into teaching, prepare them through condensed training model, then place them to teach for two years in underperforming schools. Although these programs are now commonplace across approximately sixty countries, their proliferation has raised both considerable controversy and challenging questions for researchers.

For instance, many researchers have sought to understand the effectiveness of these teachers: Are they more or less effective than other teachers? (e.g., Clark and Isenberg 2020; Redding and Henry 2019) But even this seemingly simple question sparks a number of related questions. Which cohort of teachers are best for comparison—teachers who completed a university-based teacher education program, teachers who completed other alternative teacher education programs, or both? Or which teaching subjects or grades/years should be compared? Is it appropriate to compare teachers across states or provinces within a country, or teaching effectiveness outcomes across countries?

Beyond studies of teaching effectiveness, some researchers have explored the experiences of TFAll teachers. What are their perceptions of the program? How do they understand their work as novice teachers? These studies might occur within a single national context—China (Lam 2019) or Lebanon (Nimer and Makkouk 2021), for example—or compare the experiences of TFAll teachers across two or more countries, such as New Zealand and the United States (Crawford-Garrett et al. 2021). Other researchers have compared TFAll teachers' understandings of education and professionalism with teachers completing a more traditional teacher education program in the very same higher education institution (see Southern 2021). Researchers examining the experiences and perspectives of TFAll teachers nonetheless have a range of methodological decisions to make, including what methods to employ (e.g., interviews, focus groups, participatory action research), when to collect data (i.e., once, multiple times, at set intervals), and how to analyze the data (thematic analysis, poststructural analysis, etc.).

Researchers have also explored the discourses produced by TFAll. As a large transnational network, TFAll and its national programs utilize a wide variety of communication platforms for various purposes, enabling researchers to analyze the discourses it promotes. To date researchers have compared the websites of TFAll programs (Blumenreich and Gupta 2015; Lefebvre et al. 2022), analyzed their Facebook pages and Twitter accounts (Adhikary et al. 2018; Friedrich et al. 2015), and even examined YouTube videos associated with the TFAll Talks series (Straubhaar 2021). Again, selecting which texts to examine and how to collect and organize the data—to say nothing of the theoretical lenses brought to bear—reflect key decisions made by the researchers.

Lastly, researchers have understandably been interested in how these programs and ideas flow through global networks across contexts as well as the different policy environments that enable or constrain their emergence and impact. To address these issues, researchers have commonly drawn on innovative methodologies such as network ethnography that seek to combine methods such as interviews and focus groups, participant observations in digital and in-person spaces, social network analyses, and more. While many of these studies center on a particular national context—such as Australia (Rowe 2023), India (Subramanian 2018), Taiwan (Thomas and Xu 2023), or the United Kingdom (Olmedo et al. 2013)—they typically maintain a globalized lens recognizing the powerful roles played by transnational actors and the complex ways policies are initiated, spread, and contextualized within and beyond national boundaries. Accounting for these issues remains a critical concern for researchers in the field of comparative and international education.

So, what does all this mean? Well for one, it means the TFAll phenomenon is immensely compelling, though in fairness I may be a bit biased! On a deeper level, this brief discussion of the TFAll phenomenon as a research topic exemplifies many of the difficult decisions made by researchers who want to conduct research in comparative and international education.

First, there are issues related to which aspect of the phenomenon to study, such as teaching effectiveness, teachers' perspectives, etc. Second, there are decisions concerning the context(s) to be studied. Whereas issues of commensurability emerge in comparative studies; issues of access, ethics, and local knowledge emerge in international studies, and often domestic studies, too. Third, application of various methodologies and methods requires careful deliberation, as do the analytical approaches and theories employed to help understand and explain the phenomenon. There are perhaps other decisions to be made as well, but the broader points are that engaging in research within comparative and international education can be an immensely complex (though fascinating and worthwhile) endeavor, and that seemingly simple phenomena such as Teach for All can be studied in a wide variety of ways.

References

Adhikary, R. W., B. Lingard, and I. Hardy (2018), 'A Critical Examination of Teach for Bangladesh's Facebook Page: "Social-mediatisation" of Global Education Reforms in the "Post-truth" Era', *Journal of Education Policy*, 33 (5): 632–61.

Blumenreich, M., and A. Gupta (2015), 'The Globalization of Teach for America: An Analysis of the Institutional Discourses of Teach for America and Teach for India within Local Contexts', *Teaching and Teacher Education*, 48 (May): 87–96.

Clark, M. A., and E. Isenberg (2020), 'Do Teach For America Corps Members Still Improve Student Achievement? Evidence from a Randomized Controlled Trial of Teach For America's Scale-Up Effort', *Education Finance and Policy*, 15 (4): 736–60.

Crawford-Garrett, K., S. Oldham, and M. A. M. Thomas (2021), 'Maintaining Meritocratic Mythologies: Teach For America and Ako Mātātupu: Teach First New Zealand', *Comparative Education*, 57 (3): 360–76.

Friedrich, D., M. Walter, and E. E. Colmenares (2015), 'Making all Children Count: Teach For All and the Universalizing Appeal of Data', *Education Policy Analysis Archives*, 23 (48).

Lam, S. (2019), *From Teach for America to Teach for China: Global Teacher Education Reform and Equity in Education*, London: Routledge.

Lefebvre, E. E., S. Pradhan, and M. A. M. Thomas (2022), 'The Discursive Utility of the Global, Local, and National: Teach For All in Africa', *Comparative Education Review*, 66 (4): 620–42.

Nimer, M., and N. Makkouk (2021), 'Bringing a Global Model to the Lebanese Education Context: Adaptation or Adoption?', in M. A. M. Thomas, E. R. Rauschenberger, and K. Crawford-Garrett (eds), *Examining Teach For All: International Perspectives on a Growing Global Network*, 96–114. Abingdon: Routledge.

Olmedo, A., P. L. Bailey, and S. J. Ball (2013), 'To Infinity and Beyond …: Heterarchical Governance, the Teach for All Network in Europe and the Making of Profits and Minds', *European Educational Research Journal*, 12 (4): 492–512.

Redding, C., and G. T. Henry (2019), 'Leaving School Early: An Examination of Novice Teachers' Within-and end-of-year Turnover', *American Educational Research Journal*, 56 (1): 204–36.

Rowe, E. (2023), 'Policy Networks and Venture Philanthropy: A Network Ethnography of "Teach for Australia"', *Journal of Education Policy*, 39 (1): 1–19.

Southern, A. (2020). 'Teach First Cymru: Whose Mission? Teach First and the Welsh Government's 'National Mission' for Education', in K. Crawford-Garrett et al. (eds), *Examining Teach For All*, 179–99). London: Routledge.

Straubhaar, R. (2021), 'Unpacking Teach For All's Conceptualisation of Leadership Through the "Teach For All Talks" Series', in M. A. M. Thomas, E. Rauschenberger, and K. Crawford-Garrett, *Examining Teach For All: International Perspectives on a Growing Global Network*, 243–64, London: Routledge.

Subramanian, V. K. (2018), 'From Government to Governance: Teach for India and New Networks of Reform in School Education', *Contemporary Education Dialogue*, 15 (1): 21–50.

Thomas, M. A. M., and H. Baxendale (2022), 'Wendy Kopp', in B. Geier (ed.), *The Palgrave Handbook of Educational Thinkers*, 1–16, Cham: Palgrave Macmillan.

Thomas, M. A. M., and K. Boivin, 'Teaching and Teacher Education: An Overview of Sociological Perspectives', in C. Maxwell, M. Yemini, and L. Engel (eds), *Educational Foundations, Sociological Foundations of Education*, vol. 3, London: Bloomsbury Publishing.

Thomas, M. A. M., and R. -Hao Xu (2023), 'The Emergence and Policy (Mis) alignment of Teach For Taiwan', *Journal of Education Policy*, 38 (4): 686–709.

Christina Yao and Chrystal A. George Mwangi

International Students and Education Abroad—Whether in Global or Virtual Engagements

Keywords: global education, international students, diversity, internationalization, racial (in)equity, equity audit

Opening up

As a senior international officer, you recently attended a professional development webinar on diversity, equity, and inclusion (DEI) within internationalization. You participated because you want to address race, racism, and racial (in)equity within international education at your university given recent challenges in these areas. For example, during the height of Covid-19, the front wall of the International Student Center was graffitied with the words "Kung Flu U." and since then, you have seen increased numbers of East Asian international students reporting experiences with racism and nativism on campus and in town. Additionally, the Education Abroad staff recently circulated a report of their upcoming programs, and you noticed that all the research-related programs were to Europe and Australia, while all of the service-related programs were to Africa, Latin America, and the Caribbean. Additionally, there were not any faculty-led programs being led by faculty of Color. You believe these and other examples in your international education office are interconnected and situated within the context of race, racism, and equity. You want to engage in efforts to acknowledge and address racial (in)equity but are not sure where to start. You also want to ensure any efforts go beyond performativity and a "band-aid" approach.

Historical and Contemporary Context

Global education and DEI campus efforts visibly intersected in 2020. During the Covid-19 pandemic, the global health crisis spurred more visibility of anti-Asian sentiments due to the perceived origin of the virus in China. Additionally, the murders of George Floyd, Ahmaud Arbery, and Breonna Taylor triggered a global racial reckoning and illumination of the pervasiveness of anti-Blackness around the world. These racial issues, and many others, affect all aspects of global education, including international student support and education abroad. As a result, interest in the intersections of global education and campus DEI have become a priority in more recent years.

Historically, international education and campus diversity efforts were often considered to be parallel topic areas with regard to campus priorities. For example, international students were often essentialized into one homogenous group despite their diversity of national origin, language, and other identities. University administrators in global education offices focused on supporting international students and students studying abroad, often with an emphasis on compliance, whereas staff in campus diversity offices concentrated their efforts on US domestic students. Thus, university administrators have recently been grappling with the question of where and how to start moving towards an equity approach to ensure meaningful change in global higher education.

Theoretical and practical perspectives from the field

Growing scholarship demonstrates that internationalization practices are situated within systems of oppression and can reify Western hegemony, neoliberal ideologies, and structural racism (see Buckner and Stein 2020; Castiello-Gutiérrez and Gozik 2022; Lee 2021; Stein and de Andreotti 2016). Given this context, the senior international officer (SIO) in this case should consider the equity-driven lens for higher education internationalization (George Mwangi and Yao 2021) as a framework for informing next steps. This framework has four lenses that magnify the (in)equity present within internationalization.

The first lens focuses on *constructing and deconstructing internationalization*, which will support the SIO in questioning "what counts?" and "who counts?" as internationalization. This lens considers what is made visible or invisible, center or periphery, and possible or impossible by existing internationalization terminology, structures, processes, partnerships, and initiatives. In considering the education abroad programs within this case, a narrow definition of knowledge and the perception that the Majority World should be knowledge receivers, while the United States as part of the

Minority World should be knowledge bringers (George Mwangi 2017), can influence how education abroad programs are designed.

The second lens is *defining the sociohistorical context*, which highlights that internationalization cannot be divorced from historical events and ideologies. It is evident that the US historical context of racism continues to impact campus spaces and since the early nineteenth century, East Asians in the United States have been blamed for causing various forms of educational and economic competition, disease, and immorality (Yao and George Mwangi 2022). Referred to as the Yellow Peril, this fear and mistrust of Asian individuals draws parallels to the racist-nativist treatment of East Asian international students during the pandemic as highlighted in this case.

The next lens, *connecting to contemporary forces of globalization*, highlights that campus internationalization does not exist in a vacuum, but rather is linked to the pushes and pulls of global structures, systems, and ideologies. Within this case, contemporary neoliberal pressures to produce scholarship, rather than focus on student engagement, can act as a barrier to faculty of Color leading education abroad programs. Moreover, given racial inequity, faculty of Color also experience greater demands for their service, which often goes unrecognized (Johnson et al. 2018) and can make leading an education abroad program untenable.

The final lens focuses on *integrating equity-driven conceptual and theoretical perspectives*, which can enable the SIO to more clearly see, critique and disrupt inequity and marginalization that occurs within internationalization, as well as to identify and engage in resistance of inequity and (re)imagining of internationalization. While this could include formal theory or frameworks like the equity-driven lens for internationalization, being reflective of one's own experiences, positioning and perspectives can also be powerful in identifying the assumptions and beliefs that guide one's understanding of how internationalization should be enacted.

Ideate and debate

We offer several considerations below for those who want to begin infusing an equity perspective in global higher education. Although this case study is from the perspective of the SIO, there are multiple stakeholders involved in advancing equity in global higher education on campus; thus, the considerations below are for all members of the campus community. As part of the movement towards equity, we offer some preliminary suggestions for consideration:

- Taking an equity audit of all programs, policies, and practices in global education offices.
- What have been the priorities of the office from a historical perspective?
- What are practices that are "hidden," with assumptions that everyone just "gets it"?
- Where are resources (financial and people efforts) being used in the office and what could be re/allocated to equity efforts?
- Partnering across and beyond campus: Who are campus partners and who should be included in these conversations of equity?
- How can you go beyond expected offices/departments to partner with?
- How can you leverage the knowledge in other international educators, perhaps through networking in national associations?
- Considering global forces affecting the local campus
- What is happening around the world that is affecting the decisions being made in the office?
- What are equity issues that affect participation in global education?

References

Buckner, E., and S. Stein (2020), 'What Counts as Internationalization? Deconstructing the Internationalization Imperative', *Journal of Studies in International Education*, 24 (2): 151–66.

Castiello-Gutiérrez, S., and N. J. Gozik (2022), 'Decolonizing Education Abroad: Grounding Theory in Practice', in N. J. Gozik and H. B. Hamir (eds), *A House Where all Belong: Redesigning Education Abroad for Inclusive Excellence*, 183–202, Carlisle: Forum of Education Abroad.

George Mwangi, C. A. (2017), 'Partner Positioning: Examining International Higher Education Partnerships Through a Mutuality Lens', *Review of Higher Education*, 41 (1): 33–60.

George Mwangi, C. A. and C. W. Yao (2021), 'U.S. Higher Education Internationalization Through an Equity Driven Lens: An Analysis of Concepts, History, and Research', in L. W. Perna (ed.), *Higher Education: Handbook of Theory and Research*, 549–609, Cham: Springer.

Johnson, J. M., G. M. Jones, C. A. George Mwangi, and G. A. Garcia (2018), 'Resisting, Rejecting, and Redefining the Professoriate: Faculty of Color in Higher Education', *The Urban Review*, 50 (4): 630–47.

Lee, J. J., ed. (2021), *U.S.Power in International Higher Education*, New Brunswick: Rutgers University Press.

Stein, S., and V. O. de Andreotti (2016), 'Cash, Competition, or Charity: International Students and the Global Imaginary', *Higher Education*, 72 (2): 225–39.

Yao, C. W., and C. A. George Mwangi (2022), 'Yellow Peril and Cash Cows: The Social Positioning of Asian International Students in the USA', *Higher Education*, 84 (5): 1027–44.

Illustrations/Case Studies Contributors' Affiliation

Education Finance, Equality and Equity
Iris BenDavid-Hadar

Professor, Educational Policy and Finance, Department of Educational Leadership, Administration and Policy Studies

Bar Ilan University, Ramat Gan, Israel

Internationalization and Global Education
Gerardo L. Blanco

Associate Professor and Academic Director, Center for International Higher Education

Boston College, Boston, MA, USA

Affect Theory and its Contribution to Comparative Education
Irving Epstein

Ben and Susan Rhodes Endowed Professor in Peace and Justice, Chair of Ed Studies, Director of the Center for Human Rights

Illinois Wesleyan University, Bloomington, IL, USA

Sharpening Girls' and Women's Education Agenda: Gender Responsive and Gender Transformative Approaches
Caroline "Carly" Manion

Associate Professor, Teaching Stream, Director, Comparative, International and Development Education (CIDE) Director of related research center (CIDEC).

University of Toronto, Toronto, Canada

Geopolitical Shifts and Comparative Education

Fazal Rizvi

Emeritus Professor of Global Studies in Education

University of Melbourne, Melbourne, Australia

The Implications of Commitments for Research Practice

Karen Ross

Associate Professor and Director, Graduate Programs in Conflict Resolution

University of Massachusetts Boston, Boston, MA, USA

Driving Educational Change Through Capacity-Building of Government School Leaders: A Case of India

Kathan Shukla

Associate Professor, Ravi J. Matthai Centre for Educational Innovation

Indian Institute of Management Ahmedabad, Ahmedabad, India

New Approaches in Teacher Education, and New Ways to Research Them

Matthew A. M. Thomas

Senior Lecturer, International and Comparative Education, School of Education

University of Glasgow, Glasgow, Scotland

International Students and Education Abroad— Whether in Global or Virtual Engagements

Christina Yao

Associate Professor and Educational Leadership Ph.D. Program Coordinator

University of South Carolina, Columbia, SC, USA

and

Chrystal A. George Mwangi

Associate Professor, Higher Education Program

George Mason University, Fairfax, VA, USA

References

Adams, D. (1977), 'Development Education', *Comparative Education Review*, 21 (2/3): 296–310.

Adams, D. (1988), 'Extending the Educational Planning Discourse: Conceptual and Paradigmatic Explorations', *Comparative Education Review*, 32 (4): 400–15.

Adams, D. K. (n.d.), *Faculty Files*, University Archives, Archives & Special Collections, University of Pittsburgh Library System, Pittsburgh, PA. Available online: https://historicpittsburgh.org/islandora/object/pitt:US-PPiU-uapersonalfiles

Adams, D., and Adams, J. (1968), 'Education and Social Development', *Review of Educational Research*, 38 (3): 243–63.

Adams, D., and Gottlieb, E. E. ([1993] 2017), *Education and Social Change in Korea.*, 2nd edn. London: Routledge.

Albó, X. (2018), 'Suma Qamaña or Living Well Together: A Contribution to Biocultural Conservation', in R. Rozzi et al. (eds), *From Biocultural Homogenization to Biocultural Conservation. Ecology and Ethics*, 333–42, vol 3. Springer, Cham. https://doi.org/10.1007/978-3-319-99513-7_21

Aljabreen, H., (2017), 'A Comparative Multi-Case Study of Teacher Roles in U.S. Montessori Preschool and Saudi Public Preschool', PhD Dissertation, Kent State University, Ohio USA, May 2017.

Altbach, P. (1971), 'Education and Neocolonialism: A Note', *Comparative Education Review*, 15 (2): 237–9.

Altbach, P. (2004), 'Globalisation and the university: Myths and realities in an unequal world,' *Tertiary Education and Management*, 10 (1): 3–25. http://dx.doi.org/10.1080/13583883.2004.9967114

Altbach, P. (2013), 'Brain Drain or Brain Exchange: Developing Country Implications', *International Higher Education*, (72): 2–4.

Altbach, P. G. (1977), 'Servitude of the Mind?: Education, Dependency, and Neocolonialism', *Teachers College Record*, 79 (2): 1–11.

Amin, S. (1990), *Delinking: Towards a Polycentric World*, London: Bloomsbury.

Anderson, C. A. (1961), 'Methodology of Comparative Education', *International Review of Education*, 7 (1): 1–23.

Anderson, G. L. (1989), 'Critical Ethnography in Education: Origins, Current Status, and New Directions', *Review of Educational Research*, 59 (3): 249–70.

Anderson, K. et al. (2023), 'A Systematic Methods Review of Photovoice Research with Indigenous Young People', *International Journal of Qualitative Methods*, 22. https://doi.org/10.1177/16094069231172076

Anderson-Levitt, K. (2003), *Local Meanings, Global Schooling: Anthropology and World Culture Theory*, New York: Palgrave.

Apple, M. W. (1979), *Ideology and Curriculum*. London: Routledge.

Apple, M. W. (1996), *Cultural Politics and Education*, New York: Teachers College Press.

Arnove, R. F., ed. (1980), *Philanthropy and Cultural Imperialism: The Foundations at Home and Abroad*, Bloomington: Indiana University Press.

Aronowitz, S., and H. A. Giroux (1985), *Education Under Siege: The Conservative, Liberal, and Radical Debate Over Schooling*. Hadley: Bergin & Garvey Publishers.

Arora, Payal, (2019), *The Next Billion Users: Digital Life Beyond the West*, Boston: Harvard University Press.

Arora, P. A. et al. (2022), *The Digital Leisure Divide and the Forcibly Displaced*, Rotterdam: UNHCR Innovation Services. Joint Report with Erasmus University.

Artopoulos, A. (2023), 'Knowledge Economy Meets Development Imaginaries', in R. J. Tierney, F. Rizviand, and K. Erkican (eds), *International Encyclopedia of Education*, 280–9, Amsterdam: Elsevier.

Asher, W., and J. E. Shively (1969), 'The Technique of Discriminant Analysis: A Reclassification of Harbison and Myers' Seventy-five Countries', *Comparative Education Review*, 13 (2): 180–6.

Assié-Lumumba, N. T. (2016), 'Evolving African Attitudes to European Education Resistance, Pervert Effects of the Single System and the Ubuntu Framework for Renewal', *International Review of Education*, 62 (1): 11–27.

Backer, D. I. (2021), 'History of the Reproduction-Resistance Dichotomy in Critical Education: The Line of Critique Against Louis Althusser, 1974–1985', *Critical Education*, 12 (6): 1–21.

Baghiu, Ş. (2019), 'Translating Hemispheres: Eastern Europe and the Global South Connection Through Translationscapes of Poverty', *Comparative Literature Studies*, 56 (3): 487–503.

Baimukhamedova, Z. (2022), 'The Eye of the Beholder: Applying Visual Analysis in an Historical Study of Lynxes' Representations in the Bavarian Forest Region Zhanna', in A. Franklin (ed.), *Co-Creativity and Engaged Scholarship: Transformative Methods in Social Sustainability Research*, 299–355, London: Palgrave Macmillan.

Baran, M. L., ed. (2016), *Mixed Methods Research for Improved Scientific Study*. Hershey, Pennsylvania: IGI Global publisher.

Bartlett, L., and F. Vavrus (2009), 'Introduction Knowing, Comparatively', in F. Vavrus and L. Bartlett (eds), *Critical Approaches to Comparative*

Education: Vertical Case Studies From Africa, Europe, the Middle East, and the Americas, 1–18, New York: Palgrave Macmillan US.

Bartlett, L., and F. Vavrus (2017), *Rethinking Case Study Research: A Comparative Approach*. New York: Routledge.

Bartlett, L., and Vavrus, F. (2019), 'Rethinking the concept of "context" in comparative research', in R. Gorur, S. Sellar, and G. Steiner-Khamsi (eds), *World Yearbook of Education 2019: Comparative Methodology in the Era of Big Data and Global Networks*, 185–202, Routledge.

Beck, U., and E. Grande (2010), 'Varieties of Second Modernity: The Cosmopolitan Turn in Social and Political Theory and Research', *The British Journal of Sociology*, 61: 409–43. https://doi.org/10.1111/j.1468-4446.2010.01320.x

Beech, J., M. A. Larsen, and W. Wei (2024), 'Stretching Spatial Theories in Comparative Education: New Approaches for Challenging Times', *Comparative Education Review*, 61 (2): 183–201. https://doi.org/10.1080/03050068.2024.2366760

Bhattacharjea, S., and E. J. Byker (2017), 'The ASER (Translating Policy into Practice) Toolkit: From Participatory Action Research to Evidence-Based Action', in H. Kidwai et al. (eds), *Participatory Action Research and Educational Development. South Asian Education Policy, Research, and Practice*, 75–96, New York: Palgrave Macmillan.

Bilgen, A., A. Nasir, and J. Schöneberg (2021), 'Why Positionalities Matter: Reflections on Power, Hierarchy, and Knowledges in "Development" Research', *Canadian Journal of Development Studies*, 42 (4): 519–36.

Blake, N. (1996), 'Between Postmodernism and Anti-Modernism: The Predicament of Educational Back', *British Journal of Educational Studies*, 44 (1): 42–65.

Blanco, G. L., L. E. Rumbley, and H de Wit (2021), 'Rankings and Internationalization: An Unfortunate Alliance', in E. Hazelkorn and G. Mihut (eds), *Research Handbook on University Rankings*, 137–49, Northampton: Edward Elgar Publishing.

Blumer, H. (1969), *Symbolic Interactionism: Perspective and Method*, Englewood Cliffs: Prentice-Hall.

Bodkin-Andrews, G. and Carlson, B. (2016), 'The legacy of racism and Indigenous Australian identity within education', *Race Ethnicity and Education*, 19 (4): 784–807, DOI: 10.1080/13613324.2014.969224

Boli, J., F. O. Ramirez, and J. W. Meyer (1985), 'Explaining the Origins and Expansion of Mass Education', *Comparative Education Review*, 29 (2): 145–70.

Bonala, X., C. Fontdevilab, and A. Zancajo (2013), 'The World Bank and Education in a Changing Global Arena,' in R. Tierney, F. Rizvi, and K. Ercikan (eds), *International Encyclopedia of Education*, 4th edn, 480–7, Amsterdam: Elsevier Science

Bond, P. (2023), 'BRICS: An Anti-Imperialist Fantasy and Sub-Imperialist Reality?', *CADTM* 9 October. Available online: https://www.cadtm.org/Patrick-Bond-political-economist-Professor

Boroughs, Don. (2015, March 28). 'Why South African Students Say The Statue Of Rhodes Must Fall.' NPR. Retrieved from NPR website.

Bourdieu, P., and J. -C. Passeron, (1977), *Reproduction in Education, Society and Culture*, London: Sage Publications Ltd.

Bowles, S., and H. Gintis (1976), *Schooling in Capitalist America: Educational Reform and the Contradictions of Economic Life*, New York: NY Basic Books.

Bowman, M. J. (1966), 'The Human Investment Revolution in Economic Thought,' *Sociology of Education*, 39 (2): 111–37.

Bowman, M. J. (1969), 'Economics of Education', *Review of Educational Research*, 39 (5): 641–70. https://doi.org/10.3102/00346543039005641

Braidotti, R. (2019), 'A Theoretical Framework for the Critical Posthumanities', *Theory, Culture & Society*, 36 (6): 31–61. https://doi.org/10.1177/0263276418771486

Braun, A. M. B. (2021), 'Being Seen and Heard: Using Photovoice Methodology in Inclusive Education Research', in M. J. Schuelka and S. Carrington (eds), *Global Directions in Inclusive Education: Conceptualizations, Practices, and Methodologies for the 21st Century*, London: Routledge.

Breen, L. J. (2007), 'The Researcher "in the Middle": Negotiating the Insider/Outsider Dichotomy', *The Australian Community Psychologist*, 19 (1): 163–74.

Bristow, T. (1965), 'The University of London Research Library for Comparative Education in the Institute of Education', *Comparative Education Review*, 9 (2): 213–18.

Brown, R., and M. Schweisfurth (2024), 'Making Context Matter Through Massey's Relational Space: Methodological and Theoretical Implications for Comparative and International Education', *Comparative Education Review*, 68 (3): 469–88.

Brown, R. H. (1987), *Society as Text: Essays on the Rhetoric, Reason, and Reality*, Chicago: University of Chicago Press.

Burrell, G., and G. Morgan (1979), *Sociological Paradigms and Organizational Analysis*, London: Heinemann Educational Books.

Call-Cummings, M., C. Manion, and P. P. Shah (2019), 'Interrogating and Innovating CIE Research: Setting the Stage', in C. Manion et al. (eds), *Interrogating and Innovating Comparative and International Education Research*, The Netherlands: Brill.

Campbell, H. J., and D. Vanderhoven (2016), *Knowledge that Matters: Realising the Potential of Co-production*. Manchester: N8 Research Partnership.

Carnoy, M. (1974), *Education as Cultural Imperialism*, New York: David McKay Company.

Carnoy, M. (1985), 'The Political Economy of Education', *International Social Science Journal*, 37 (104).

Chiang, T (2010), *The Lifecycle of Software Objects*, Burton: Subterranean Press.

Chin, M. et al. (2022), 'Navigating Researcher Positionality in Comparative and International Education Research: Perspectives From Emerging Researchers', *The International Education Journal: Comparative Perspectives*, 21 (2): 21–36. http://iejcomparative.org

Chisholm, L., and A. Chissale (2024), BRICS, sub-imperialism and education in Mozambique. Comparative Education, 61 (2): 225–43. https://doi.org/10.1080/03050068.2024.2372209

Chisholm, L., and G. Steiner-Khamsi, eds (2008), *South-South Transfer: Cooperation and Unequal Development in Education*, New York: Teachers College Press.

Chowdhury, S. R. (2017), 'Why Children do Well in "Street Maths" but not in the Classroom: Researchers Fault Teaching Methods', *Scroll.in*, online October 15. https://scroll.in/article/850763/why-children-do-well-in-street-maths-but-not-in-the-classroom-researchers-fault-teaching-methods

Clifford, J. (2013), *Returns: Becoming Indigenous in the Twenty-First Century*, Boston: Harvard University Press.

Coleman, J. S. (1988) 'Social Capital in the Creation of Human Capital', *American Journal of Sociology*, 94 (Supplement): S95–S120.

Colletta, N. J. and M. L. Cullen (2000), 'Violent Conflict and the Transformation of Social Capital: Lessons from Cambodia, Rwanda, Guatemala, and Somalia', Washington DC: World Bank, Report Number 20564: vol 1. https://documents.worldbank.org

Colletta, N. J., and M. Sutton (1989), 'Achieving and Sustaining Universal Primary Education: International Experience Relevant to India', *Policy, Planning and Research Department Working Papers*, no. WPS 166 Washington: World Bank.

Collins, P. H. (2015), *Intersectionality as Critical Social Theory*, Durham: Duke University Press.

Comaroff, J., and J. Comaroff (2012), *Theory from the South: Or How Euro-America is Evolving Toward Africa*, London: Paradigm Publishers.

Connell, R. (2007), *Southern Theory: Social Science and The Global Dynamics of Knowledge*, Hoboken: Wiley

Connell, R., and N. Dados (2014), 'Where in the World Does Neoliberalism Come From? The Market Agenda in Southern Perspective', *Theory and Society*, 43 (2): 117–38.

Cornbleth, C., and D. Waugh (1995), *The Great Speckled Bird: Multicultural Politics and Education Policymaking*, New York: St Martin's Press.

Cortina, R. (2019), '"The Passion for What is Possible" in Comparative and International Education', *Comparative Education Review*, 63 (4): 463–79.
Cottrell, M. (2010), 'Indigenous Education in Comparative Perspective: Global Opportunities for Reimagining Schools', *International Journal for Cross-Disciplinary Subjects in Education*, 1 (4): 223–7.
Cowen, R. (2000), 'Comparing Futures or Comparing Pasts?', *Comparative Education*, 36 (3): 333–42.
Cowen, R. (2017), 'Toward a Postcolonial Comparative and International Education', *Comparative Education Review*, 61 (S1): S1–24.
Cowen, R. (2018), 'Embodied Comparative Education', *Comparative Education* 54 (1): 10–25. doi:10.1080/03050068.2017.1409554.
Crăciun, D. (2018), 'National Policies for Higher Education Internationalization: A Global Comparative Perspective', in A. Curaj et al. (eds), *European Higher Education Area: The Impact of Past and Future Policies*, 95–106, New York: Springer.
Crossley, M., and G. Vulliamy (1984), 'Case-Study Research Methods and Comparative Education', *Comparative Education*, 20 (2): 193–207.
Curtis, S. M. S. et al. (2024), *The Technological-Industrial Complex and Education: Navigating Algorithms, Datafication, and Artificial Intelligence in Comparative and International Education*, Cham: Springer Nature.
Dados, N., and R. Connell (2012), 'The Global South,' *Contexts*, 11 (1): 12–13. https://doi.org/10.1177/1536504212436479
Daniel, A. & Platzky Miller, J. (2024), 'Imagination, Decolonization, and Intersectionality: The #RhodesMustFall Student Occupations in Cape Town, South Africa.' *Third World Quarterly*, 45 (5), 506–28. https://doi.org/10.1080/01436597.2024.2419011
Darling, S. B. (2023), 'Tackling Wicked Sustainability Problems,' *ACS Sustainable Resource Management*, 1:4–5.
de Moralis, M. G. (2005), 'South to South Cooperation Policy Transfer and Best Practicing Reasoning: The Transfer of Solidarity in Literacy Program from Brazil to Mozambique', Working *Paper No. 416*, The Hague: Institute of Social Studies.
de Sousa Santos, B. (2018), *The End of the Cognitive Empire: The Coming of Age of Epistemologies of the South*, Durham: Duke University Press.
Deer, F., and R. Heringer (2023), 'Indigenous Perspectives at the Cultural Interface: Exploring Student Achievement through School/Community-Based Interventions', *Canadian Journal of Education*, 46 (1): 33–55. https://doi.org/10.53967/cje-rce.5707
Desai, R. (2013), *Geopolitical Economy: After US Hegemony, Globalization and Empire (the Future World of Capitalism)*, London: Pluto Press.
Dhara, C., and V. Singh (2021), 'The Elephant in the Room: Why Transformative Education Must Address the Problem of Endless

Exponential Economic Growth', in R. Iyengar and C. Kwauk (eds), *Charting an SDG 4.7 Roadmap for Radical, Transformative Change in the Midst of Climate Breakdown*, 120–43, The Netherlands: Brill Publishers.

Dillabough, J. (2001), 'Gender Theory and Research in Education: Modernity Traditions and Emerging Contemporary Themes', in B. Francis and C. Skelton (eds), *Perspectives Investigating Gender: Contemporary in Education*, 11–26, Philadelphia: Open University.

Dos-Santos, T. (1970), 'The Structure of Dependence', *American Economic Review*, 60 (2): 231–6.

du Plessis, G. E. (2019), 'Gendered Human (In)security in South Africa: What Can Ubuntu Feminism Offer?', *Acta Academica*, 51 (2): 41–63.

Durst, J., and Á. Bereményi (2024), 'False Promises and Distinct Minority Mobility Paths: Trajectories and Costs of the Education-Driven Social Mobility of Racialized Ethnic Groups', *Compare* 54 (3): 355–67.

Dyson, A., and L. Todd (2010), 'Dealing with Complexity: Theory of Change Evaluation and the Full Service Extended Schools Initiative', *International Journal of Research & Method in Education*, 33 (2): 119–34.

Eckstein, M. A. (1970), 'On Teaching a "Scientific" Comparative Education', *Comparative Education Review*, 14 (3): 279–82.

Edding, F. (1965), 'The Use of Economics in Comparing Educational Systems', *International Review of Education*, 453–65.

Edwards, Jr. D. B. (2017), 'Unpacking the Problematic Statistical Foundations of Knowledge Production in Global Education Governance', in C. Manion et al. (eds), *Interrogating and Innovating Comparative and International Education Research*, 206–24, The Netherlands: Brill Publishers.

Elkins, K. (2024), 'A(I) University in Ruins: What Remains in a World with Large Language Models?', *PMLA/Publications of the Modern Language Association of America*, 139 (3): 1–7.

Enslin, P., and K. Horsthemke (2004), 'Can *Ubuntu* Provide a Model for Citizenship Education in African Democracies?', *Comparative Education*, 40 (4): 545–58.

Epstein, I. (2019), *Affect Theory and Comparative Education Discourse: Essays on Fear and Loathing in Response to Global Educational Policy and Practice*, London: Bloomsbury Academic.

Escobar, A. (1992), 'Imagining a Post-Development Era? Critical Thought, Development and Social Movements', *Social Text*, 31/32: 20–56.

Escobar, A. ([1995] 2011), *Encountering Development: The Making and Unmaking of the Third World*, 2nd edn, Princeton: Princeton University Press.

Espinoza, O., and N. McGinn (2023), 'Six Decades of Development: The Impact of Structural Adjustment Programs on Education in Developing

Countries', in R. Tierney, F. Rizvi, and K. Ercikan (eds), *International Encyclopedia of Education*, 4th edn, 205–17, Amsterdam: Elsevier.

Ethridge, I., and M. Rabiee (2023), 'GIS and Storytelling for Sustainable Development Education', in R Iyengar and O. K. Caman (eds), *Rethinking Education for Sustainable Development: Research, Policy and Practice*, London and New York: Bloomsbury Academic.

Farrell, J. P. (1979), 'The Necessity of Comparison in the Study of Education: The Salience of Science and the Problem of Comparability', *Comparative Education Review*, 23 (1): 3–16.

Foster, P. (1960), 'Comparative Methodology and the Study of African Education,' *Comparative Education Review*, 4 (2): 110–17.

Foster, P. (1965), 'The Vocational School Fallacy in Development Planning', in A. A. Anderson and M. J. Bowman (eds), *Education and Economic Development*, 142–66, Chicago: Aldine.

Foucault, M. (1970), *The Order of Things*, New York: Random House.

Foucault, M. (1979), *Archaeology of Knowledge: And the Discourse on Language*, New York: Vintage Paperbacks

Foucault, M. (1982), *Archaeology of Knowledge*. San Fernando, CA: Vintage Classics.

Frank, A. G. (1966), 'The Development of Underdevelopment', *Monthly Review*, 18 (4): 17–31.

Franklin, A. (2022), *Co-creativity and Engaged Scholarship: Transformative Methods in Social Sustainability Research*, Cham: Springer Nature.

Fraser, S. E. (1964), *Jullien's Plan for Comparative Education 1816–1817*, New York: Teachers College, Columbia University.

Fraser, S. E., and W. W. Brickman (1968), *A History of International and Comparative Education*, Northbrook: Scott Foresman.

Freire, P. (1996), *Pedagogy of the Oppressed*. New York: Continuum Pub. Company.

Galtung, J. (1971), 'A Structural Theory of Imperialism', *Journal of Peace Research*, 8 (2): 81–117.

Garfinkel, H. (1979), *Studies in Ethnomethodology*, New Jersey: Prentice Hall.

Garfinkel, H. (1984), *Studies in Ethnomethodology*, Cambridge: Polity Press.

Gee, J. P. (1996), *Social Linguistics and Literacies: Ideology in Discourses*, 2nd edn, London: Taylor & Francis.

George Mwangi, C. A., and C. W. Yao (2021), 'U.S. Higher Education Internationalization through an Equity Driven Lens: An Analysis of Concepts, History, and Research,' in L. W. Perna (ed.), *Higher Education: Handbook of Theory and Research*, 549–609, Cham: Springer.

Ghosh, A. (2016), *The Great Derangement: Climate Change and the Unthinkable*, Chicago and London: The University of Chicago Press.

Goebel, J. G., E. Fischman, and I. Silova (2019), 'Why Measure Un-Sustainable Education?', in *Innovations in Global Learning Metrics*, June 8th, 2024, symposium. Arizona State University. https://resources.norrag.org/resource/546/

Gorostiaga, J. M. (2017), 'Prespectivism and Social Cartography: Contribution to Comparative Education,' *Educação & Realidade*, 42 (3): 877–98.

Gorur, R. (2019), 'Patterns: In Search of Patterns: With Enough Data, Do the Numbers Speak for Themselves?', in R. Gorur, S. Stellar, and G. Steiner-Khamsi (eds), *World Yearbook of Education 2019: Comparative Methodology in the Era of Big Data and Global Networks*, 53–8, New York: Routledge.

Gottlieb, E. E. (1989), 'The Discursive Construction of Knowledge: The Case of Radical Education Discourse', *International Journal of Qualitative Studies in Education*, 2 (2): 131–44.

Gottlieb, E. E. (1991), 'Global Rhetoric, Local Policy: Teacher Training Reform in Israeli Education', *Educational Policy*, 5 (2) 178–92. doi.org/10.1177/0895904891005002

Gottlieb, E. E. (2000), 'Are We Postmodern Yet? Historical and Theoretical Explorations in Comparative Education', in M. Ben-Peretz, S. Brown, and B. Moon (eds), *International Companion to Education*, 125–76, London: Routledge.

Gottlieb, E. E., and T. J. LaBelle (1990), 'Ethnographic Contextualization of Freire's Discourse: Consciousness-Raising, Theory and Practice', *Anthropology & Education Quarterly*, 21 (1): 3–18.

Gottlieb, E. E., S. Ben-Asher, and K. Alsraiha (2022), 'When is an Academic Degree the Best Vocational Education? Bedouin Professionals Reflect on Their Life Choices', *Diaspora, Indigenous, and Minority Education*, 17 (3): 168–81. https://doi.org/10.1080/15595692.2022.2149486

Grant, C. (2017), *The Contribution of Education to Economic Development*, UK Department for International Development, K4D_HDR. Available online: https://assets.publishing.service.gov.uk

Grassini, S. (2023), 'Shaping the Future of Education: Exploring the Potential and Consequences of AI and ChatGPT in Educational Settings', *Education. Science*, 13 (7): 692. doi.org/10.3390/educsci13070692

Günbayı, I., & Sorm, S. (2018), 'Social Paradigms in Guiding Social Research Design: The Functional, Interpretive, Radical Humanist and Radical Structural Paradigms', *International Journal on New Trends in Education and Their Implications*, 9 (2): 57–76.

Halls, W. W. (1977), 'Comparative and International Education Society: An Historical Analysis', *Comparative Education Review*, 21(2/3): 396–404.

Hans, N. A. (1958), *Comparative Education: A Study of Educational Factors and Traditions*, London: Routledge.

Haraway Donna, J. (1991), *Simians, Cyborgs, and Women: The Reinvention of Nature*, New York: Routledge.

Harris, J., V. A. Brown, and J., Russell, eds (2010), *Tackling Wicked Problems: Through the Transdisciplinary Imagination*, Abingdon: Taylor & Francis.

Hayhoe, R. (2007), 'The Use of Ideal Types in Comparative Education: A Personal Reflection', *Comparative Education*, 43 (2): 189–205.

Hayhoe, R., and K. Mundy (2008), 'Introduction to Comparative and International Education: Why Study Comparative Education?', in K. Mundy et al. (eds), *Comparative and International Education: Issues for Teachers*, Toronto: Canadian Scholars' Press.

Heryadi, R. D., S. Darmastuti, and A. A. Rachman (2024), 'Advancing South-South Cooperation in Education: Indonesian Experience with South Africa', *F1000Research*, 11: 982. doi.org/10.12688/f1000research.123311.3

Heyman, R. (1979), 'Comparative Education from an Ethnomethodological Perspective', *Comparative Education*, 15 (3): 241–9.

Høgmo, A. (2018), 'Distance Education System Thinking Policy Comparison Between South Africa and Norway,' MA Thesis, Sweden: Stockholm University, Department of Education. doi:10.13140/RG.2.2.17657.93288

Holmes, B. (1981), *Comparative Education: Some Considerations of Method*, London: Unwin Hyman.

Huaman, E. S. (2022), 'How Indigenous Scholarship Changes the Field: Pluriversal Appreciation, Decolonial Aspirations, and Comparative Indigenous Education', *Comparative Education Review*, 66 (3): 391–416.

Husserl E. (1970), 'Syllabus of a Course of Four Lectures on "Phenomenological Method and Phenomenological Philosophy', *Journal of the British Society for Phenomenology*, 1 (1): 18–23.

Inkeles, A. (1969), 'Making Men Modern: On the Causes and Consequences of Individual Change in Six Developing Countries', *American Journal of Sociology*, 75 (2) 208–225.

Iyengar, R. (2015), 'ICT in Education Impact Study', New York: Columbia University Center for Sustainable Development, Earth Institute. Available online: https://www.ericsson.com/assets/local/news/2013/11/ict-in-education-study-spread.pdf

Iyengar, R., and O. K. Caman, eds (2022), *Rethinking Education for Sustainable Development: Research, Policy and Practice*, London: Bloomsbury.

Iyengar, R., S. Jain, and U. Ewaldsson (2017), 'How Information and Communications Technology can Accelerate Action on the Sustainable Development Goals', New York: Columbia University Earth Institute. Available online: https://onestoneadvisors.-com/wp-content/. uploaded/2017/09/ICT-and-the-SGCs.pdf

Iyengar, R., and M. A. Witenstein (2019), 'Amplifying Indian Women's Voices and Experiences to Advance their Access to Technical and Vocational

Education Training', in C. Manion et al. (eds), *Interrogating and Innovating Comparative and International Education Research*, 72–85, Leiden: Brill.

Jabbar, Z. K. (1976), 'A Critical Study of Educational Implications of Existentialism', PhD (Education), AMU, Third Survey of Research in Education. NCERT, 41.

Jackson, P. T., and D. Nexon (2016), 'Globalization, the Comparative Method, and Comparing Constructions', in R. T. Green (ed.), *Constructivism and Comparative Politics*, 88–120, London: Routledge.

Jameson, F. (1991), *Postmodernism, or, The cultural logic of late capitalism*, Durham, NC: Duke University Press (Original work published 1984).

Jameson, F. (1998), *Postmodernism, or The Cultural Logic of Late Capitalism*, Durham: Duke University Press

Jamison, D. T. et al. (1981), 'Improving Elementary Mathematics Education in Nicaragua: An Experimental Study of the Impact of Textbooks and Radio on Achievement', *Journal of Educational Psychology*, 73 (4), 556–67. https://doi.org/10.1037/0022-0663.73.4.556

Jules, t. d., and Sá e Silva, M. M. (2008), 'How Different Disciplines Have Approached South-South Cooperation and Transfer', *Society for International Education Journal*, 5(1): 45–64.

jules, t. d., R. Shields and M. A. M. Thomas, eds (2021), *The Bloomsbury Handbook of Theory in Comparative and International Education*, London: Bloomsbury.

Kandel, I. L. (1961), 'Comparative Education and Underdeveloped Countries: A New Dimension', *Comparative Education Review*, 4 (3): 130–5.

Kell, M., and P. Kell (2010), 'International Testing: Measuring Global Standards or Reinforcing Inequalities', *International Journal of Learning*, 17 (4): 477–89.

Kelly, G. P., and P. Altbach (1986), 'Comparative Education: Challenge and Response', *Comparative Education Review*, 30 (1): 89–107.

Kelly, G. P. (1979), 'The Relation Between Colonial and Metropolitan Schools: A Structural Analysis', *Comparative Education*, 15 (2): 209–15.

Kelly, P. (2014), 'Intercultural Comparative Research: Rethinking Insider and Outsider Perspectives', *Oxford Review of Education*, 40 (2): 246–65.

Kelly, P. (2020), 'Comparing Post-Socialist Transformations: Purposes, Policies and Practices in Education', *Journal of Education for Teaching*, 46 (2): 253–6.

Kern, S. (2015), *The Culture of Time and Space, 1880–1918*, 2nd edn, Cambridge: Harvard University Press.

Kern, S. (2025), *Time and Space on the Internet Age*, New York: Routledge.

Kidwai, H. et al., eds (2017), *Participatory Action Research and Educational Development: South Asian Perspectives*, Cham: Palgrave Macmillan.

Khavenson, T., and M. Carnoy (2016), 'The Unintended and Intended Academic Consequences of Educational Reforms: The Cases of Post-Soviet Estonia, Latvia and Russia', *Oxford Review of Education*, 42 (2): 178–99.

Kim, B. S. (1984), *Schooling and Social Achievements*, Seoul: KEDP Press.

King, E. (1958), *Other Schools and Ours: A Comparative Study for Today*, London: Holt, Rinehart and Winston.

Klees, S. J. (1986), 'Planning and Policy Analysis in Education: What Can Economics Tell Us?', *Comparative Education Review*, 30 (4): 574–607.

Klees, S. J., J. Samoff, and N. P. Stromquist, eds (2012), *The World Bank and Education Critiques and Alternatives*, Cham: Springer

Kneller, G. F. (1963), 'The Prospects of Comparative Education', *International Review of Education*, 9: 396–406.

Kobayashi, T. (1973), 'Foreword', in R. Edwards et al. (eds), *Relevant Methods in Comparative Education: Report of a Meeting of International Experts*, UNESCO Paris: Institute for Education.

Kurlansky, M. (2003), *1968: The Year that Rocked the World*, New York: Random House.

Kvamme, O. A. (2023), 'Curriculum and the United Nations' sustainable development goals', in R. J. Tierney, F. Rizvi, and K. Erkican (eds), *International Encyclopedia of Education*, 4th edn, 406–13, Amsterdam: Elsevier.

Landri, P. (2014), 'The Sociomateriality of Education Policy', *Discourse: Studies in the Cultural Politics of Education*, 36 (4): 596–609. doi.org/10.1080/01596 306.2014.977019

Lave Jr, R. E., and D. W. Kyle (1968), 'The Application of Systems Analysis to Educational Planning,' *Comparative Education Review*, 12 (1): 39–56.

Lee, A. (1992), 'Poststructuralism and Educational Research: Some Categories and Issues', *Issues in Educational Research*, 2 (1): 1–12.

Lee, J. J., D. Adams, and C. Cornbleth (1988), 'Transnational Transfer of Curriculum Knowledge: A Korean Case Study', *Journal of Curriculum Studies*, 20 (3): 233–46.

Lee, Valerie V. E. et al. (2011), 'School Resources and Academic Performance in Sub-Saharan Africa', *Comparative Education Review*, 55 (3): 369–97.

Levin, H. M. (1978), 'The Dilemma of Comprehensive Secondary School Reforms in Western Europe', *Comparative Education Review*, 22 (3): 434–51.

Levin, H. M. (2002), 'A Comprehensive Framework for Evaluating Educational Vouchers', *Educational Evaluation and Policy Analysis*, 24 (3): 159–74.

Li, W. L. (1971), 'A Demographic Model of Student Progression', *International Review of Education*, 408–24.

Little, A. (2010), 'International and Comparative Education: What's in a Name?', *Compare*, 40 (6): 845–52.

Loomba, A. (1998), *Colonialism/Postcolonialism*, London: Routledge.

Loomba, A. (2002), *Colonialism/Postcolonialism*, London: Routledge.

Lyotard, J. F. (1984), *The Postmodern Condition: A Report on Knowledge*, G. Bennington, & B. Massumi (trans), Minneapolis: University of Minnesota Press.

Manion, C. et al., eds (2020), *Interrogating and Innovating Comparative and International Education Research*, Leiden: Brill.

Manzon, M. (2018), 'Origins and Traditions in Comparative Education. Challenging Some Assumptions', *Comparative Education*, 54 (1): 1–9.

Marcus, G. E., and D. Cushman (1982), 'Ethnographies as Texts', *Annual Review of Anthropology*, 11: 25–69.

Marginson, S., and M. Mollis (2001), 'The Door Opens and the Tiger Leaps. Theories and Reflexivities of Comparative Education for a Global Millennium', *Comparative Education Review*, 45 (4): 581–615.

Marini, R. M. (1972), 'Brazilian Subimperialism', *Monthly Review*, 23 (9): 14–24.

Martin T. J. (2003), 'Divergent Ontologies with Converging Conclusions: A Case Study Comparison of Comparative Methodologies', *Comparative Education*, 39 (1): 105–17.

Martin, S., and D. Dandekar, eds (2022), *Global South Scholars in the Western Academy: Harnessing Unique Experiences, Knowledges, and Positionality in the Third Space*, London: Routledge.

Masemann, V. (1976), 'Anthropological Approaches to Comparative Education', *Comparative Education Review*, 20 (3): 368–80.

Masemann, L. V. (1991), 'Ways of Knowing: Implications for Comparative Education', *Comparative Education Review*, 34 (4): 465–73.

Mayberry, M. (1998), 'Reproductive and Resistant Pedagogies: The Comparative Roles of Collaborative Learning and Feminist Pedagogy in Science Education', *Journal of Research in Science Teaching*, 35 (4): 443–59.

Mazrui, A. A. (1975), 'The African University as a Multinational Corporation: Problems of Penetration and Dependency', *Harvard Educational Review*, 45 (2): 191–210.

McHale, B. (1989), *Postmodernist Fiction*, Routledge, London.

McHale, B. (2015), *The Cambridge Introduction to Postmodernism*, Cambridge: Cambridge University Press.

McMahon, E., and L. O. Milligan (2021), 'A Framework for Ethical Research in International and Comparative Education', *Compare*, 53 (1): 72–88.

Mead, P. (2003), 'The American Model II', in Romana Huk, ed., *Assembling Alternatives: Reading Postmodern Poetries Transnationally*, 169, Middletown: Wesleyan UP.

Menashy, F. (2019), *International Aid to Education. Power Dynamics in the Era of Partnership*, New York: Teachers College Press.

Menashy, F., and R. Read (2016), 'Knowledge Banking in Global Education Policy: A Bibliometric Analysis of World Bank Publications on Public-Private Partnerships', *Education Policy Analysis Archives*, 24 (95): 1–24.

Menashy, F., and Z. Zakharia (2022), 'White Ignorance in Global Education', *Harvard Educational Review*, 92 (4): 461–85.

Meyer, J. W., J. Boli-Bennett, and C. Chase-Dunn (1975), 'Convergence and Divergence in Development,' *Annual Review of Sociology*, 1: 223–46.

Meyer, J. W., F. O. Ramirez, and Y. N. Soysal (1992), 'World Expansion of Mass Education, 1870–1980,' *Sociology of Education*, 65 (2): 128–49.

Meyer, J. W., J. W. Boli-Bennet, G. M. Thomas, and F. Ramirez (1997), 'World Society and the Nation State,' *American Journal of Sociology*, 103 (1): 144–81.

Mignolo, W. (2011), *The Darker Side of Western Modernity: Global Futures, Decolonial Options*, Princeton: Duke University Press.

Mignolo, W. D. (1993), 'Colonial and Postcolonial Discourse: Cultural Critique or Academic Colonialism?' *Latin American Research Review*, 28 (3): 120–34.

Mignolo, W. D. (2007), 'DELINKING,' *Cultural Studies*, 21 (2): 449–514

Ministry of Foreign Affairs of Japan (2011), 'BEGIN: Basic Education for Growth Initiative'. Available online: https://www.mofa.go.jp/region/africa/education3.html

Mirón, L. F., and M. Lauria (1998), 'Student Voice as Agency: Resistance and Accommodation in Inner-city Schools,' *Anthropology & Education Quarterly*, 29 (2): 189–213.

Mitchell, W. J. T., ed. (1980), *The Language of Images*, Chicago: University of Chicago.

Mitter, W. (1992), 'Educational Adjustments and Perspectives in a United Germany,' *Comparative Education*, 28 (1): 45–52.

Miyoshi, M., and H. D. Harootunian (2002), *Learning Places: The Afterlives of Area Studies*, Durham: Duke University Press.

Mohanty, C. T. (1984), 'Under Western Eyes: Feminist Scholarship and Colonial Discourses,' *Boundary*, 2 (12/13): 333–58.

Moraru, Christian (2011), *Cosmodernism: American Narrative, Late Globalization, and the New Cultural Imaginary*, Ann Arbor: University of Michigan Press.

Moraru, C., A. Terian, and A. Matei (2002), *Theory in the "Post" Era A Vocabulary for the 21st-Century Conceptual Commons*, New York: Bluesberry.

Moreton-Robinson, A. (2013), 'Towards an Australian Indigenous Women's Standpoint Theory: A Methodological Tool,' *Australian Feminist Studies*, 28 (78): 331–47.

Musoni-Chikede, F. (2022), 'Transcending Colonial Rule and Reimagining Rhodesia's Future: The Rockefeller Foundation and the University College of Rhodesia and Nyasaland, 1950–1980,' in K. Monkman and A. Frkovich (eds), *Belonging in Changing Educational Spaces*, 183–99, New York: Routledge.

Mwamwenda, T. S., and B. B. Mwamwenda (1987), 'School Facilities and Pupils' Academic Achievement,' *Comparative Education*, 23 (2), 225–35.

Noah, H. J., and M. A. Eckstein (1969), *Towards a Science of Comparative Education*, New York: Macmillan.

Nordtveit, B. H. (2023), 'Transition and Change: A Decade of Comparative and International Education, 2013–2023', *Comparative Education Review*, 67 (4): 701–9.

Ogbu, J. U. (1990), 'Minority Education in Comparative Perspective', *The Journal of Negro Education*, 59 (1): 45–57.

Pánek, J. (2013), 'The Commercialization of Public Data – How Does Participatory Datamining Look on a Global Scale?', *South African Journal of Geomatics*, 2 (3): 231–45.

Paulston, R. G. (1994), 'The Perspectivist Turn in Comparative Education', Paper presented at CIES, San Diego, California, 21–24 March 1994.

Paulston, R. G., ed. (1996), *Social Cartography: Mapping Ways of Seeing Social and Educational Change*, New York: Garland.

Paulston, R. G. (1999), 'Mapping Comparative Education After Postmodernity', *Comparative Education Review*, 43 (4): 438–63.

Perrotta, D. V. (2016), 'Regionalism and Higher Education in South America: A Comparative Analysis for Understanding Internationalization', *Journal of Supranational Policies of Education*, 4 (1): 54–81.

Peters, M. (1998), *Naming the Multiple: Poststructuralism and Education*, Westport: Bergin & Garvey.

Phelan, J. (2023), *Narrative Medicine a Rhetorical Rx*, New York: Routledge.

Phillps, D., and M. Schweisfurth (2014), *Comparative and International Education An Introduction to Theory, Method, and Practice*, London: Bloomsbury Academic.

Popkewitz, T. S. (2008), *Cosmopolitanism and the Age of School Reform: Science, Education, and Making Society by Making the Child*, New York: Routledge.

Psacharopoulos, G. (1982), 'The Economics of Higher Education in Developing Countries', *Comparative Education Review*, 26 (2): 139–59.

Ramirez, F. O., and J. Boli, J. (1987), 'Global Patterns of Educational Institutionalization', in G. M. Thomas, J. W., Meyer, F. O. Ramirez, and J. Boli (eds), Institutional Structure: Constituting the State, Society and the Individual, 150–172, Newbury Park, CA:

Ramirez, F. O., and J. W. Meyer (2012), 'Toward Post-National Societies and Global Citizenship,' *Multicultural Education Review*, 4 (1): 1–28.

Rappleye, J. (2010), 'Compasses, Maps, and Mirrors', in M. A. Larson (ed.), *New Thinking in Comparative Education*, 57–79, Rotterdam: Sense Publishers.

Rappleye, J. (2020), 'Comparative Education as Cultural Critique', *Comparative Education*, 56 (1): 39–56

Rappleye, J. (2021), 'Origins of the Faith: The Untold Story of Hugh Wood, American Development Assistance in the 1950s, and Nepal's Modern

Education', in L. Parajuli, D. Uprety, and P. Onta (eds), *School Education in Nepal*, 71–102, Nepal: Martin Chautari Publisher.

Refiti, A. L. (2017), 'How the Tā-Vā Theory of Reality Constructs a Spatial Exposition of Samoan Architecture', *Pacific Studies*, 40 (1/2): 267–88.

Reitz, T. (2022), 'Back to the Drawing Board: Creative Mapping Methods for Inclusion and Connection', in A. Franklin (ed.), *Co-Creativity and Engaged Scholarship: Transformative Methods in Social Sustainability Research*, 323–56, London: Palgrave Macmillan. https://doi.org/10.1007/978-3-030-84248-2_10

Ringel, F. (2022), 'The Time of Post-socialism: On the Future of an Anthropological Concept', *Critique of Anthropology*, 42 (2): 191–208. doi.org/10.1177/0308275X221095930

Rizvi, F. (2006), 'Imagination and the Globalization of Educational Policy Research', *Globalization, Societies and Education*, 4 (2): 193–205.

Rizvi, F., and B. Lingard (2010), *Globalizing Education Policy*, London: Routledge.

Robertson, S. L. (2012), 'Placing Teachers in Global Governance Agendas', *Comparative Education Review*, 56 (4): 584–607.

Robinson-Pant, A. (2016), *Exploring the Concept of Insider-Outsider in Comparative and International Research: Essentialising Culture or Culturally Essential?*, Oxford: Symposium Books.

Rogers, R., ed. (2004), *An Introduction to Critical Discourse Analysis in Education*, Mahwah: Lawrence Erlbaum Associates Publishers.

Rosenberg, D., and A. Grafton (2010), *Cartographies of Time*, New York: Princeton Architectural Press.

Rubalcaba, L. (2022), 'Understanding Innovation in Education: A Service Co-Production Perspective', *Economies*, 10 (5): 96. https://doi.org/10.3390/economies10050096

Rudolph, S. (2019), *Unsettling the Gap: Race, Politics and Indigenous Education*, New-York: Peter Lang Publishing.

Said, E. W. (1978), *Orientalism*, New York: Pantheon Books.

Said, E. W. (2000), 'Identity, Authority and Freedom: The Potentate and the Traveler', in *Reflections on Exile and Other Essays*, Cambridge: Harvard University Press.

Samoff, J., and N. P. Stromquist (2001), 'Managing Knowledge and Storing Wisdom? New Forms of Foreign Aid?', *Development and Change*, 32 (4): 631–56.

Sander, B. (1985), 'Education and Dependence: The Role of Comparative Education', *Prospects*, xv (2): 195–201.

Schriewer, J. (1992), 'The Method of Comparison and the Need for Externalization: Methodological Criteria and Sociological Concepts', in J. Schriewer and B. Holmes (eds), *Theories and Methods in Comparative Education*, 25–83, Frankfurt: Peter Lang.

Schriewer, J., ed. (2006), 'Comparative Methodologies in the Social Sciences – Cross-Disciplinary Inspirations', *Comparative Education*, 42 (3).

Schultz, T. W. (1961), 'Investment in Human Capital', *The American Economic Review*, 51 (1): 1–17.

Sellar, S., G. Thompson, and D. Rutkowski (2017), *The Global Education Race: Taking the Measure of PISA and International Testing*, Edmonton: Brush Education Inc.

Setty, R., and M. A. Witenstein (2017), 'Defining PAR to Refine PAR: Theorizing Participatory Action Research in South Asian Educational Contexts', in H. Kidwai et al. (eds), *Participatory Action Research and Educational Development: South Asian Perspectives*, 13–47, Cham: Palgrave Macmillan.

Silova, I. (2010a), 'Rediscovering Post-Socialism in Comparative Education', *International Perspectives on Education and Society*, 14: 1–24.

Silova, I., ed. (2010b), *Post-Socialism is not Dead(Re)Reading the Global in Comparative Education*, Leeds: Emerald Group Publishing.

Silova, I. (2021), 'Facing the Anthropocene: Comparative Education as Sympoiesis', *Comparative Education Review*, 65 (4): 587–616.

Simola, H. (2005), 'The Finnish Miracle of PISA: Historical and Sociological Remarks on Teaching and Teacher Education', *Comparative Education*, 41 (4): 453–70.

Simone Curtis, M. S. et al. (2024), *The Technological-Industrial Complex and Education: Navigating Algorithms, Datafication, and Artificial Intelligence in Comparative and International Education*, Cham: Palgrave Macmillan.

Soudien, C. (2008), 'What are the Questions that Post-Colonialism asks of Comparative Education?', *Comparative Education Bulletin*, 11: 3–20.

Spratt, R., and E. Coxon (2020), 'Decolonising "Context" in Comparative Education: The Potential of Oceanian Theories of Relationality,' *Beijing International Review of Education*, 2 (4), 519–36. https://doi.org/10.1163/25902539-02040007

Sriprakash, A., D. Nally, K. Myers, and P. Ramos-Pinto (2020), *Learning with the Past: Racism, Education and Reparative Futures*, Paris: UNESCO.

Stein, S. (2017), 'The Persistent Challenges of Addressing Epistemic Dominance in Higher Education: Considering the Case of Curriculum Internationalization', *Comparative Education Review*, 61 (S1), S25–50.

Steiner-Khamsi, G. (2004), *The Global Politics of Educational Borrowing and Lending*, New York: Teachers College Press.

Streck, D. R., M. J. Abba, and C. S. Souza (2019), 'Tendencies and Challenges in Researching Comparative Education: Interview with Jürgen Schriewer', *Eccos Revista Científica*, 50 (July/September): 1–20.

Stromquist, N. P. (1995), 'Romancing the State: Gender and Power in Education', *Comparative Education Review*, 39 (4): 423–54.

Stromquist, N. P. (2011), 'A Social Cartography of Gender in Education', in J. C. Weidman and W. J. Jacob (eds), *Beyond the Comparative*, 173–92, Rotterdam: Sense Publishers.

Strong, K. et al. (2023), 'Learning From the Movement for Black Lives: Horizons of Racial Justice for Comparative and International Education', *Comparative Education Review*, 67 (S1): S1–24.

Takayama, K., (2019), 'An Invitation to "Negative" Comparative Education', *Comparative Education*, 56 (1): 79–95.

Takayama, K., A. Sriprakash, and R. Connell (2017), 'Toward a Postcolonial Comparative and International Education', *Comparative Education Review*, 61 (S1), S1–24.

Tatto, M. T. (2022), 'The Need for Comparative Studies in Teacher Education', in I. Menter (ed.), *The Palgrave Handbook of Teacher Education Research*, 1–22, Cham: Springer International Publishing.

te Riele, K. (2006), 'Schooling practices for marginalized students—practice-with-hope', *International Journal of Inclusive Education*, 10 (1), 59–74. https://doi.org/10.1080/13603110500221750

Thomas, M. A. M., and R. -H. Xu, (2023), 'The Emergence and Policy (Mis) Alignment of Teach for Taiwan', *Journal of Education Policy*, 38 (4): 686–709.

Tikly, L. (1999), 'Postcolonialism and Comparative Education', *International Review of Education*, 45, 603–21.

Tran L. T. and D. T. B. Nguyen (2023), 'Global Processes: Global Trade in International Education and the International Education-Migration Nexus', in: R. J. Tierney, F. Rizvi and K. Erkican (eds.), *International Encyclopedia of Education* 4th edn, 250–9, Amsterdam: Elsevier.

Tröhler, D. (2023), 'Curriculum Theory and Education History', in R. J. Tierney, F. Rizvi, and K. Erkican (eds), *International Encyclopedia of Education*, 4th edn, 117–25, Amsterdam: Elsevier.

UNESCO (2011), 'The hidden crisis: armed conflict and education; gender overview', Education for All global monitoring report. Paris: UNESCO.

UNESCO (2020), State of the Education Report for India: Vocational Education First. Paris: UNESCO.

UN Women (2024), 'Gender Equality Progress 2024', *Gender equality UNGA 79* UN: https://www.unwomen.org

UNDP (2022), 'What is Just Transition? And Why is it Important?' Available online: https://climatepromise.undp.org/news-and-stories/what-just-transition-and-why-itimportant

UNICEF (2019), 'Climate Migration and Education: Are we Making our Education System Future Proof', https://www.unicef.org.uk/policy/climate-migration-and-education/

University of Pittsburgh Archives Personal Files, *Adams, Don. K.* University Archives, Archives & Special Collections, University of Pittsburgh Library System.

Vavrus, F. (2005), 'Adjusting Inequality: Education and Structural Adjustment Policies in Tanzania', *Harvard Educational Review*, 75 (2): 174–201.

Vavrus, F., and L. Bartlett (2006), 'Comparatively Knowing: Making a Case for the Vertical Case Study', *Current Issues in Comparative Education*, 8 (2): 95–103.

Vavrus, F., and M. Seghers (2010), 'Critical Discourse Analysis in Comparative Education: A Discursive Study of "Partnership" in Tanzania's Poverty Reduction Policies', *Comparative Education Review*, 54 (1): 77–103.

Venugopal, R. (2015), Neoliberalism as concept. Economy and Society, 44(2): 165–187. https://doi.org/10.1080/03085147.2015.1013356

Wallerstein, I. (1974), *The Modern World-System*, 1st edn, Cambridge: Academic Press Inc.

Wallerstein, I. (1990), 'Culture as the Ideological Battleground of the Modern World-System', *Theory, Culture & Society*, 7 (2–3): 31–55.

Wallerstein, I. (2023), 'The Rise and Future Demise of the World Capitalist System: Concepts for Comparative Analysis,' in *Imperialism*, 141–69, Routledge.

Wang, C., and M. A. Burris (1997), 'Photovoice: Concept, Methodology, and Use for Participatory Needs Assessment', *Health Education & Behavior*, 24 (3): 368–87.

Wexler, P. (1987), *Social Analysis of Education: After the New Sociology*, London: Routledge.

Willis, P. (1979), *Learning to Labor: How Working-Class Kids Get Working-Class Jobs*, Farnham: Ashgate Publishing.

Wirt, F. M. (1980), 'Comparing Educational Policies: Theory, Units of Analysis, and Research Strategies', *Comparative Education Review*, 24 (2): 174–91.

Witenstein, M. A., and J. Abdallah (2023), 'Composite Storytelling Affiliated College Faculty Narratives in India to Propose Curriculum and Exam Policy Revisions', *Journal of Higher Education Policy and Leadership Studies*, 4 (2): 92–105.

Witenstein, M., and R. Iyengar (2023), 'Policies, Practices and the Future of Technical and Vocational', *Diaspora, Indigenous, and Minority Education*, 17 (3):163–7.

Wolhuter, C. C. (2008), 'Review of the Review: Constructing the Identity of Comparative Education', *Research in Comparative and International Education*, 3 (4): 323–44.

Wolhuter, C. C., N. Popov, B. Leutwyler, and K. Skubic Ermenc, eds (2008), *Comparative Education at Universities World Wide*, Sofia: Bureau for Educational Services.

World Bank (1998), *Project Appraisal Document on a Proposed Loan in the Amount of US$62.5 Million to The Federative Republic of Brazil for The School Improvement Project—FUNDESCOLA I*, Washington: Report No: 17402-BR.

Young, M. F. D., ed. (1971), *Knowledge and Control: New Directions for the Sociology of Education*, London: Collier-Macmillan.

Zawacki-Richter, O., V. I. Marín, M. Bond, and F. Gouverneur (2019), 'Systematic Review of Research on Artificial Intelligence Applications in Higher Education—Where Are the Educators?', *International Journal of Educational Technology in Higher Education*, 16 (1): 1–27.

Zuzovsky, R. (2021), 'Failing the Test or the Failure of the Test: The Case of Environmental Education in Israel', *Education Policy Analysis Archives*, 29 (123): 1–29.

Index

Abrams, E. S. 197
Active School 140
Adams, Don 8, 21–2, 43, 132–4, 189
affect theory 73, 205–7
  assemblage 206
  intensity of encounter 205
  meaning making 206
Afro-Anglo-American Teacher
    Education 15
AI 182
alienation 58
Allende, Salvador 29
American Education Research
    Association (AERA) 167
Amin, Samir 51, 155
analytical comparative studies 17–18
Anderson-Levitt, K. 100
Apple, Michael 49, 59
Arbery, Ahmaud 233
Archival research 97
Area Studies 11, 20, 174, 189
  method 14, 103, 110
Arnold, C. 15
Arora, Payal 183
artificial intelligence (AI) 183
  and CIE 185
  prospects 184–7
Asian Development Bank (ADB) 12, 27, 134
assemblage theory 73, 206
Australia International Comparative
    Education Society 169
Australia New Zealand Comparative and
    International Education Society 169

Bartlett, Lesley 101, 105, 136, 146
Beauvoir, Simone de 60
Beech, J. M. A. 116
BEGIN (Basic Education for Growth
    Initiative) 160–1
BenDavid-Hadar, Iris 197–200
Berlant, Lauren 73
Bhattacharjea, S. 176
Bilgen, A. 99, 175
Black Lives Matter 34
Blake, Nigel 77
Blanco, Gerardo L. 188, 202–4
Bloody Monday 19
Boli-Bennett, John 94
Bologna Process 33
Bond, P. 154
Boroughs, Don 138
Botswana 88–9
Bourdieu, Pierre 56–7
Bowman, Mary Jean 15, 46, 139
BRAC 173–4
Braidotti, R. 71
Braun, A. M. B. 109–10
Brazil 21, 29, 55, 140–1, 153–5, 163
Brazil Scientific Mobility Program
    (BSMP) 33
Brentano, Franz 59
Brickman, William W. 131
BRICS (Brazil, Russia, India, China,
    South Africa) 29, 55, 153–5, 163
Bristow, Thelma 193
British Comparative and International
    Education Society 168
British Council 14

Brown, Richard H. 107, 135, 136
Buen Vivir 158–9, 164
Bulletin of Japan Comparative Education Society 170
Burrell, G. 39, 40, 42, 117
Bush, George W. 148
　war on terror 30, 148
Butler, Judith 206
Byker, E. J. 176

Call-Cummings, M. 73, 98–9
Carnegie Foundation 171–2
Carnoy, M. 57, 90, 104
case studies in comparative and international education 97, 100–2
Capability Theory 119
cartography
　critical 120, 117
　social 15, 75, 94, 96, 111, 114, 116–18, 120, 126
Center for Development Education 15
Chenery, Hollis 20
Chiang, Ted 185
China 14, 24, 29, 153–5, 163
China Comparative Education Society (CCES) 14
Chisholm, L. 56, 152, 154–5
Chissale, A. 56, 154–5
Clifford, James 138, 143, 157
Cold War 2, 14, 16–17, 26, 40, 126, 147, 212
Coleman, James 47
Colletta, N. J. 81–2
Collins, Patricia Hill 73
Colombia 123, 140
colonialism 49–50
colonization 12, 54, 80, 130, 164, 185
Columbia University 12
Columbia University, Teachers College 15, 130
Comaroff, J. 156

Compare: A Journal of Comparative and International Education 170
Comparative Education Review 131, 168, 170, 172
comparative and international education (CIE) building blocks
　academic activity—springboards 187–8
　academic careers 173–4
　artificial intelligence (AI) prospects 183–5
　digital learning 182–5
　ethics 174–7
　future 177–8
　green skilling 181
　just transition 180–1
　organizational 167–72
　Sustainable Development Goals (SDGs) 178–80
　University of London Research Library for Comparative Education 166–7
comparative and international education (CIE) histories
　1945–1960s 11–18
　1968 18–19
　1970s–1980s 19–23
　1980s–2000 23–5
　1990s 26–30
　2000s 30–5
　academic activities—springboards 35–7
　background 7–9
　international comparisons of education 9–11
comparative and international education (CIE) methods
　academic activities—springboards 123–4
　cross-paradigm methods 110–21
　functionalist research methods 80–9
　interpretive methods 102–5

262 Index

participatory action research 106–10
radical humanist paradigm 95–102
radical structuralist paradigm 90–4
comparative and international education (CIE) practices
   academic activities—springboards 162–4
   BRICS nations 153–5
   Buen Vivir, Ubuntu, va, and ta-va 158–9
   directions 126–7, 146–7
      East–West direction 147–9
      North–South direction 149–51
      South–North direction 150–1
      South–South direction 151–3
      West–East direction 147–9
      indigenous culture and education 159–60
comparative and international education (CIE) shapes 155
   Shaping the Global Order 155
   Southern Theory 155
   Re-Shaping 157
      Buen Vivir, Ubuntu, Vā, and Tā-vā 158
      Indigenous Culture and Education 159
comparative and international education (CIE) theories
   academic activities—springboards 76–8
   affect theory 73
   functionalist paradigm 40, 41–8
   interpretive paradigm 41, 60–3
   intersectionality 72–3
   postcolonialism(s) 68–9
   posthumanism 70–2
   postmodernism 66–8
   post-socialism 69–70
   poststructuralism 64–6
   radical humanist paradigm 41, 57–60
   radical structuralist paradigm 40, 48–57
comparative education 7

Comparative Education 13, 170
Comparative Education: A Study of Educational Factors and Traditions (Nicholas) 13
Comparative Education Center 15
Comparative Education Review 170
Comparative Education Society in Europe (CESE) 168
Comparative Education Society of the US 167–8
Comparative International Education Society (CIES) 172
comparativists 189
Compare: A Journal of Comparative and International Education 170
Connell, R. 151, 156–7
contingency 206
core (system) 52
cosmodernism 144
Cottrell, Michael 159–60
Cowen, Robert 30, 129, 217
critical
   cartography 117
   discourse analysis 108–9
   ethnographic methods 99–102
   theory 58–9
      alienation 58
      Paolo Freire 58
Crossley, M. 100
cross-paradigm methods 110–21
cross national comparative analysis 91
Cultural
   Capital 56–7
   Globalization 53
   Imperialism 95
Curtis, S. M. S. 185
Cushman, D. 99

Dados, N. 151
Dandekar, Deepre 150
data visualization 114–16
decolonization 15, 135, 160, 213
   decolonizing methods 98–9
   post decolonization 68

deconstruction 65, 123–4
Deer, F. 160
DEI 232–3
Deleuze, Gilles 205
delinking
  colonial past 155
  de-Westernizing 151
Democratic Convention (1968) 19
Deng Xiaoping 29
dependency 50–2
development 42–4, 50
  economic 10
developmentalism 23–5, 215
development education 34–5, 130, 132–3, 134
Development in Practice 171
Dewey, John 13
digital learning 182–5
directions 126–7, 146–7
discourse analysis 107–9
discursive practices 65
document analysis 97
Dodds, K. 214
Dos Santos, Theotônio 50, 51
Dowde, C. 209–10
Du Bois, W. E. B. 150
du Plessis, G. E. 159

Eastern bloc 24
East Germany 23
East–West direction of comparative and international education (CIE) 147–9
Eckstein, M. A. 13, 83
ecological scientific literacy 178
ecological validity 100
economic 10
  dependency 16, 30, 51
  development 15, 20, 41–6, 52, 95
    stages 50
    pre-take-off, take-off, post-take off 20–3, 33
    national 21
    growth rates 18, 24, 46–7

  prosperity 9
economics 81, 167, 174, 190
  education economics 33, 44, 46, 51, 122
  globalization economics 91
  neoclassical economics 84
education abroad 148, 174
  diversity and equity context 233–5
  in practice 232–5
educational achievement distribution (EAD) 198
educational transfer and borrowing 92–3
  context 143, 145
  unit of analysis 92
education and development 21–3
education attainment 20–3
Education Cannot Wait 145
education finance 197–200
"Education for All" 25, 141–2, 171, 179, 180
  social cohesion 31
  social good 25
education planning 1, 4, 11–12, 65, 146
  and policy 108, 146, 156
  colonialism 12
  advising, and consulting 129–33, 140
  histories of 1–2
Education for Sustainable Development 178
Edwards, D. B., Jr. 82
Enslin, P. 158, 187
Environmental Education 178
Epstein, Irving 72–3, 205–7
equality and equity 197–200
  gender (and inequity/inequality) 113, 178, 179, 180, 209–11
  higher education 148, 233
  inequality as theory 20
  PISA 85
  Racial inequity 234
  social equality (and inequality) 48, 72, 74
Escobar, Arturo 43, 65, 76–7, 123, 215
Escola Ativa 140

ethics 77, 106, 174–7
Ethiopia 29–30, 163
ethnomethodology 61–2, 103
European Union (EU) 28, 29, 80, 214
existentialism 57, 60, 96
externalization 103

Floyd, George 233
Focus Groups 97
Ford Foundation 171–2
Foreign Education Journal 170
Forum for African Women Educationalists (FAWE) 209–10
Foster, Philip 15, 82, 90, 175
Foucault, Michel 64–5, 66, 67, 136
foundations 171–2
Frank, Andre G. 51
Frankfurt School 13, 58
Freire, Paolo 28, 58
  alienation 58
functionalist paradigm 40, 41–8, 82–3
functionalist research methods 80–9

Galtung, J. 53–4
Garfinkel, Harold 62
Gaulle, Charles de 19
Gee, J. P. 108
Gender and Development 171
gender/feminist studies 112–14
gender responsive education 209–10, 211–12
gender transformative education (GTE) 114, 210–12
Geographic Information System (GIS) 114–16
geopolitics 8, 12, 25, 213–17
George Mwangi, Chrystal A. 91, 144, 148, 176–7, 232–5
German Society 170
Germany 10, 14, 19, 23, 29, 58, 60, 147
Ghosh, Amitav 71
girls' education 166, 208–12
global 31

economy 26, 32, 70, 80, 141, 151, 153
education 11, 148, 174, 176, 181, 202–4, 232–5
  citizenship 2, 159, 179, 180, 187, 191
  order 26, 145
  rankings 1
Global Monitoring Report 142
globalization 26–7, 53, 141–5, 156, 157, 202–4
Globalization, Education, and Societies 170
Global North 2, 45, 127, 145, 149–50, 151, 155, 156, 169, 173, 175, 176, 180, 184, 191, 203
Global Partnership for Education (GPE) 146
Global South 2, 16, 29, 33, 64, 67, 69, 75, 82, 100, 104, 127, 133, 145, 147, 149–50, 151–2, 156–7, 169, 173, 175, 176, 181, 183, 191
glonacal 144
Goethe Institute 14
Gorostiaga, J. M. 111, 118
Gorur, R. 86
Gottlieb, E. E. 48, 93, 96, 103, 107–8, 121, 125, 175–6
Gramsci, Antonio 58
Green, A. 178
green skilling 165, 180–1, 191
Guattari, Felix 205

Halls, W. D. 172
Hans, Nicholas A. 13, 151
Haraway, Donna 70, 71–2, 187
Hegel, Georg Wilhelm Friedrich 59
Heidegger, Martin 60
Heringer, R. 160
Heryadi, R. D. 153
Heyman, R. 62, 63
Hiratsuka, Masunori 168
Høgmo, Astrid 118–19, 138
Hofmann, Hans-Georg 23

Holmes, Brian 13, 84
Horsthemke, K. 158, 187
human capital 23, 28, 45-7, 76, 81, 82, 87-8
Humphrey, Hubert 19
Husserl, E. 59

Iberoamerican Society 169
ICT 142, 146, 179, 182-3
imperialism 1, 8, 16, 31, 53-4
    neo-imperialism 1, 8, 55, 138, 162
    sub-imperialism 31, 55-6, 154
India 12, 24, 26, 29, 47, 54, 55, 81-2, 89,
    105, 107, 148, 153, 155, 163,
    173, 180-1, 221-6, 229
    ASER 173, 176, 222
India school system 221-6
indigenous culture and education 150,
    159-60
    ways of knowing 100, 127, 162, 190
    peoples 67, 70-1, 159-60, 164
Individual Modernity 95
Inkeles, Alex 45, 82
inquiry teaching methods 93
intensity of encounter 205
International and Development
    Education Program (IDEP),
    University of Pittsburgh 15
international comparisons of education
    9-11
international education 32-4, 138-43
*International Educational Journal:
    Comparative Perspectives* 170
International Education Assessments
    (IEA) 142, 143, 178
International Finance Corporation 29
Internationalists 189
internationalization 202-4, 233
*International Journal of Educational
    Development* 170
International Monetary Fund (IMF) 30,
    45, 140, 141, 145, 155
International Review of Education 170
international students 8, 11, 26, 32-3, 98,
    144, 174, 181, 186, 232-5

economic benefit and impact 33, 148,
    181
International Year Books 18
internet 116, 122, 134, 149, 173, 182,
    183
interpretive methods 31, 102-5
interpretive paradigm 41, 60-3, 74,
    103-5
intersectionality 41, 72-3, 114, 210
Item Response Theory (IRT) 85-6
Iyengar, R. 47, 72-3, 179-81, 183

Jameson, Fredric 66-7, 126, 136
Jamison, D. T. 88
Japan 2, 14, 24, 86, 93, 118, 130, 132, 149,
    151, 160-1, 168, 170, 172
Japan and comparative international
    education 14
Japan Comparative Education Society
    (JCES) 7, 168, 170
Jewish-Palestinian binational education
    218-20
Johnson, Lyndon B. 19
jules, t. d. 34, 152
Jullien, Marc-Antoine 9
just transition 4, 165, 180-1, 191

Kandel, Isaac 13, 35-6, 129
Kant, Immanuel 59
Kelly, Gail 31
Kennedy, Robert F. 19
Kent State University 15, 19
Kern, Stephen 183
Kidwai, H. 106-7
Kim, B. S. 88
King, Edmund 13-14, 36
King, Martin Luther, Jr. 19
Klees, S. 82, 84
Kneller, George F. 13
Knowledge Society 141
Kobayashi, Torasaburo 161, 172
Korea 21, 24, 26, 32, 93, 119, 132-3, 138,
    147, 163, 181
Kvamme, Ole Andreas 177

Landri, P. 146
Large Language Models (LLMs) 185
Latin American education national societies 168–9
Latour, Bruno 206
Leadership Studies 105
Lee, J. J. 93
Lee, V. 89
Lerner, Daniel 44
Levin, Henry 87–8, 89, 197
liberty 197–8
Little, Angela 178, 192
Lyotard, J. F. 66

macro level of analysis 80
Making Men Modern 45
Malawi 89
Mapping 111
    CIE paradigms and theories 75
    creative mapping method 120
    gendered spaces 114
    transfer 93
    social 116–21, 149
        participatory method 106
        Visualization method 115
Mandela Washington Fellowship for Young African Leaders (YALI) 154–5
Manion, Caroline "Carly" 73, 208–12
Mao Zedong 14
Marcel, Gabriel 60
Marcus, G. E. 99
Marginson, S. 97
Marini, Ruy Mauro 55
Martin, Staci 150
Martin, T. J. 39
Marx, Karl 49–50
Marxist theory 49–50
Masemann, Vandra 62
mass education 93–4
McEwan, Patrick J. 87
McHale, B. 67
McMahon, E. 175
Mead, Margaret 62

Mediterranean Journal of Educational Studies 170
Mediterranean Society of Comparative Education 170
Menashy, F. 145, 176
meso level of analysis 80
Metcalfe, Amy Scott 204
Methods 79–80, 121–3
    interpretive methods 102–5
Meyer, John W. 94, 100, 139, 141
micro level of analysis 80
Mignolo, W. D. 155
Milligan, L. O. 175
Mitchell, W. J. T. 127
Mixed methods 98
modernization 44–6, 157
    alternative 52
    critique 51, 64, 113
    method (research) 82–3
    national 92
    theory 23
Mohanty, Chandra Talpade 65
Mollis, M. 97
Moraru, Christian 41, 63, 144
Morgan, G. 39, 40, 42, 117
Mozambique 30, 153, 154
Mwamwenda, B. B. 88–9
Mwamwenda, T. S. 88–9
My Lai Massacre 19

Narrative Medicine 104
Namibia 89
National Aeronautics and Space Administration (NASA) 17
national education 138–41
nation-state unit of analysis 84–7
neocolonialism 12
neo-imperialism 54–5
neoliberalism 27–30, 53
    neoliberal economic policies 30
Nepal 118, 131
networks 47
New Era in Education: A Comparative Education (Kandel) 13

New York University 12, 15
Nicaragua 88
Nixon, Richard 19
Noah, H. J. 13
Non-Aligned Movement 153
Nordtveit, B. H. 184
norms 47
North–South direction of comparative and international education (CIE) 149–51
Norway 118, 119

Obama, Barack 154
Oceania 159
Oceania Comparative and International Education Society (OCIES) 169
OECD 29
offshore campuses 33–4
organizational building blocks 167–72
Organization for Economic Co-operation and Development (OECD) 18, 29, 141
organizations 171–2
Orientalism 65, 68, 148
Oxfam 170–1

Palestinian-Jewish binational education 218–20
Parsons, Talcott 44
participatory action research 106–10
participant observation 97
Passeron, Jean-Claude 56
Paulston, Rolland 75–6, 117, 118, 120–1
Pedagogy, Culture and Society 170
periphery (system) 52
Phelan, James 104
phenomenology 59
Phillips, D. 189
photovoice 109–10
Pinochet, Augusto 29
Plan International 211
Popper, Karl 13
positionality 175, 177
postcolonial 30, 50, 69, 99, 104

theories 34
postcolonial culture 104
postcolonialism(s) 41, 68–9
posthumanism 70–2
postmodernism 66–8
post-socialism 69–70
poststructuralism 64–6
post-take-off 21
Prague Spring 18
Pratham 173
pre-takeoff 20–1
problems of education 35–6
professional associations 168
professional journals 169–71
Program for International Student Achievement (PISA) 24–5, 85, 86, 124
Progress in International Reading Literacy Study (PIRLS) 24–5, 85
Prospects 170
protest 76–7
Putin, Vladimir 163

quantitative-to-qualitative transition 97–8

racism 176
radical humanist paradigm 41, 57–60, 95–102
radical structuralist paradigm 40, 48–57, 90–4
Ramirez, Francisco 94, 141
Rappleye, J. 92–3, 117–18, 151
rate of return on education 87–8
rate-of-return on investment 81
Rawls, J. 199
Reagan, Ronald 29
Reed, Gerald 168
Reflexive journaling 97
Reitz, Talitta 120
research
    context 134, 157
    knowledge hierarchies 176
    research practice 218–20

Research in Comparative and International Education 170
Research Institute of Comparative Education and Culture 14
Research Society of Foreign Education 14
Rhodes, Cecil 137
Rhodesia 137
Ringel, F. 69, 70
Rizvi, Fazal 145, 213–17
Rockefeller Foundation 171–2
Rogers, Rebecca 108
Ross, Karen 99, 218–20
Rostow, Walt 20
Rudolph, S. 175
Russia 29, 153, 163

Sadaka Reut: Arab Jewish Youth Partnership 218–20
Said, Edward 65, 68, 161
Samoa 159
Samoff, J. 27
Sartre, Jean-Paul 60
Schöneberg, J. 175
school provision 88–9
Schriewer, Jürgen 13, 103
Schultz, Theodore 45, 81, 87
Schweisfurth, M. 135, 189
Second World War 16, 20, 23, 32, 42, 60, 80, 92, 146, 215
  colonial space 130, 136
  post (after) 10, 129, 147, 215, 192
Sedgwick, Eve 73
Seghers, M. 109
Sellar, S. 86
semi-peripheral 52
September 11, 2001, terrorist attacks 30
Setty, R. 107
Shah, Dawood 133
shapes 127, 155, 157–8
Shukla, Kathan 221–6
Silova, Iveta 69, 71, 104
social
  capital 47, 183
  cartography 116–21

development 43
mobility 95
political theory 144
Soudien, C. 68
South Africa 29, 118–19, 153, 163
South Asia 24
Southern theory 155–7
South Korea 21, 24, 26, 32, 93, 119, 132
  Korean Educational Development Institute (KEDI) 132
South–North direction of comparative and international education (CIE) 150–1
South–South direction of comparative and international education (CIE) 151–3
South-to-South Collaboration 2
Southern Theorizing 2
Soviet Union 24, 147
space race 147
spaces (where CIE is practiced) 126, 135–46
  Beyond Globalization 143
  Colonial Space 136
  International and Global 141
  National and International 138
spatial turn 135, 136
Sputnik 17, 147
stages of development 20–3
Stanford University 15
Steiner-Khamsi, G. 143, 152
Sternberg, Robert 89
Stiglitz, E. J. 200
Stromquist, N. P. 27, 114
study abroad 148
sub-imperialism 55–6, 154
Suez Canal crisis (1956) 54
SUNY Albany 15
SUNY Buffalo 15
Sustainable Development Goals (SDGs) 177, 178–80, 199
Sustainable Development Solutions Network (SDSN) 179
Sutton, M. 81–2

symbolic interaction 62
Syracuse University, Center for Development Education 15
Syrquin, Moises 20

Takayama, K. 151
ta-va 159
Taylor, Breonna 233
teacher education 227–30
Teachers College, Columbia University 15, 130
Teach for All 173, 228–30
Teach for America 228
Technical Vocational Education Training 180–1
Tertium Comparationis 170
Tet Offensive 18
textbooks 12–14
Thatcher, Margaret 29
Theory of Justice 199
Theories in the "post" 41
Third World 16, 42, 65
Thomas, Matthew A. M. 124, 227–30
time 126, 127–9
timeline 128
    ancient time 128
    imperial time 126–8
Times Higher Education 179
transcendental phenomenology 61
Transform Education 211
traveling theory 150
Trends in International Mathematics and Science Study (TIMSS) 24–5, 85, 124

Ubuntu 158–9
Uganda 89
UNESCO 17–18, 27, 170, 171, 177–8
UNICEF 211
United Nations 171
United Nations Development Programs 27
United Nations Girls' Education Initiative (UNGEI) 211
universal primary education (UPE) 81
University of Cape Town 137
University of Hong Kong Comparative Education Research Center 170
University of London Research Library for Comparative Education 166–7
University of Michigan 15
University of Oregon 131
University of Pittsburgh 132, 133
University of Pittsburgh, International and Development Education Program (IDEP) 15
University of Wisconsin 15
UN organizations 171–2
UN Universal Declaration of Human Rights 25
US Agency for International Development (USAID) 178
US education system 17
US State Department AID agency 130, 148–9

va 159
values 47
Vavrus, Frances 101, 105, 109, 136, 146
vertical case study 101–2
Vietnam War 18–19
Vulliamy, G. 100

Wallerstein, Immanuel 41, 52, 90
War on Terror 30
Weber, Max 49
West–East 126, 146, 147
West–East and East–West 147–9
Western Sydney University 179
Wetherell, Margaret 206
Wexler, Philip 107
white supremacy 176
Witenstein, M. A. 47, 72–73, 105, 107, 180–1
Wolhuter, C. C. 84, 161
Women in Development (WID) 112–13

women's education 208–12
Wood, Hugh 131, 133
World Bank 27, 29, 81, 140–1, 141–2
World Council of Comparative Education Societies (WCCES) 14, 51, 168
World Council of Comparative Education (WCCE) 14, 51
World Culture System 52–3, 57
World Culture Theory 53, 90
world economic system 52–3
World Surveys of Education 18

World-Systems theory 52–3, 93–4, 139
World Trade Organization 29
World War II. *See* Second World War
World Yearbook of Education 17–18

Yamamoto, Yuzo 160
Yao, Christina 144, 148, 176–7, 232–5
Yellow Peril 234

Zakharia, Z. 176
Zawacki-Richter, O. 183
Zuze, L. 89